What's hidden in these feathers?
Turn to the last page.

100 WAYS TO SEE INDIA

100 WAYS TO SEE INDIA

STATS, STORIES, AND SURPRISES

ROHIT SARAN

WITH
SAJEEV KUMARAPURAM

HarperCollins *Publishers* India

First published in India by HarperCollins *Publishers* 2026
HarperCollins *Publishers* India, Cyber City, Building 10-A,
Gurugram, Haryana—122002, India
www.harpercollins.co.in

2 4 6 8 10 9 7 5 3 1

P-ISBN: 978-93-6989-447-5
E-ISBN: 978-93-6989-508-3

Typeset in 10/14.5 Work Sans
Designed by Sajeev Kumarapuram

Printed and bound at
Archana Advertising Pvt. Ltd.

MIX
Paper
FSC FSC® C010615

This book is produced from independently certified FSC® paper to ensure responsible forest management.

*

HarperCollins *Publishers*, Macken House, 39/40
Mayor Street Upper, Dublin 1, D01 C9W8, Ireland

WELCOME TO THE VISUAL DISCOVERY OF INDIA

Some of the most revealing stories about India today are hidden in plain sight—in government surveys, academic reports, private studies, and international databases being published every day. But being available isn't the same as being accessible.

Datasets are often so dry, dense, or fragmented that it takes the endurance of a camel and the patience of a saint to find the right data, clean it, visualise it, and build compelling stories around it. Try glancing at Bihar's caste Census or the periodic labour force survey—two reports dealing with India's most urgent problems, caste and jobs. You'll quickly see why the camel-and-saint metaphor is no exaggeration.

Never before have we had so much data—and such urgent need to make sense of it. We are flooded with numbers, but starved for insight.

That is what *100 Ways to See India* attempts to address. This book tries to transform the raw, the dull, and the overlooked into what we call 'Idea Graphs'—charts that don't just inform but make you pause, think, and say, 'I didn't know that.'

Data feels like the ultimate truth. But even the truest number can mislead.

WHY THIS BOOK

Data Is Abundant, Meaning Is Scarce

THE POWER AND PERIL OF A NUMBER

Data Is Easy to Understand —And Misunderstand

Take averages, for instance. In 2025, the average age of world leaders reached an all-time high. But look closely and the rise is driven by authoritarian regimes; in most democracies, leaders are actually younger today than in the 1970s.

Or consider crime. Delhi and Kerala top India's crime charts—until you realise they also record crimes better. Jharkhand, which ranks lowest in overall crime, has the highest murder rate. A data success can easily be dressed up as a crisis.

The democratisation of media, without corresponding gains in numeracy, has further complicated our relationship with data. A viral social media post once claimed a 22% surge in murders in one Delhi neighbourhood—blamed, falsely, on a migrant influx. The fact behind the fiction? Murders rose from 18 to 22—an absolute increase of four.

The challenge is to bridge the gap between data's potential and its pitfalls—to ensure that it serves as a tool for clarity, not confusion.

FACTS DON'T TAKE SIDES

But They Can Be Made to Look like They Do

In a world increasingly shaped by ideological echo chambers, *100 Ways to See India* takes no side. It does not take a position on politics, religion, or policy debates. What it offers instead are carefully sourced facts—designed to speak to readers of any belief or persuasion.

In fact, many of the charts will challenge assumptions on both ends of the ideological spectrum. As British economist Joan Robinson once said: 'Whatever you can rightly say about India, the opposite is also true.'

Much of this book lives in that contradiction.

Too often, people mistake inefficiency for conspiracy. A gap in government data or a fuzzy definition is read as deception. This book won't end that habit—but it might help. When the official unemployment rate falls, it might simply reflect a rise in self-employment—often low-paying or unpaid. That's a flaw in definition, not a cover-up.

By highlighting such nuances, this book aims to make readers not just more informed, but more discerning. Facts don't take sides. But they can help you see all sides more clearly. And then take a side—or better understand your side.

WHAT THIS BOOK IS

Charts as the New Paragraph

This is a book of visual text, not visuals *plus* text. That's a deliberate distinction. Often, visuals and text run in parallel lanes. Here, they are fused—each chart blended with a narrative that deepens it, rather than merely paraphrasing it. This is a reader's book as much as a visual one—with charts that complement the text, not repeat it.

Each chapter spans just two or four pages. Open the book anywhere, and you'll find a self-contained story—complete in itself, yet tightly linked to others for deeper exploration. This respects modern reading habits: dip in anywhere, finish something, and come away with a spark of discovery.

In tone, it assumes nobody is dumb for not knowing. It doesn't condescend to the lay reader nor bore the expert. This book is meant to be your thinking partner—welcoming, honest, and often surprising.

From the shape of our population pyramid to the languages we speak, the time we spend working to the water we consume—this book covers the deep structure of India, one chart at a time.

A LIVING BOOK

Data Is Dynamic, so Is This Book

Data almost never ages well. Even a minor update can shift a story's direction. That's why the tables behind each chart will be available to readers online—and updated regularly.

This ensures three things:

1. You can go deeper. Most tables contain more data than the charts can show.
2. The data is transparent and verifiable.
3. The book's shelf-life is extended—both online and offline.

We hope this is especially useful for students, teachers, researchers, and policy professionals. Too many Indian textbooks rely on outdated numbers. With this book, readers will not only access the latest available data but also find linked research reports, source surveys, and context for each topic.

Our broader goal is to build data confidence—where readers learn to ask better questions, spot misleading claims, and use data not to reinforce cynicism but to unlock clarity.

We like to think of this book as a box of chocolates: you never quite know what you'll get next, only that it's small, different, and meant to be savoured.

PS: **About that 100 on the cover.** We began this project with a working title, *India in 100 Charts*. It took only a couple of chapters to realise that most stories needed more than one chart. The result: nearly 300 visuals, 85-plus chapters, and roughly a hundred distinct 'ways' of seeing India—each built around a question and a story. If you feel like counting and get a different total, we'll happily accept your number.

WHERE DO I START?

Think of these contents pages not as a map, but as a menu. You don't have to read this book linearly, though you can do that too. Flip, dip, explore. Come back and connect the dots later.

Small Charts, Big Surprises

MILLION OR LAKH? Crore or billion? This book mostly uses Indian number units (lakh, crore) and currency (rupees), except in chapters where dollar values or global comparisons are central to the story.

100000	=1 lakh
1000000	=10 lakh =1 million
10000000	=10 million =1 crore
100000000	=10 crore =100 million
1000000000	=100 crore =1 billion

Why not convert everything to just rupees or just dollars? Because sometimes, converting currency shifts the context or even misleads.

That's why this book uses rupee values when local relevance matters, and dollar values where global comparison is the point.

Since Independence, the average age of Indians has gone up by almost:

- 50%
- 75%
- 100%

Answer on Page 40

Life

THE REAL LANGUAGE MAP

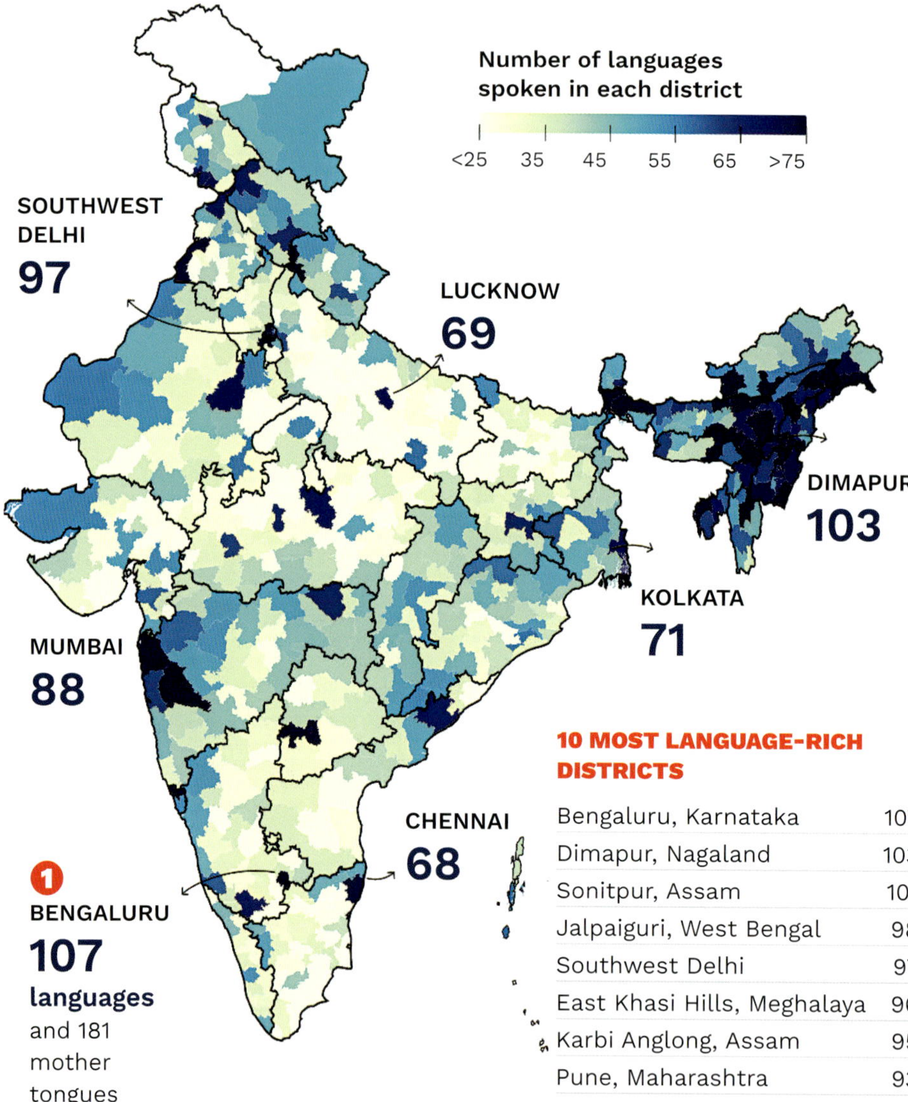

10 MOST LANGUAGE-RICH DISTRICTS

District	Languages
Bengaluru, Karnataka	107
Dimapur, Nagaland	103
Sonitpur, Assam	101
Jalpaiguri, West Bengal	98
Southwest Delhi	97
East Khasi Hills, Meghalaya	96
Karbi Anglong, Assam	95
Pune, Maharashtra	93
Darjeeling, West Bengal	91
Mumbai Suburban, Maharashtra	88

Multiple mother tongues and dialects are clubbed into 121 Scheduled and Non-Scheduled Languages. For example, Bhojpuri, Magadhi, and Rajasthani are clubbed as Hindi.
Only counting the first language of a speaker
Data source: Census 2011, statsofindia.in

01

How Bengaluru Became the Language Capital of India

India is the most exciting treasure hunt of languages on the planet. Words and sounds change every few kilometres. The ultimate destination on this treasure hunt is Bengaluru district. People here spoke 107 languages in 2011—the highest in the country. Dimapur was home to 103 languages, making it the second most language-diverse district.

The numbers are even more impressive for mother tongues: people in Bengaluru spoke 181, Pune 176 and Southwest Delhi 149. Several districts have over 100 mother tongues. Why is the number of mother tongues higher than the number of languages? The answer lies in how languages are classified in Census surveys. Hindi, for instance, is made up of at least 56 dialects or mother tongues, the largest of which is Bhojpuri.

Languages move with people and people move for, and with, jobs. That's why some of the most language-rich districts are also the biggest migrant hubs—and job creation engines. These are the places where India's famed diversity meets unity, making our diversity more purposeful and less (potentially) divisive.

A few Northeast districts are also among the language toppers, which speaks to their historic demographic diversity.

KNOW MORE

How fast does India's crime clock tick? • Page 36

CAN YOU FIND YOUR HINDI HERE?

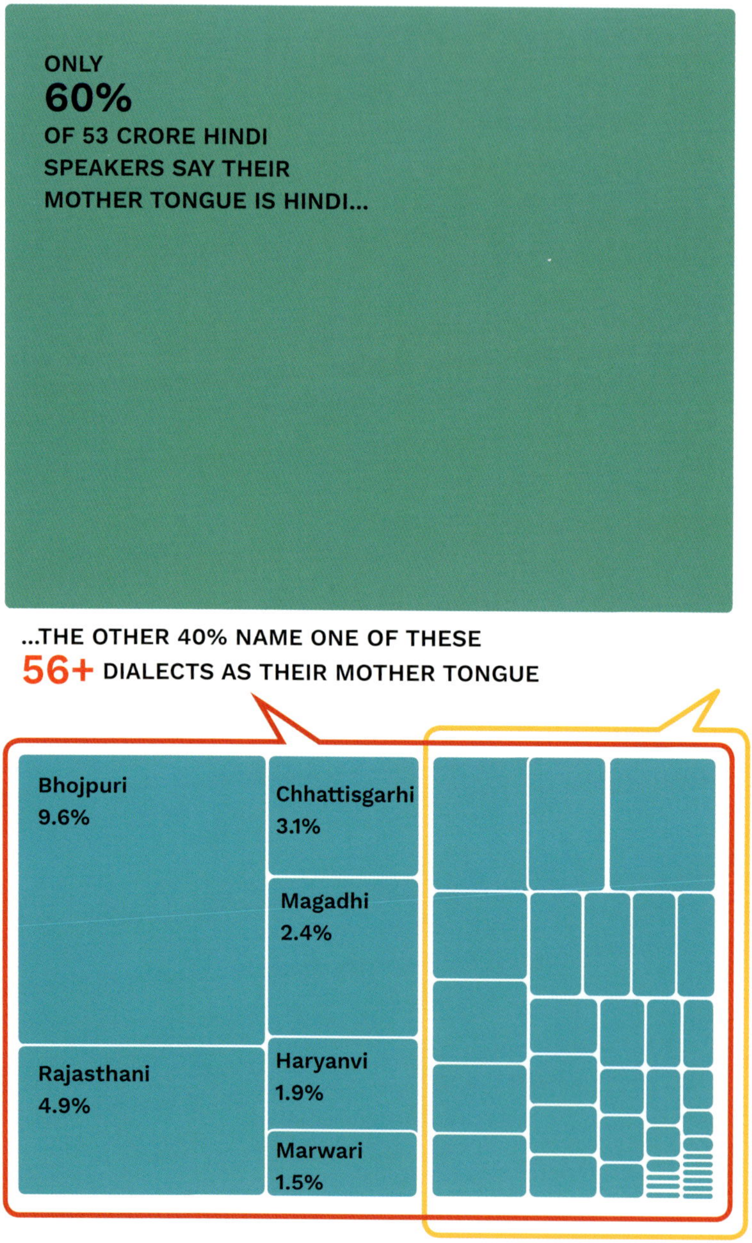

Bundeli
Malvi
Sadan
Mewari
Awadhi
Lamani
Pahari
Hara
Khortha
Bagheli
Garhwali
Nimadi
Surjapuri-
Kumauni
Surgujia
Banjari
Brajbhasha
Dhundhari
Gojri
Kangri
Mewati
Nagpuria-
Mandeali
Pawari
Kurmali Thar
Panch Pargania
Bagri-
Rajasthani
Sondwari
Kulvi
Bharmauri
Sugali
Lodhi
Jaunpuri
Chambeali
Sirmauri
Bhadrawahi
Laria
Churahi
Khari Boli
Handuri
Palmuha
Bhagoria
Gawari
Pangwali
Padari
Baghati
Pando
Puran
Bishnoi

Data source: Census publication called 'Language' released in 2018.
Census records first, second, and third languages spoken by people.
The terms 'mother tongue' and 'dialect' are often used interchangeably.

02

56 Mother Tongues—and They Are All Hindi

When the 2011 Census data on languages was first collated, it showed there were 19,569 mother tongues spoken in India. A 'thorough linguistic scrutiny, edit, and rationalization' brought that down to a more manageable 1,369. That was still too many. The 'inventory' of mother tongues was then grouped under 121 official languages of India—of which 22 are scheduled languages and 99 are unscheduled. By now, there were 270 mother tongues, of which 123 were part of the 22 scheduled languages, and 147 under unscheduled languages.

The problem with such drastic 'rationalization' is that it brought hundreds of mother tongues under a single name—Hindi. Today, there are more than 56 mother tongues under what the Census calls Hindi, but speakers call these Awadhi, Bhojpuri, Haryanvi, Rajasthani... What does this mean? It means that 40% of the 52.8 crore Indians who speak Hindi according to the 2011 Census actually speak a multitude of different languages. Bhojpuri (9.6%) was the second-largest spoken mother tongue under the Hindi umbrella.

Quick note: some 1.7 crore Indians report a mother tongue that is not on the list of 56; the Census calls them all Hindi too. So, the next time someone starts talking about Hindi imposition, ask which Hindi they are talking about.

KNOW MORE

- After Hindi, Odia has the largest number of mother tongues—9—among the 22 scheduled languages

INDIA'S QUIETEST REVOLUTION

NUMBER OF ANNUAL **BIRTHS** AND **DEATHS** IN INDIA SINCE 1950

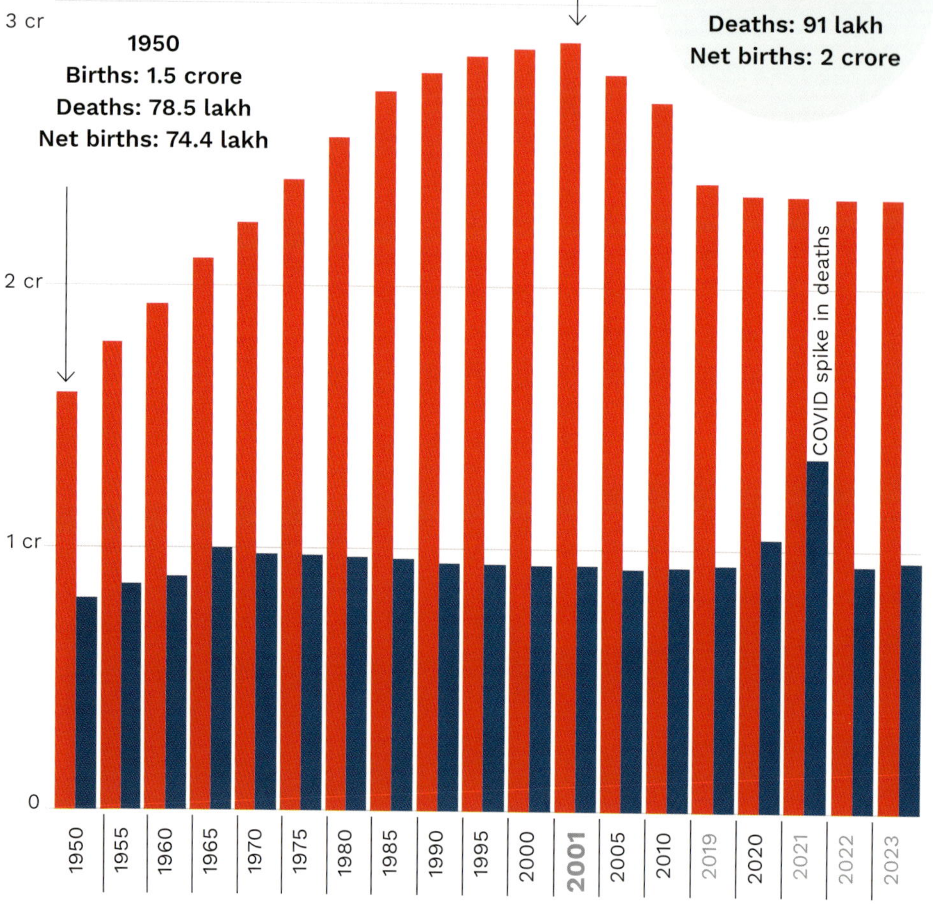

CHINA'S BABY BUST

Starting 2021, number of **deaths** exceed number of **births** in China

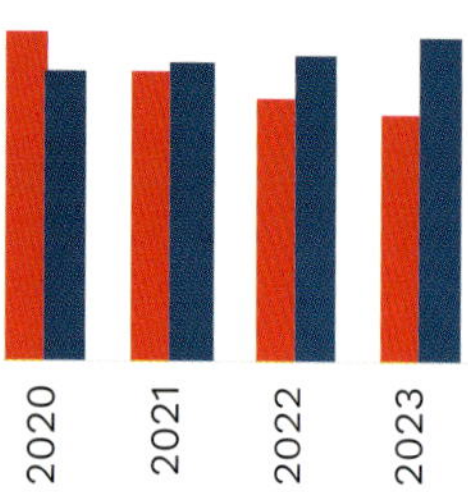

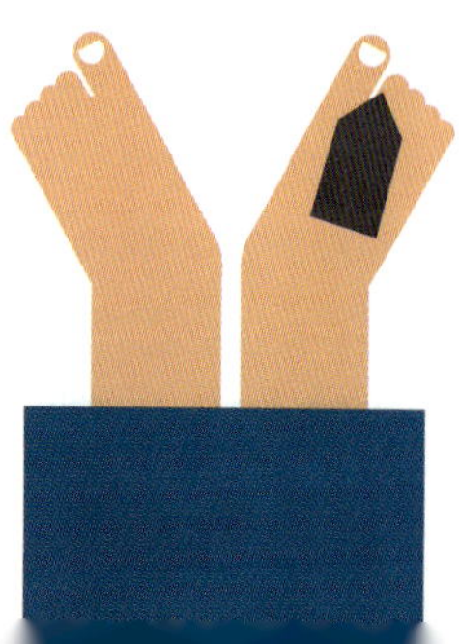

Data source: UN, World Population Prospects (2024), Ourworldindata

03

India's Baby Boom Is Over. You Just Haven't Noticed Yet.

Here's a quiet revolution you may have missed: India's baby boom ended in 2001. Since then, the number of children born each year has been falling steadily. In 2023, an estimated 2.3 crore babies were born—17,000 fewer every day than in 2001. So why is India's population still growing? Because births still outnumber deaths. In 2023, there were around 2.3 crore births and just over 95 lakh deaths. That surplus keeps the population rising—but at a slower rate.

By or before 2050, India's population will begin to shrink—just like China and over 30 other countries. In China, there are fewer births than deaths. Some parts of India are already on that path. Several districts have shrinking populations (see Page 144), though states like Delhi still grow rapidly due to migration. This shift has far-reaching implications. Slower population growth can ease pressure on resources—but it also raises questions about workforce shortages and aging. India now has a window to make the most of its demographic peak. And like most windows, it will close eventually.

KNOW MORE
Are companies getting bigger than countries?
● Page 104

1 million=10 lakh; 10 million=1 crore; details on Page xv

If all Indians lived as densely as people in Delhi do (11,320 persons per sq km) they would fit in the orange area—just **3.25%** of India

If all Indians lived as densely as people in Northeast Delhi do (36,155 persons per sq km) they would fit in the yellow area—just **1.02%** of India

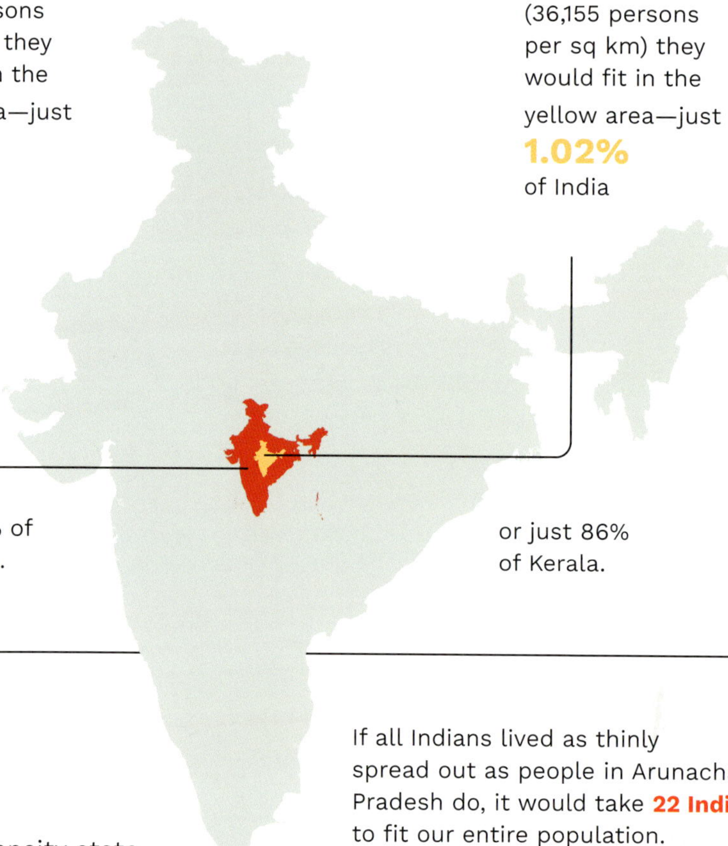

or just 82% of Tamil Nadu.

or just 86% of Kerala.

Highest density state	
Delhi	**11,320**
Highest density district	
Northeast Delhi	**36,155**
Lowest density state	
Arunachal Pradesh	**17**
Lowest density district	
Dibang Valley	**1**
India	**368**

If all Indians lived as thinly spread out as people in Arunachal Pradesh do, it would take **22 Indias** to fit our entire population.

If all Indians lived as thinly spread out as people in Dibang Valley, Arunachal Pradesh, do, it would take **368 Indias** to fit our entire population.

All calculations based on 2011 Census data
Data source: Sample Registration System (SRS) bulletin 2022; statsofindia.in

04

Yes, All of India Can Fit into Kerala

If this headline conjures up an image of a billion people packed into 'God's Own Country', it's only slightly exaggerated. If every Indian lived as densely as the residents of Northeast Delhi, India's most crowded district, the entire population would fit in just 86% of Kerala. That's because in Northeast Delhi there are over 36,000 people in every square kilometre—but you won't realise it walking around the area. If you take the average density of Delhi as a whole—the densest state in India—then all of India would fit into Tamil Nadu.

But density isn't just about land and people. It's a window into how Indians live, move, and find work. Crowded cities like Delhi keep attracting migrants because of the opportunities they offer. The Indo-Gangetic belt—running through UP, Bihar, and Bengal—makes up just 13% of India's geography but houses 35% of its population. It is fertile land, settled over centuries. At the other extreme lies Dibang Valley in Arunachal Pradesh, where just 0.8 people live per square kilometre. If all of India were spread out that thin, it would take 368 Indias to fit us all. Where we live reflects far more than just how many we are—it reflects the story of where India is going.

KNOW MORE
When chess joined cricket at the top • Page 164

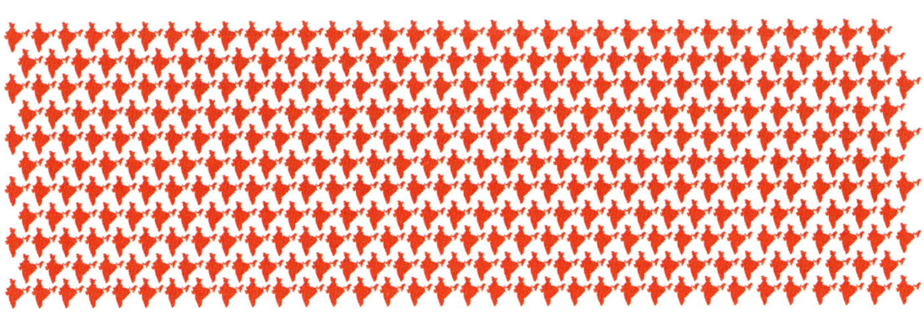

1. IN ALL EXCEPT 4 STATES, MOST EAT MEAT

Share of Indian adults who eat egg, fish, chicken, or meat, 2021

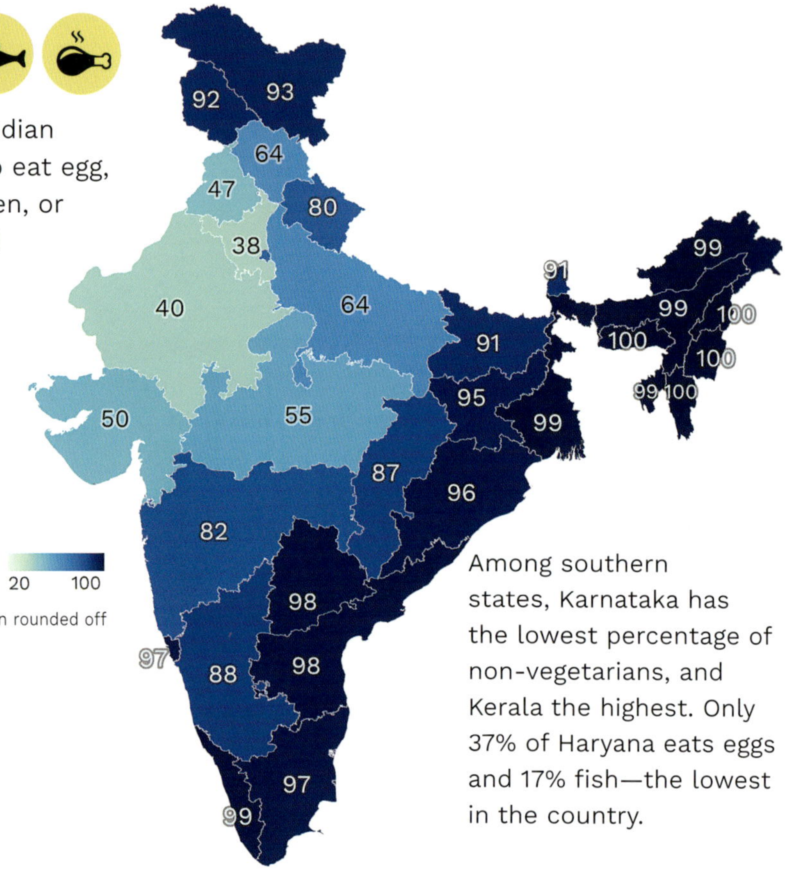

Figures have been rounded off

Among southern states, Karnataka has the lowest percentage of non-vegetarians, and Kerala the highest. Only 37% of Haryana eats eggs and 17% fish—the lowest in the country.

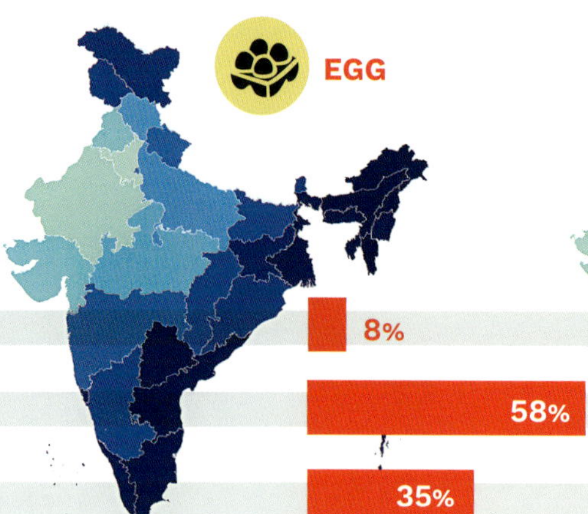

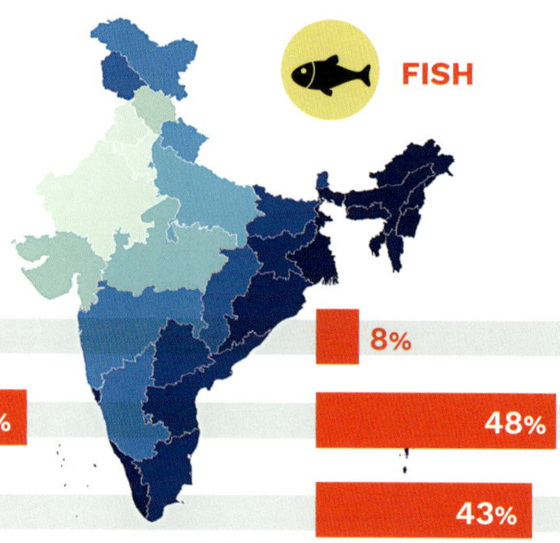

05

India's Vegetarian Perception—and Non-Vegetarian Reality

Nowhere does India's famed—and confusing—diversity show up as starkly as it does on the dinner plate. That explains the ignorance, sometimes willful, about how many Indians eat meat. According to the National Family Health Survey, 87% of men and 75% of women are non-vegetarian. And yet, 67% of Jains and 21% of Hindus avoid even root vegetables, while 60% of Buddhists say they wouldn't eat at places serving both veg and non-veg food.

In India, meat is not just a diet—it's also a cultural code, a religious boundary, and, sometimes, a political identity. Unlike most meat-eating countries, non-vegetarianism in India doesn't mean daily meat consumption. Many eat meat only once a week—or even once a month. Religious festivals, caste customs, and

2. INFREQUENTLY NON-VEG:
Daily meat consumption is rare, with most eating meat only weekly or monthly, influenced by religious festivals, customs, and fasting days.

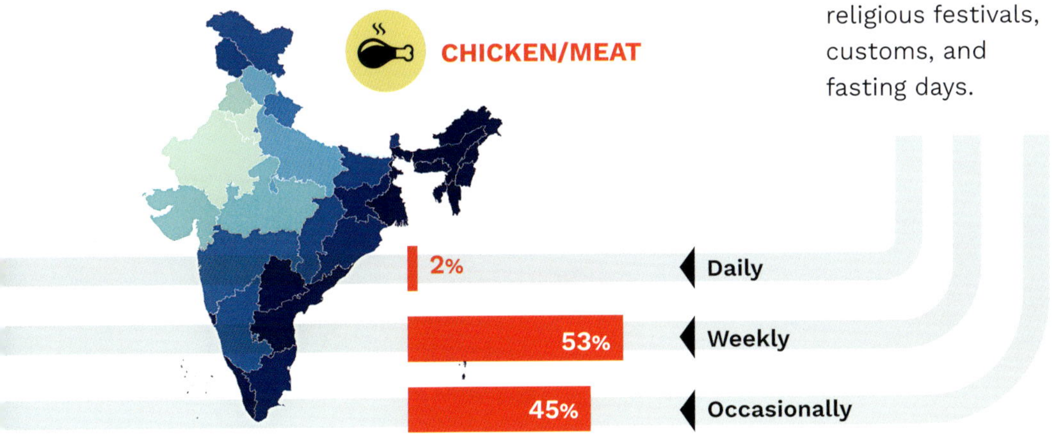

3. ACROSS GENDER AND YEARS, NUMBER OF NON-VEGETARIANS IS RISING

Share of Indian adults who eat meat

fasting days influence what's eaten and when. Even among non-vegetarians, many avoid beef or pork, creating an intricate pattern of preferences. Geographical variation is just as stark. In states like Nagaland and Kerala, nearly everyone eats meat. In Rajasthan and Punjab, vegetarians dominate. Within religions too, patterns vary: most Hindus eat meat but avoid beef; most Muslims eat meat but not pork; Christians tend to consume meat more frequently. These regional, religious, and personal variations defy easy categorisation.

Affordability plays a role too. In some regions, a daily vegetarian diet is more expensive and less accessible than a non-vegetarian one—a reason why India's richest households report the highest share of vegetarians. The gender gap (chart above), however, is shaped less by affordability than by norms and household choices—especially in rural homes. In India, food is far more than nourishment. Like faith, it is deeply personal—and widely political.

KNOW MORE

What kills Indian men, women the most ● Page 150

4. PREFERENCE FOR MEAT FALLS AS INCOME RISES

Share of Indian adults who eat meat, by wealth group (2021)

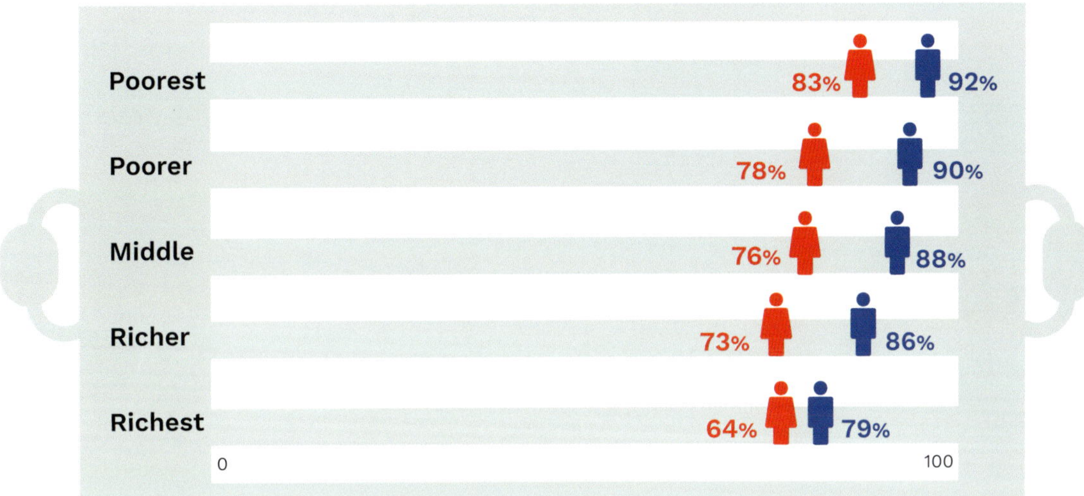

5. HUGE VARIATION ACROSS RELIGIONS ON WHEN AND WHICH MEAT IS CONSUMMED

% of Indian adults who say they are...

	VEGETARIAN	NON-VEGETARIAN				
		Any restriction on meat	Abstain from eating meat on certain days	Abstain from eating certain meats	Both these restrictions	No restriction
Hindu	44	83	6	4	29	16
Muslim	8	67	7	14	39	32
Christian	10	66	10	16	30	33
Sikh	59	82	3	4	16	16
Buddhist	25	84	14	8	38	15
Jain	92	97	1	0	4	3

Data source: National Family Health Survey (2019–21), Dataforindia.com, Pew Research
Data is for people aged 15–49. The survey records food consumption separately for men and women. Religion-wise data may not exactly match the government's NFHS survey data shown in other charts.

ENTRY TEST OR ELIMINATION TEST?

In 2024,
9.9 lakh
applied for civil services exams

But 4.1 lakh applicants didn't sit for the prelims

5.8 lakh
appeared for the prelims

5.6 lakh failed to qualify

98.5% of applicants were out before the main exams

14,627
appeared for the main exam

2,845
appeared for the interview

1,009
qualified

Only 0.1% of applicants and 0.2% of those who appeared in the prelims cleared all three levels.

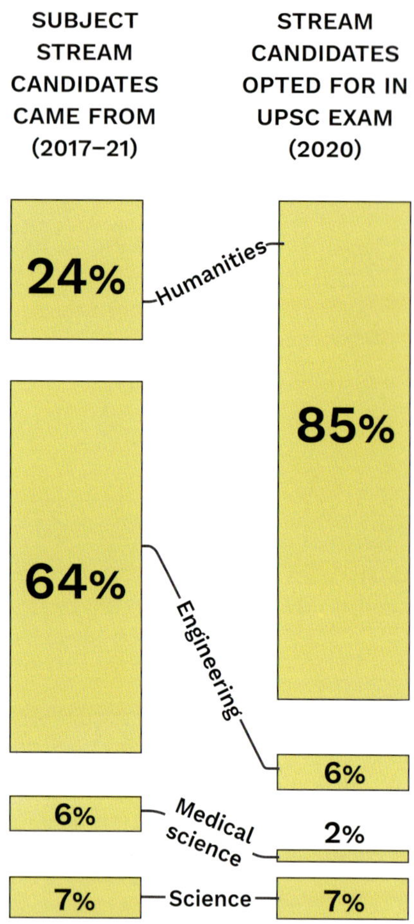

56% SUCCESS CAME FROM JUST 4 SUBJECTS

Political science and international relations	18.5%
Sociology	13.8%
Anthropology	12.0%
Geography	11.4%

Data source: UPSC annual reports

06

When Engineers and Doctors Choose Political Science

What are the chances of flipping a coin 10 times and getting heads each time? About the same as cracking India's civil services exam—roughly 0.1%. In 2024, nearly 10 lakh aspirants competed for just 1,009 posts. Statistically that makes it harder to become a civil servant in India than to get into Harvard, Oxford, or even NASA's astronaut programme. But what sets this exam apart isn't just how tough it is. The route people take to crack it is puzzling. Between 2017 and 2021, over 76% of aspirants came from science, engineering, or medical backgrounds. And yet, 85% of those who succeeded chose a humanities subject for their main papers.

Just 4 of the 41 optional subjects—political science, sociology, geography, and anthropology—accounted for over half the successful candidates. The 2025 topper, for example, held a post-graduate degree in biochemistry but opted for political science for her main exam. The reasons are part academic, part structural. The general studies papers overlap heavily with humanities which makes preparation easier, and the coaching ecosystem for humanities is better developed. But it raises a broader question: is India misallocating its technical talent chasing the prestige and power of a government job? Or is this a good way to build a bureaucracy equally fluent in science and statecraft?

KNOW MORE
What 25 pyramids say about India's future • Page 140

07

One Real Love, Three Fake Crimes

MURDER FOR LOVE

30,012 women were killed for being in romantic relationships during 2013–22. The three reported causes were:

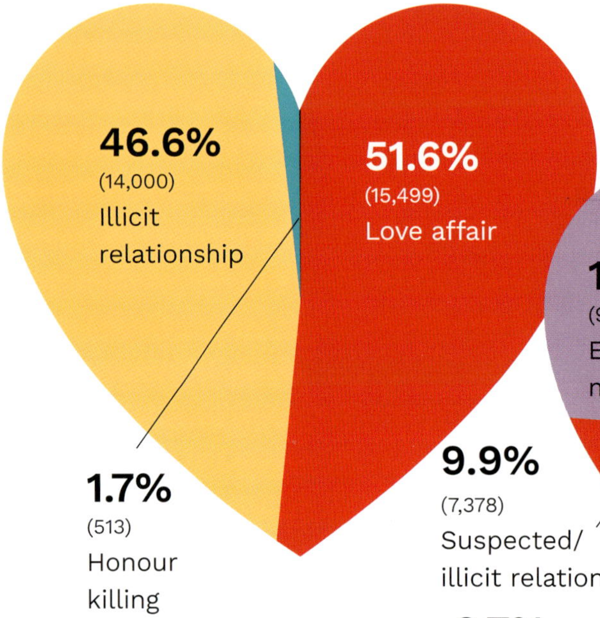

SUICIDE FOR LOVE

74,180 women died by suicide during the same 10 years for being in an 'unapproved' relationship. Four reported causes were:

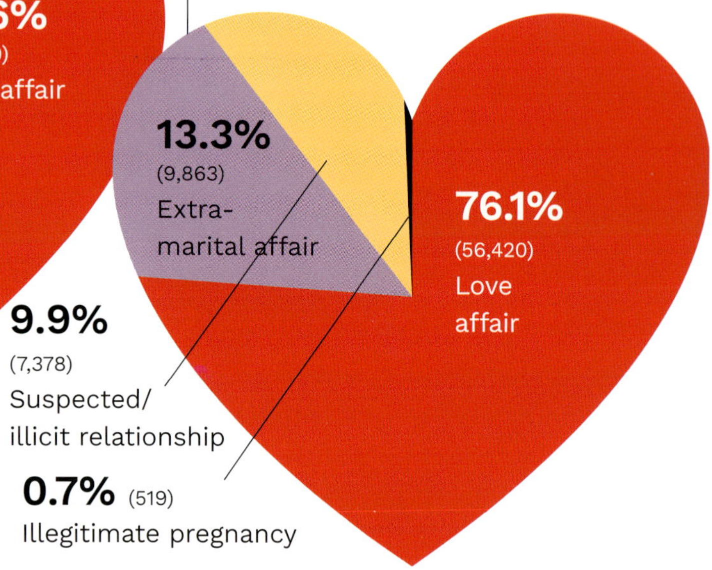

Love in India creates hundreds of thousands of crimes each year—fake ones. A woman marries a man of her choosing, against her family's wishes. She elopes. Days or months later, the couple is caught—not by chance, but by the police. Why? Because her parents filed a case of kidnapping (fake crime no. 1). The man is charged with rape (fake crime no. 2). If the woman was under 18—even by a few days—it also becomes a POCSO case. That's up to three crimes where there was just a relationship.

But that's not the worst outcome. Some love stories don't end in courtrooms. They end in murder. Between 2013

8. India slayed its deadliest tiny killer

Malaria cases per 1 lakh people

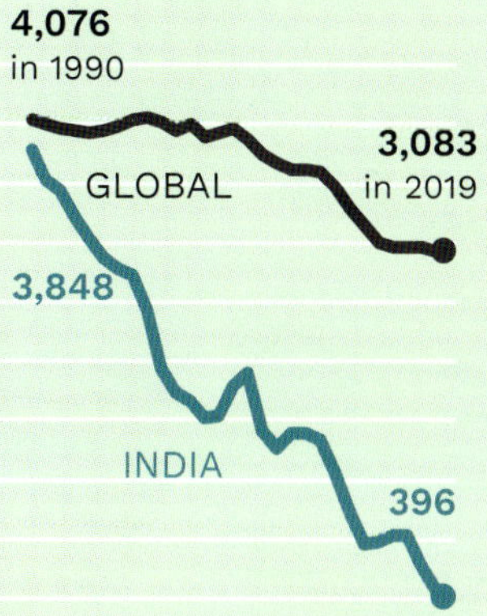

9. A habit change that improved individual and family health

Prevalance of tobacco use

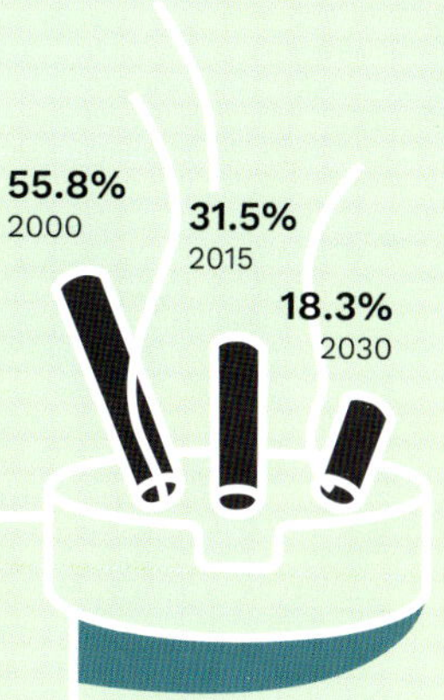

10. New-age Indian businesses turned billion-dollar stories

Number of unicorns

2011	1	2020	30+
2012	2	2021	70–80
2013	3	2022	100–107
2014	7–10	2023	108+
2016-17	10–15	2024	110–117
2018-19	18–24	2025 (August)	120+

GAPS

2. Millions of missing women

6.3 crore women either not born due to sex-selection abortions or died prematurely from neglect due to society's preference for a son

4. Overfed and undernourished, at the same time

Obesity in ages 5–9

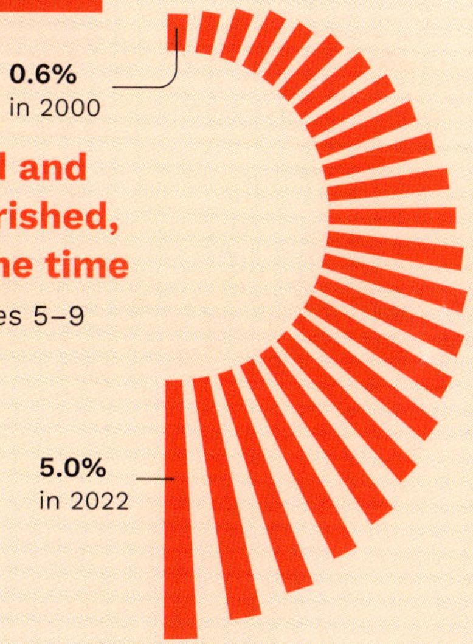

3. 1 in 4 Indian children is too short for their age (0–5 years)

37.1% of children are stunted

5.5% are wasted

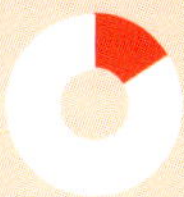
15.9% are underweight

5. The price of mobility shouldn't be life

26% of all deaths of men aged 15–29 is due to road accidents

4.5 lakh road accidents

1.5 lakh casualties (NCRB)

3.3 lakh casualties (SRS)

Data for 2022

6. Innocent until proven guilty—but still in jail

Undertrial prisoners as % of total (2022)

7. Some court cases may outlive the complainants

Pending cases (Juy 2025)

86,844 Supreme Court

63.3 lakh High courts

4.7 crore District and subordinate courts

8. One in four families in few state still don't use toilet facilties

Share of households that do not use a toilet facility (2021)

Bihar	38.9%
Odisha	33.9%
Jharkhand	33.6%

9. Life-threatening air

No. of years added to life if pollution is within WHO limits

	India	Delhi
2018	4.2	9.8
2019	4.1	9.2
2020	4.1	9.2
2021	3.7	7.9
2022	3.9	8.6
2023	3.9	8.6
2024	3.5	7.8
2025	3.5	8.2

10. Safe water should not come with a price tag

Bottled water as a source of drinking water in **rural** and **urban** India

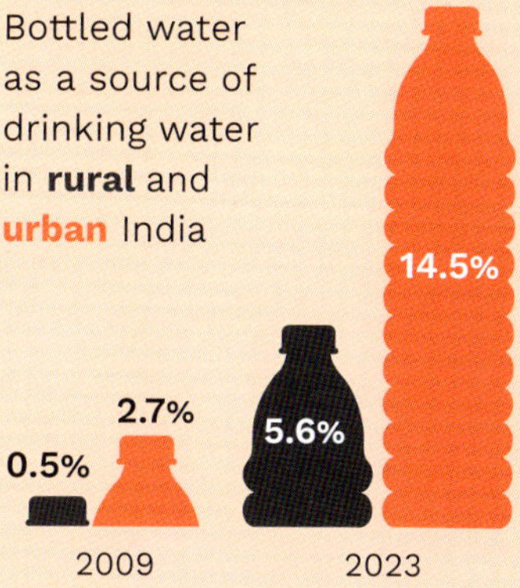

Data source: PMJSY dashboard, dataforindia.com, TRAI, pmjdy.gov.in, Ministry of Rural Development, humancapital.worldbank.org, WHO and UNICEF's washdata.org, NPCI, Global Burden of Disease (GBD), Tracxn, PIB, UNICEF's global database on school-age children and adolescents' nutrition, Ministry of Women and Child Development, njdg.ecourts.gov.in, NFHS (2019-21), Sample Registration System (SRS), National Crime Records Bureau (NCRB)

DISPOSAL OF CRIMES AGAINST WOMEN CASES IN 2022

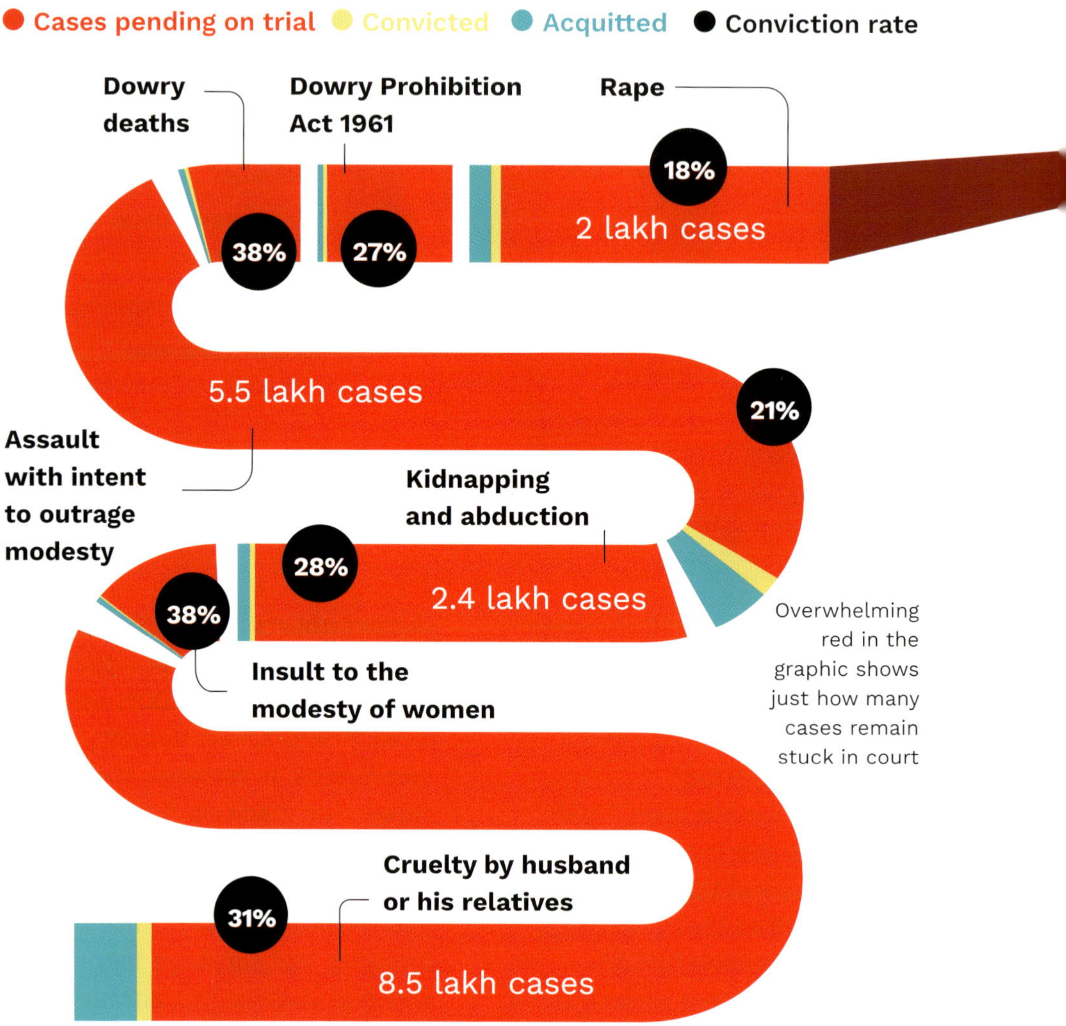

Overwhelming red in the graphic shows just how many cases remain stuck in court

Crime	Cases sent for trial in 2022	Total no. of cases on trial	Cases convicted in 2022	Cases acquitted in 2022	Rate of conviction (%)
Rape	26,508	1,98,285	5,067	12,062	18
Dowry Prohibition Act 1961	12,547	75,302	1,847	3,236	27
Dowry deaths	6161	60,577	1,231	2,189	38
Assault to outrage modesty	71,630	5,48,354	8,056	22,084	21
Kidnapping and abduction	33,847	2,41,445	3,452	6,459	28
Insult to modesty of women	7621	52,113	524	2,100	38
Cruelty by husband/his relatives	1,23,297	8,52,598	8,307	35,998	31

08

The Justice Gap in Crimes Against Women

One of the deadliest years in recent history brought an unlikely reprieve for women in India: crimes against them dropped sharply across most of the 50-plus categories tracked by the police. In 2020, when overall crime in India surged by nearly 30%, cases of rape, dowry deaths, and domestic cruelty declined sharply. The reason? Lockdowns and social distancing. But the lull was short-lived. By 2022, these crimes were up again: rape cases rose by 12%, cruelty by family by 26%, dowry-related crimes by 30%, and kidnappings by 37%. (As explained on Page 16, many kidnapping cases are elopements, registered mostly by the woman's parents.)

But how do the police and courts respond to these crimes? Let's look at rape cases. In 2022, over 3 lakh rape-related cases were reported. Fewer than 45,000 progressed to investigation, and only 60% of those resulted in charge sheets. The visual in this chapter focuses on the final step of the justice chain—court disposals in seven types of crime against women. In 2022, fewer than 8% of reported rape cases reached a verdict. Of the nearly 20,000 decided that year, just 5,000 ended in convictions, while 12,000 ended in acquittals. A high acquittal-to-conviction ratio does not by itself prove bias or injustice—especially if the trial was fair and evidence insufficient. But when stacked against rising crimes and 2 lakh pending cases of just one crime (rape), it reveals how hard justice can be to reach.

COVID RELIEF AND THE BOUNCE BACK

The pandemic offered a respite, but in many crimes, the rebound was sharp

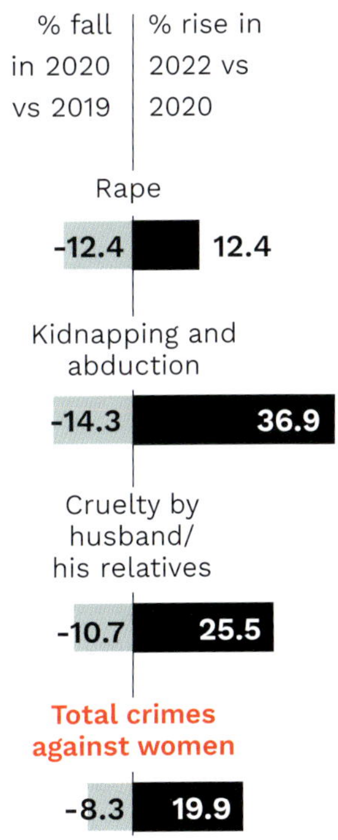

Data source: Women and Men in India 2024, NCRB

TOP 5 LANGUAGES IN EACH STATE

	1	2	3	4	5
Uttar Pradesh	Hindi	Urdu	Punjabi	Bengali	Sindhi
Rajasthan	Hindi	Bhili/Bhilodi	Punjabi	Urdu	Sindhi
Uttarakhand	Hindi	Urdu	Punjabi	Bengali	Nepali
Madhya Pradesh	Hindi	Bhili/Bhilodi	Marathi	Gondi	Urdu
Haryana	Hindi	Punjabi	Urdu	Bengali	Lahnda
Himachal Pradesh	Hindi	Punjabi	Nepali	Kinnauri	Kashmiri
NCT of Delhi	Hindi	Punjabi	Urdu	Bengali	Maithili
Chhattisgarh	Hindi	Gondi	Odia	Halabi	Kurukh/Oraon
Bihar	Hindi	Maithili	Urdu	Bengali	Santali
Chandigarh	Hindi	Punjabi	Urdu	Nepali	Bengali
Jharkhand	Hindi	Santali	Bengali	Urdu	Ho
Daman and Diu	Gujarati	Hindi	Marathi	Bengali	Odia
D&N Haveli	Bhili/Bhilodi	Hindi	Gujarati	Marathi	Konkani
Jammu and Kashmir	Kashmiri	Hindi	Dogri	Punjabi	Bhotia
A&N Islands	Bengali	Hindi	Tamil	Telugu	Nicobarese
Maharashtra	Marathi	Hindi	Urdu	Gujarati	Bhili/Bhilodi
Punjab	Punjabi	Hindi	Urdu	Bengali	Lahnda
Gujarat	Gujarati	Hindi	Sindhi	Marathi	Bhili/Bhilodi
Sikkim	Nepali	Hindi	Bhotia	Limbu	Lepcha
West Bengal	Bengali	Hindi	Santali	Urdu	Nepali
Odisha	Odia	Hindi	Kui	Santali	Urdu
Goa	Konkani	Marathi	Hindi	Kannada	Urdu
Assam	Assamese	Bengali	Hindi	Bodo	Miri/Mishing
Andhra Pradesh	Telugu	Urdu	Hindi	Tamil	Marathi
Tripura	Bengali	Tripuri	Hindi	Mogh	Odia
Lakshadweep	Malayalam	Tamil	Hindi	Bengali	Telugu
Arunachal	Nissi/Dafla	Adi	Bengali	Hindi	Nepali
Meghalaya	Khasi	Garo	Bengali	Hindi	Nepali
Puducherry	Tamil	Telugu	Malayalam	Urdu	Hindi
Karnataka	Kannada	Urdu	Telugu	Tamil	Marathi
Nagaland	Kontak	Ao	Lotha	Angami	Chakru/Chokri
Manipur	Manipuri	Mao	Thado	Tangkhul	Kabui
Mizoram	Lushai/Mizo	Bengali	Lakher	Tripuri	Pawi
Tamil Nadu	Tamil	Telugu	Kannada	Urdu	Malayalam
Kerala	Malayalam	Tamil	Tulu	Kannada	Konkani

Colours are used to aid navigation, and do not imply a formal category.
States/UTs listed per their status in 2011.
Data source: Census publication called 'Language' released in 2018.

09

How Many Indians Speak Hindi? Fewer than You Think

As the map shows, Hindi is the first language of over 90% of people in only seven Indian states—all in the heart of the Hindi belt. Include Delhi, and the count rises to eight. Hindi is also spoken by over 50% of people in another nine states—but here, it's often not the mother tongue.

That's clear from the table on the left, which shows the top five languages spoken in every Indian state. Punjabi in Punjab, Marathi in Maharashtra, Bengali in West Bengal, and Konkani in Goa—Hindi is widely understood but not native to the majority. These states highlight how language familiarity doesn't always translate into language identity.

In the 2011 Census, 69.2 crore Indians (57% of the population) were recorded as Hindi speakers. But only 52.8 crore spoke it as their first language. The rest—16.3 crore—knew it as a second or third language. Among second-language Hindi speakers, Marathi speakers topped the list, while Telugu speakers dominated third-language Hindi users. These patterns show how Hindi travels with education, migration, and media—not birth.

The next Census is overdue, but it's likely that Hindi-speaking ability has grown. After all, half of India's newborns are now from Hindi-majority states (see Page 138).

% OF PEOPLE WHO SPEAK HINDI

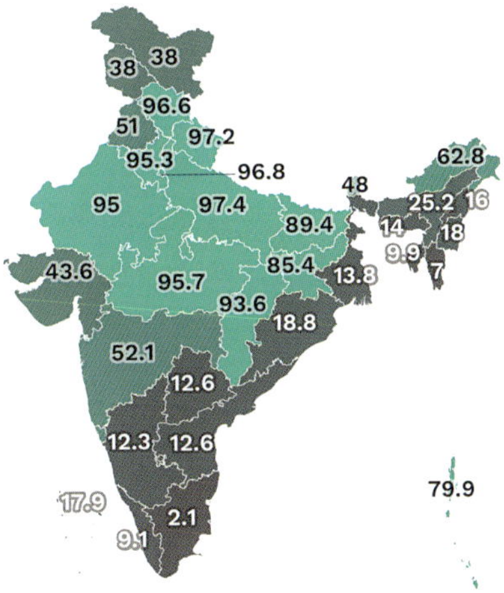

KNOW MORE

Which of these Hindis is India's national language?
● Page 4

THE 470 LOK SABHAS OF INDIA

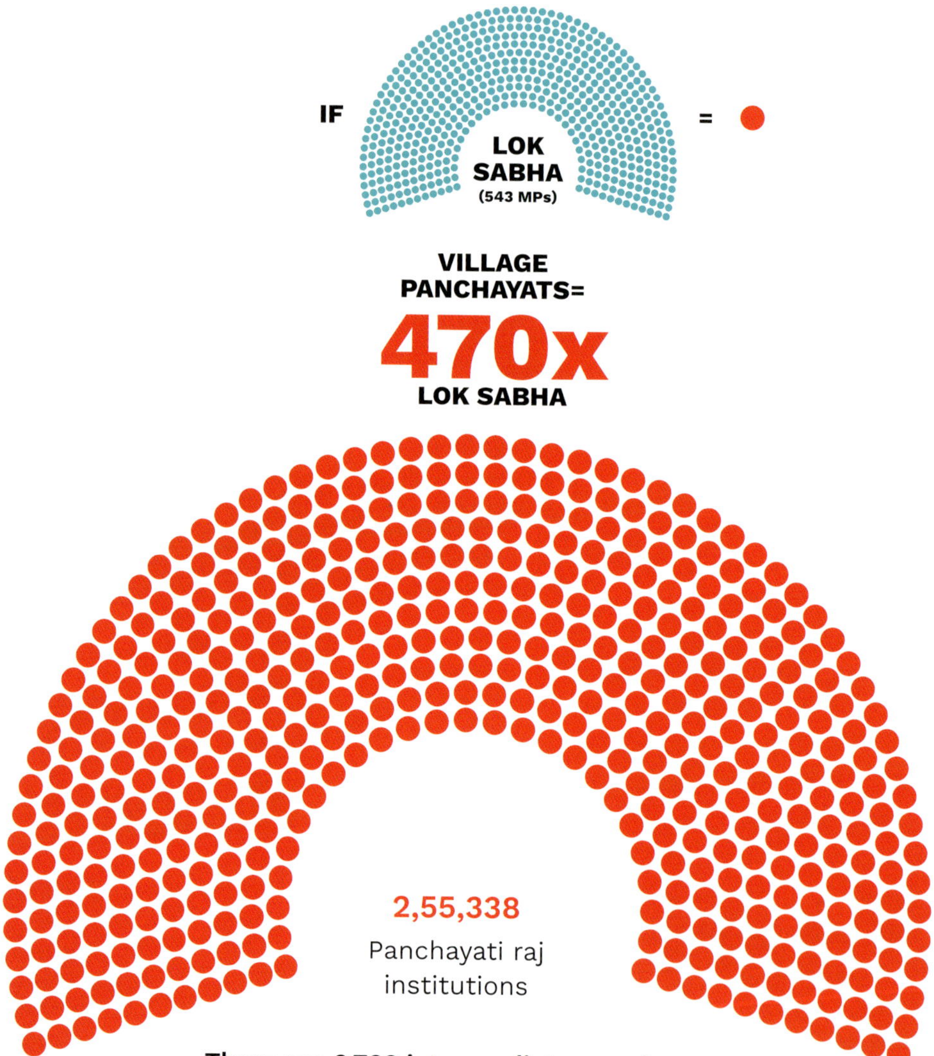

There are 6,733 intermediate panchayats and 674 district panchayats. Together with PRIs, they make up 2,62,745 local self-governments in India.

Data source: Ministry of Panchayati Raj, 'Local Government Directory' accessed on 28 July 2025
*TN sarpanch example quoted from Shruti Rajagopalan's IndiasofIndia podcast (3 July 2025).
China's local level spending source: Karthik Muralidharan, *Accelerating India's Development*.

10

India's Largest—and Least Empowered—Democracy

India is rightly celebrated as the world's largest democracy. But its most remarkable democratic feat is also its least appreciated: the 2.5 lakh Panchayati raj institutions (PRIs) that represent almost every village in India. Every 5 years, over 30 lakh citizens are elected to these local bodies—far more than the number of MPs and MLAs combined. This vast network of village governments isn't just massive, it's also inclusive: nearly 44% of panchayat seats are held by women, with some states reserving up to 50%.

Panchayats bring democracy closer to the people. A Tamil Nadu sarpanch told an economist: 'When I step out of the house, neighbours ask: What happened to that water pipe? That road? Which MLA or MP faces that kind of accountability?'* And yet, these institutions —enshrined in the Constitution since the 73rd Amendment in 1992—remain underpowered. They have responsibility but almost no resources. While China spends nearly half of its public budget at the local level, India spends just 3%. For a country aiming to be both democratic and developmental, that's a contradiction.

The result? India's most participatory political space remains its weakest. The village is where democracy is most visible, but least supported. Fixing this gap—by devolving real financial and administrative power—won't just improve rural governance; it will strengthen India's federal future from the grassroots up.

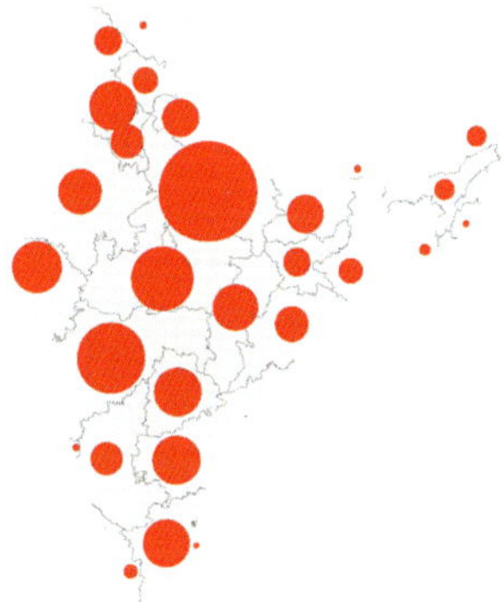

Uttar Pradesh has the most PRIs, 57,695, followed by Maharashtra (27,962) and Madhya Pradesh (23,011).

July 2025 data

KNOW MORE

Why India's Parliament hasn't changed since 1971
● Page 154

1. NO GOVERNMENT HAS REPRESENTED 50% INDIANS

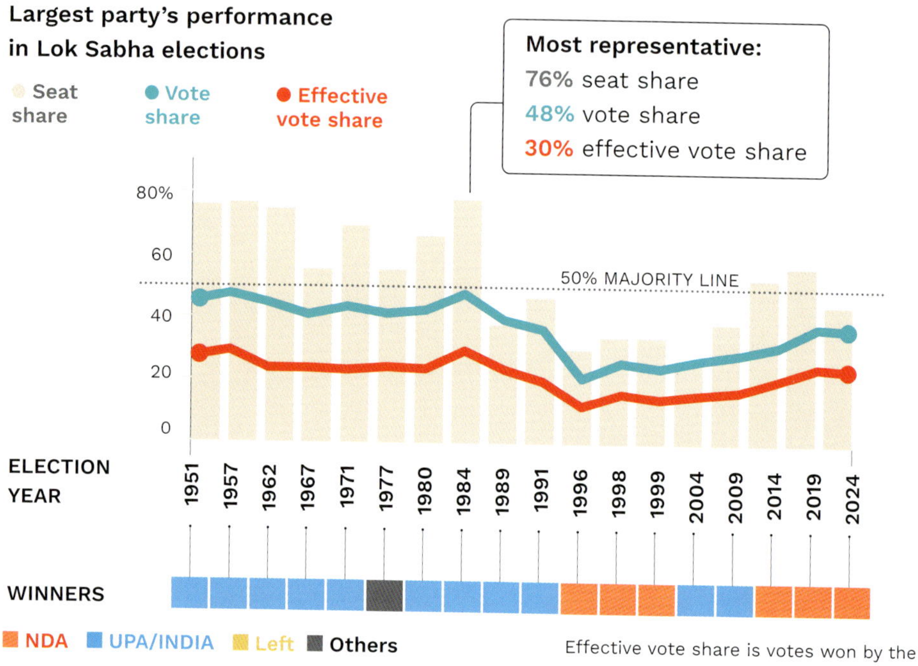

Effective vote share is votes won by the party as % of total voting population

2. BJP'S 10X RISE AND CONGRESS'S 50% FALL

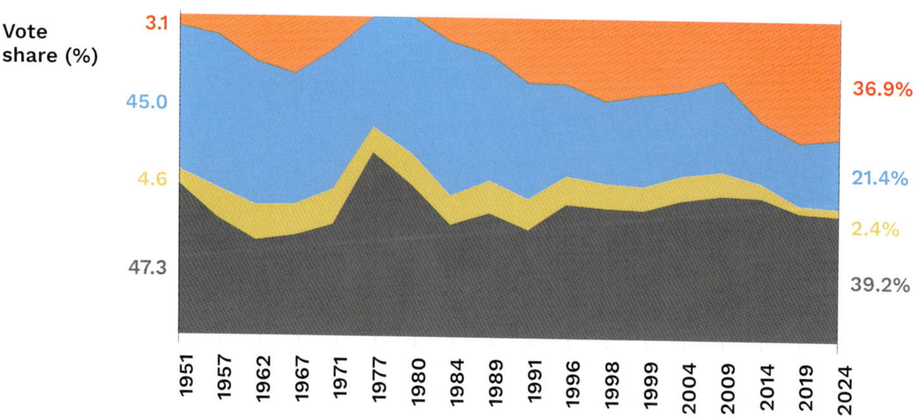

BJP seats and vote share from 1951–1971 are for Jan Sangh. The party did not exist in 1977 and 1980. Left parties include seat and vote share of CPI, CPM, RSP, and AIFB. For 2024, CPI (ML) is included.

11

5 Surprising Truths about How India Elects Its Governments

India's most decisive election came in 1984, when Congress won a record 414 Lok Sabha seats—over 76% of the House. Yet, even then, more than half of the voters did not vote for the party. That's the paradox of Indian democracy: no party has ever won even 50% of the polled votes—let alone a majority of eligible voters.

At typical turnout levels, about a third of Indians don't vote at all. This means that even in its strongest wave, a winning party's effective vote share—counting all eligible voters—was just 30%. Put another way: no Indian government has ever represented 70% of its people.

The coalition era that began in the 1990s changed things—for worse, and for better. Parties with just 20% votes (11.5% effective votes) led governments, but as part of coalitions that together garnered over 40%—making those governments more representative and democratic.

Another way to assess how representative Indian elections are is to look at the combined vote share of the top 2 candidates in each constituency (see chart 4). That share has risen since

1 billion voters

India will cross 100 crore eligible voters in the next Lok Sabha election.

3. WOMEN NOW VOTE MORE THAN MEN

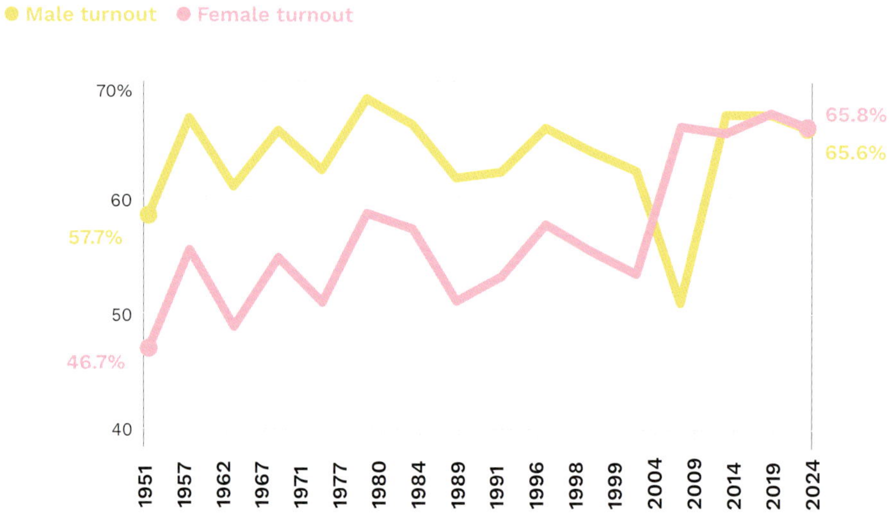

4. ELECTIONS NOW MORE BIPOLAR, AGAIN

Number of seats to first and second party in each election

Vote share of first and second party	1977	1991	1996	1998	1999	2004	2009	2014	2019	2024
Less than 40%	0	0	2	0	0	0	1	0	0	1
40%–60%	1	52	50	6	29	38	62	15	3	10
60%–80%	25	173	225	208	144	146	208	279	76	108
Above 80%	514	309	266	329	370	359	272	249	464	424

Data source: Election Commission, Lokniti, PIB

2014, thanks to more pre-poll alliances—making contests more bipolar. In most seats, the winner and runner-up now together get over 80% of the vote.

Indian democracy is also getting more gender-equal. Since 2000, women's voter turnout has risen by over 10 percentage points. In the last two general elections, more women voted than men.

Even as political divides deepen, voting patterns suggest growing clarity, competitiveness—and, for many, new reasons to believe in the promise of democratic opportunity.

5. THREE LEVELS OF PARTIES

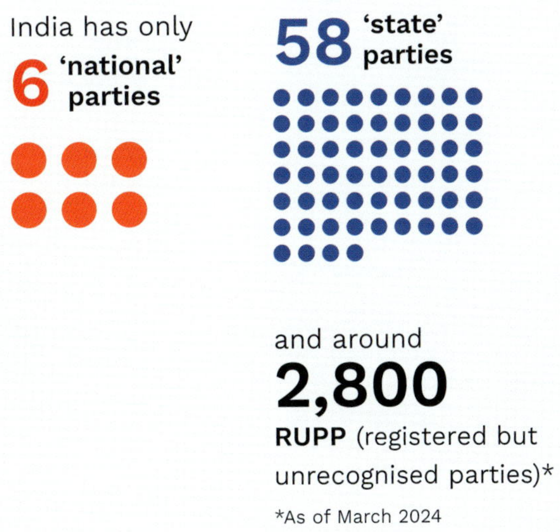

LIVESTOCK POPULATION

Change from 1951 to 2019, in crore

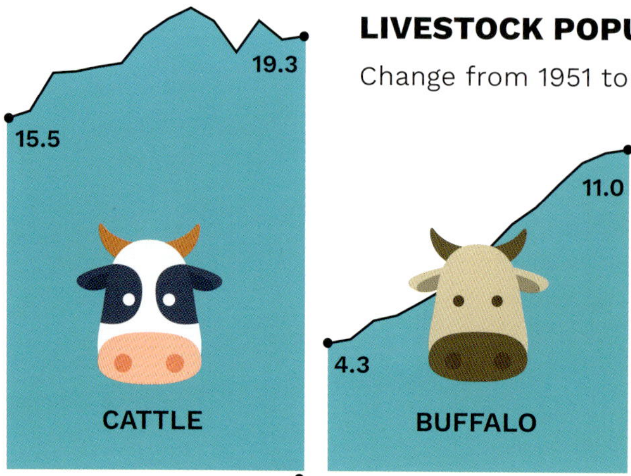

Buffaloes were 28% of the cattle population in 1951. By 2019, they had risen to 57%.

POULTRY

7.4 crore
in 1951

In 1951, there were two cattle for every chicken. By 2019, there were nearly 5 chickens for every cow. A complete reversal in the pecking order.

1 million=10 lakh; 10 million=1 crore; details on Page xv
Data source: Livestock Census, MoFAHD, DAHD, GoI

12

Decline of the Cow, Rise of the Chicken

The charts in this chapter map a quiet revolution in India's domestic animal kingdom—and with it, changing stories of rural life, food, faith, and farming. India's total livestock population has nearly doubled since Independence, but not all animals have prospered equally. Cattle, once the backbone of the rural economy, declined 6% since 1992 after growing by 32% before that. Buffaloes surged ahead, prized for their milk, resilience, and lower social-political-religious baggage. Calves, once 71% of cattle, now make up only 58%—a sign that the decline in cows may continue.

The runaway winner? Chickens. Poultry has exploded more than 12-fold, thanks to urban diet and industrial farming. Goats—low-investment, high-return animals—have quietly tripled since 1951. Pigs grew till the 1990s but are now down 30%. Female livestock now outnumber male—a flip in gender ratios that shows they are reared almost exclusively for milk and not for farming or transport.

And then there are dogs. For the first time, the 2019 livestock Census counted them—but barely. While courts and cities battle over stray dog attacks and rabies, the data remains poor. The Census underway in mid-2025 covers only 3 breeds of dogs, versus 53 for cattle and 39 for goats. Cats don't even make the list. How we eat, pray, farm, and fear now shapes India's animal population—and will continue to shape it for decades to come.

KNOW MORE
Everywhere to see, few to care, nobody to solve • Page 38

SPIRITS, SHAME, AND STATISTICS: INDIA'S ALCOHOL PUZZLE

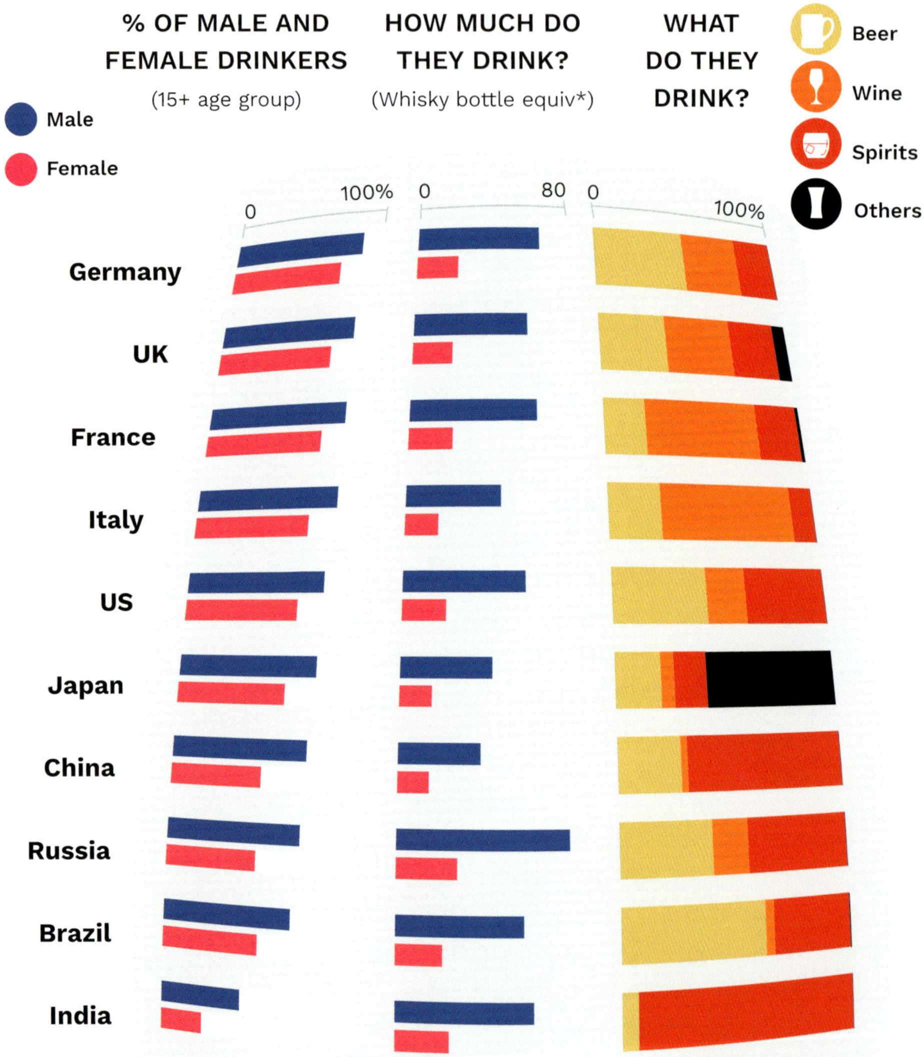

Fewer people in India drink: **41%** men, **21%** women

But they drink a lot: Men- **62** whisky bottle equivalent in a year, women-**24**

92.8% Indians prefer spirits, 7.1% beer

*Whisky bottle equivalent—based on calculation for 750 ml bottle with 42.8% pure alcohol.
What people are drinking is based on recorded consumption; other data is for recorded and estimated consumption.

Data source: WHO's Global Information System on Alcohol and Health. Atul Thakur's estimates for *The Times of India*

13

Fewer Indians 'Drink', but They Drink a Lot and Drink Hard

Call it a dilemma or duplicity, but India's relationship with alcohol is full of contradictions. Far fewer Indians drink compared to most large countries—less than half of men and just a fifth of women. No other country in the top 10 has such a skewed gender ratio. But those who do drink, drink heavily. India's per-drinker alcohol consumption is higher than the US, China, or even Italy. And there's no gender gap in quantity consumed. Worse, over 93% of Indians who drink prefer spirits—typically 3 to 8 times stronger than beer or wine. Roughly, 350 ml of light beer or 145 ml of wine equals 45 ml of spirits in alcohol content.

Why so much, and why so strong? In part, because alcohol is taboo. It's rarely social. For many, drinking happens in secret—men drinking alone, often outside the home. That secrecy, stigma, and shame amplify overuse and misuse. The social cost is high: alcohol abuse has been a major cause of domestic violence and financial ruin in families. Gujarat has had prohibition since its formation, and Bihar joined it in 2016 citing financial and health implications.

The WHO data doesn't include country liquor or local brews—except probably in the case of Japan which has sake in 'others'. Nor does it capture a quiet and recent shift among young Indians away from hard drinks. Perhaps this isn't a contradiction—just another face of India's diversity.

BIGGER BILLS

Alcohol spending nearly tripled in 12 years

Data source: National Accounts Statistics, MoSPI May 2025

KNOW MORE

What shifts in consumption spending shows
● **Page 114**

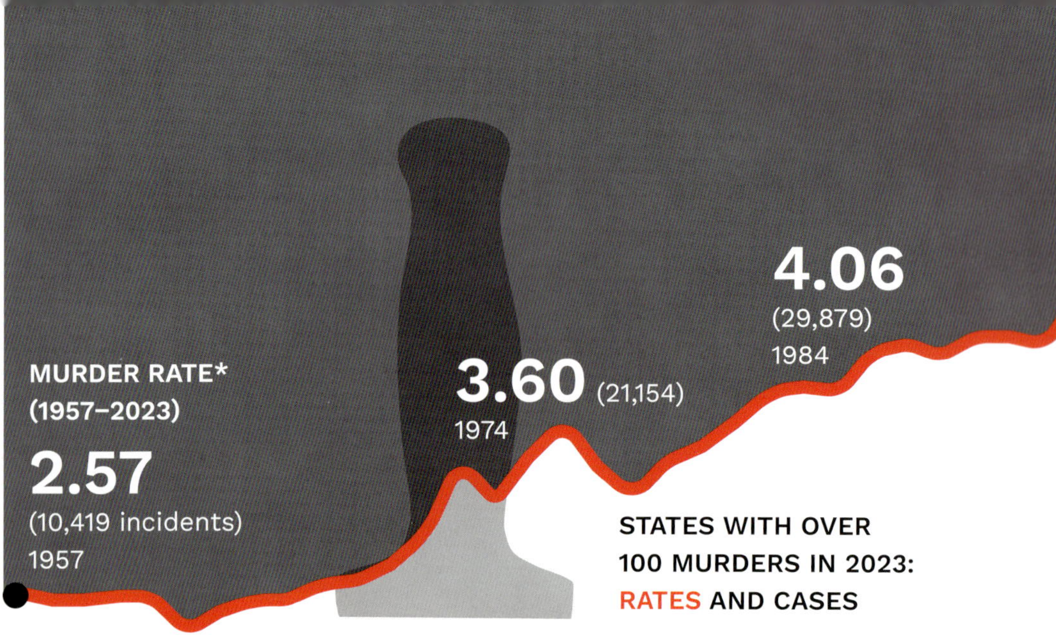

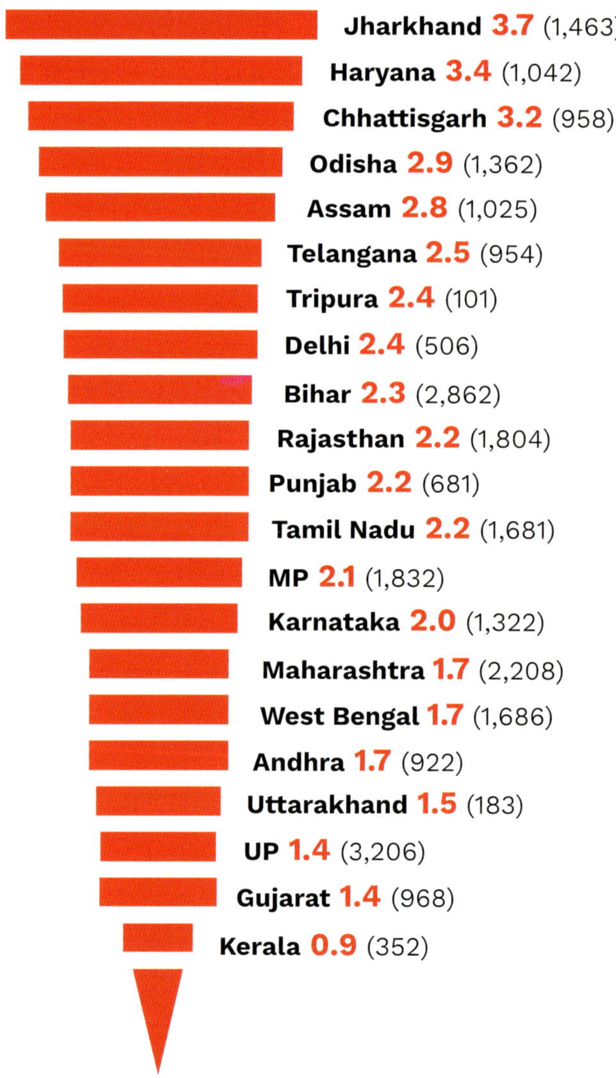

*Number of murders per lakh population

KNOW MORE

India's first trillion-dollar state may not be the one you think ● Page 63

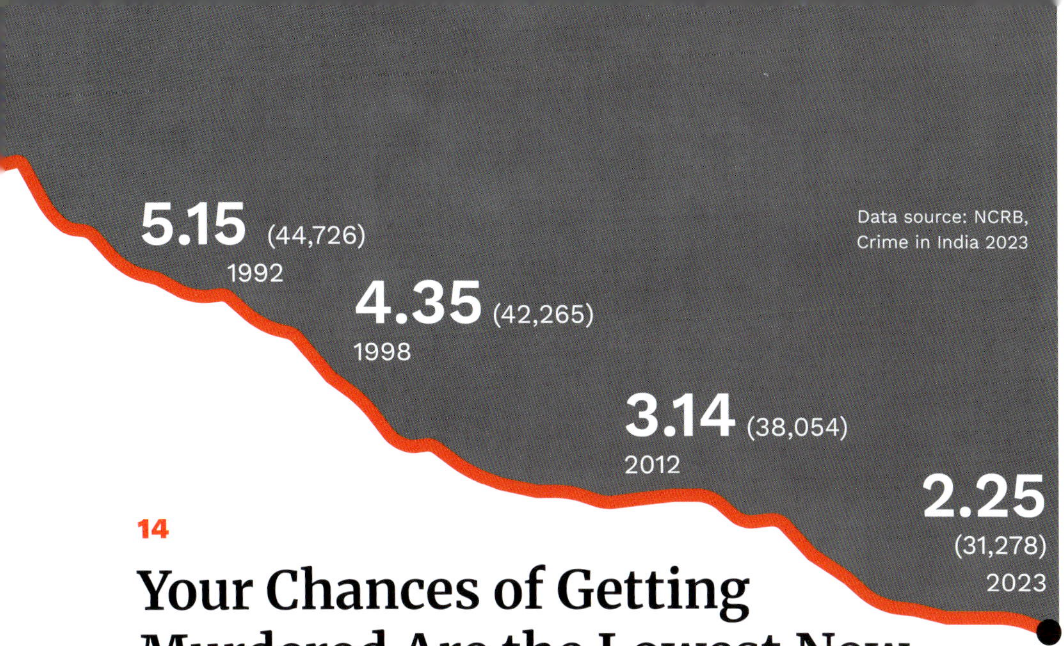

14

Your Chances of Getting Murdered Are the Lowest Now

You don't have to be a news junkie to feel we're living in dangerous times. Graphic reports of murders—over road rage, family feuds, or 'affairs' gone wrong—are everywhere. But the data tells a different story. India's murder rate (number of murders per lakh people) is now the lowest since 1957, as far back as official records go. In 1992, India's murder rate peaked at 5.15. By 2023, it had fallen to less than half: 2.25. In absolute terms, that's 13,500 fewer murders than 30 years ago—an average of 37 lives saved every day.

The national trend, however, hides wide differences between states. Jharkhand had the highest murder rate in 2023—nearly twice the national average and four times higher than Kerala, which had the lowest. Delhi, often called India's 'crime capital', actually ranks better than many states. Even UP—long stereotyped for lawlessness—is now among the least murder-prone. India is not alone. Since the 1990s, murder rates have been falling across much of the world—even as crime reporting has improved. The steady decline defies the usual theories of crime and punishment. The drop has continued despite economic instability, rising inequality in some regions, and a global trend away from capital punishment. If harsher penalties or booming economies were the main deterrents, we wouldn't see this pattern. Something else—perhaps better policing, surveillance, demography, or urbanisation—is at play.

WHAT INDIANS SPEAK MOST, AS FIRST, SECOND, AND THIRD LANGUAGE

(In crore)

	1st	2nd	3rd	Total
Hindi	52.8	13.89	2.43	69.12
English	0.026	8.27	4.56	12.85
Bengali	9.72	0.91	0.11	10.75
Marathi	8.30	1.30	0.30	9.91
Telugu	8.11	1.22	0.12	9.45
Tamil	6.90	0.67	0.09	7.66
Urdu	5.08	1.13	0.11	6.32
Gujarati	5.55	0.40	0.08	6.03
Kannada	4.37	1.36	0.14	5.88
Odia	3.75	0.47	0.04	4.26

English is the second most spoken language, but for **99.97%** of its speakers, it's not their first.

19% of Tamil speakers and 16% of Hindi speakers spoke English.

Only top 10 spoken languages shown; all languages, except English, have multiple dialects.

1 crore= 10 million.
Data source: Census 2011, Language Report released in 2018

15

Nobody's Mother Tongue, Everybody's Language

It is India's oldest, quietest, largest—and fastest-growing—import. Except that it isn't an import anymore. English may have arrived with colonial rule, but it now belongs to India as much as cricket does. The country is home to the world's second-largest population of English speakers, and is on track to become the largest in under a decade.

That this can happen in a country with 2,843 officially recorded dialects is nothing short of a linguistic miracle. According to the 2011 Census—whose detailed language data was released only in 2018—English was the second most spoken language in India, ahead of Bengali. More than 99% of its users spoke it as a second or third language—not their first. Nearly 2 crore more Indians knew English than Bengali in 2011. That gap has likely doubled since. Tamil speakers made up the largest group of those who also knew English (19%), followed by Hindi speakers. English is India's most-popular third language by a wide margin. And in 2011, it ranked just behind Hindi as the second language—a position it has likely tied or even overtaken by now.

In a country where language is identity, it is remarkable that a 'foreign' tongue is quietly winning over more minds and mouths than any other local language. It has done so by becoming a practical passport to jobs, migration, digital access, and social mobility. And in some form, English has done this in much of the world.

KNOW MORE

India's largest, and least empowered, democracy
• Page 22

FREQUENCY OF 11 MAJOR CRIMES

CASES IN 2023

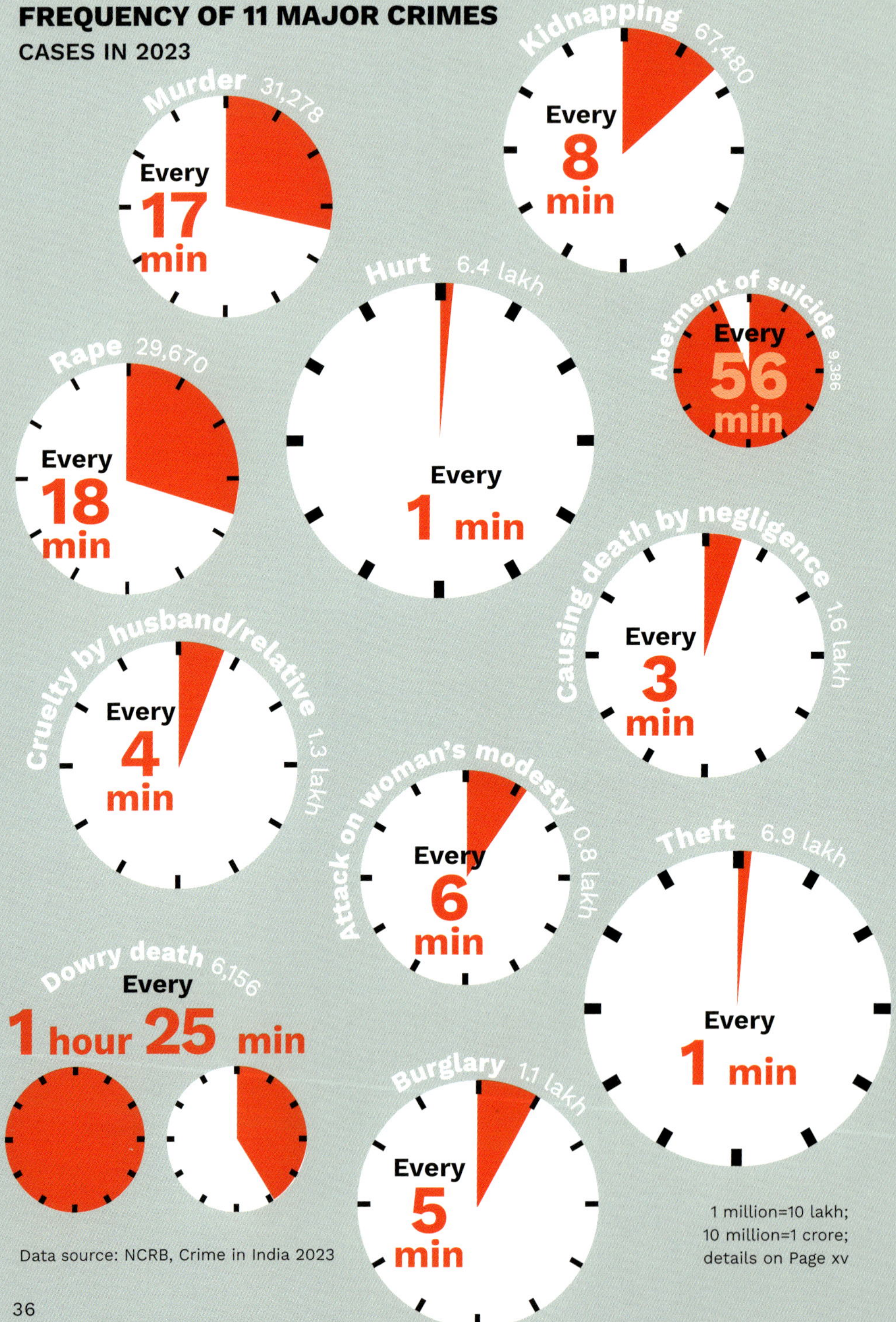

1 million=10 lakh;
10 million=1 crore;
details on Page xv

Data source: NCRB, Crime in India 2023

16

How Fast Does India's Crime Clock Tick?

In 2023, India recorded over 62 lakh crimes, the latest year with official data. About 61% were serious crimes under the Indian Penal Code (IPC); the rest fell under Special and Local Laws (SLL). That's about 7 IPC crimes and 5 SLL crimes every minute. There are 191 types of cognisable crimes—those where police can arrest without a prior warrant and can begin investigations without permission from a magistrate. Some are shockingly frequent: one rape every 18 minutes, one murder every 17 minutes, one incident of cruelty by a husband or his family every 4 minutes. Less visible but equally widespread are the 12 legal categories of 'hurt', ranging from simple assault (over 5 lakh cases) to acid attacks (207). The eleven clocks in this chapter show how often major crimes occur in India. In July 2024, the IPC was replaced by the Bharatiya Nyaya Sanhita (BNS). However, the most recent national crime data available is for 2023.

Between 2020 and 2023, total reported crimes fell by 13%. But that hides wide state-wise and crime-wise variation. Murder rates have dropped (Page 32), while crimes against women and road accident deaths have risen. These are only reported crimes. In 2023, police received 1.8 crore complaints, but only 34% (62 lakh) were registered as cases. Better policing often improves reporting—creating the illusion of rising crime, when what's rising may be accountability. For example, the US reported 1.4 crore crimes in 2023—more than twice the cases registered in India, despite having just 25% of India's population.

Police received **1.8 crore complaints** in 2023, of which **38 lakh cases** were registered under the Indian Penal Code (IPC)

24 lakh cases of cognisable crimes were registered under Special and Local Laws (SLL)

KNOW MORE

The 1990s was India's most murderous decade • Page 32

DATA DIVERSITY OR DATA DILUTION?

Rabies and snakebite estimates differ wildly.

Stray cattle (2019)

50 lakh

Stray dogs

1.5 crore

(Livestock Census, 2019)

DOG BITES

(2024)

37.2 lakh

5 lakh

ANIMAL BITES

(Other than dog, including monkey; 2024)

RABIES DEATHS EVERY YEAR

18,000-20,000

(WHO)

5,726

(ICMR, 2023)

180

(Parliament Q&A)

Stray cats

80 lakh

SNAKE BITES

50 lakh

(WHO)

10,144

(NCRB, 2023)

69%

of dogs and cats are homeless

SNAKE BITE DEATHS

10,118

(NCRB, 2023)

17

Everywhere to See, Few to Care, Nobody to Solve

In very few countries do people live as close to their animals as in India. Cows in traffic, dogs at chai stalls, monkeys on balconies, snakes in the fields, pigeons on every ledge. Much of this coexistence is affectionate and almost invisible. The toll is not.

India accounts for roughly a third of the world's rabies deaths. The WHO estimates 18,000–20,000 deaths a year; one ICMR study suggests a few thousand. At the time of publication of this book, some aspects of stray dog management were sub judice before the Supreme Court of India.

Snakebites kill more people in India than anywhere else, yet even those numbers are stitched together from hospital records that miss those who never make it to a ward. Stray dogs are now among the leading causes of animal-related road accidents in big cities. For monkeys, pigeons, and feral cattle, the data gaps are even wider than the potholes they share with us.

Faith and fear walk in step. The same lane that feeds a cow or a pack of dogs may erupt in fury after a bite, a fall, or a child mauled. Laws protect animals (rightly so); politics protects sentiment; municipal capacity struggles to protect either species.

In the end, a 'stray' is a failure twice over—of planning for people, and of caring for animals. The streets are simply where both show up.

150%

rise in pigeon density

(2000-2023)

Data source: Livestock Census 2019, Accidental Deaths and Suicides in India 2023, National Rabies Control Programme, State of Pet Homelessness Project, World Health Organization

HOW LIFE EXPECTANCY CHANGES WITH AGE

HOW MANY YEARS THE AVERAGE INDIAN CAN EXPECT TO LIVE AT AGE:

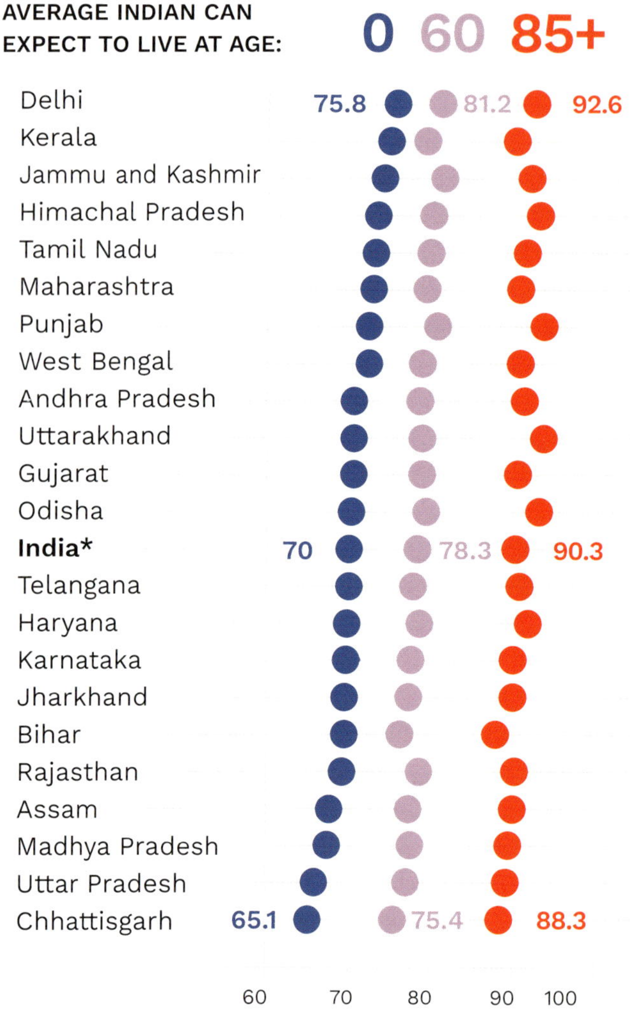

State	Difference between life expectancy at 0 and at 85 (no. of years)
Delhi	16.8
Kerala	15.3
Jammu and Kashmir	17.6
Himachal Pradesh	19.6
Tamil Nadu	18.4
Maharashtra	17.7
Punjab	21.1
West Bengal	18.5
Andhra Pradesh	20.7
Uttarakhand	22.9
Gujarat	19.9
Odisha	22.8
India*	**20.3**
Telangana	20.7
Haryana	21.8
Karnataka	20.2
Jharkhand	20.4
Bihar	18.4
Rajasthan	20.8
Assam	22.1
Madhya Pradesh	22.0
Uttar Pradesh	23.1
Chhattisgarh	23.2

States with high infant mortality have the longest gap between life expectancy at birth and at 85.

Data source: SRS-based abridged life tables 2016–20, released October 2022. Updates for life expectancy after 2011 Census available only for 23 states

HEALTHY LIFE EXPECTANCY vs LIFE EXPECTANCY

18

Two Lifetimes in One: How Long India Now Lives

An average urban woman in Himachal Pradesh now lives 81 years. If she reaches 85, she's likely to live till 96.5—the highest life expectancy currently recorded in India across all categories. In 75 years, India has doubled its life expectancy, turning one lifetime into two. But where you live, your gender, and whether you're urban or rural still decides how long that second life lasts.

States like Kerala, Delhi, and Himachal Pradesh consistently lead on life expectancy across all age brackets. In contrast, Uttar Pradesh and Chhattisgarh start low at birth, mostly due to high infant mortality, but gain more years later. Bihar trails throughout. Urban Indians live longer than rural Indians almost everywhere—except in Kerala, where the rural edge remains. One of the most striking shifts since Independence is gendered: except in Bihar and Jharkhand, women now outlive men in every Indian state. This wasn't true till a few decades ago when men lived longer. The reversal is both a medical achievement and a quiet social revolution.

This lengthening of life is one of India's less appreciated triumphs. The only decade when life expectancy fell was during World War I. But living longer doesn't always mean living well. India's 'healthy' life expectancy is 10 years shorter than its total—meaning millions spend their final decade in poor health, or without support. To truly celebrate India's gains in longevity, we must focus not just on adding years to life, but adding life to those years.

LIFE EXPECTANCY AT BIRTH SINCE 1901

KNOW MORE

What kills Indians the most • Page 150

CASTE IDENTIFICATION ACROSS RELIGIONS

% of Indians who identify as

- Brahmin
- Other general category
- Scheduled Caste
- Scheduled Tribe
- Other backward class

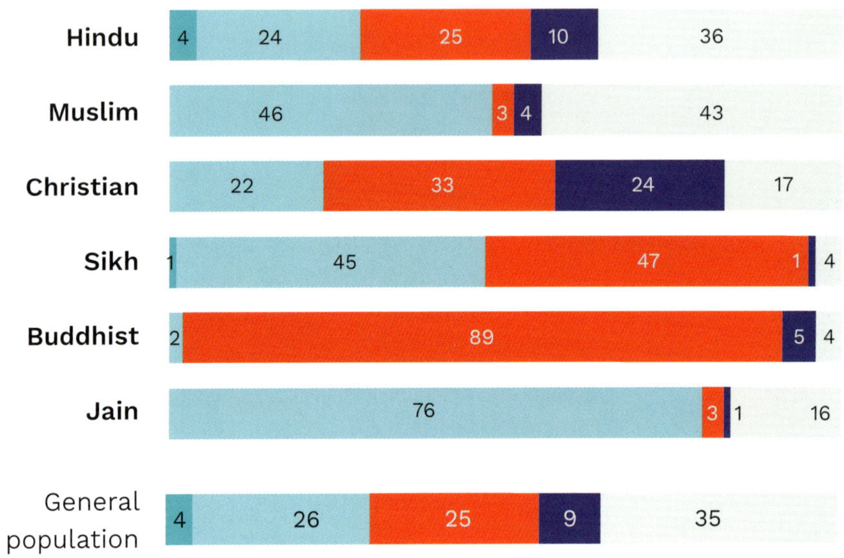

Caste identification across education level (%)

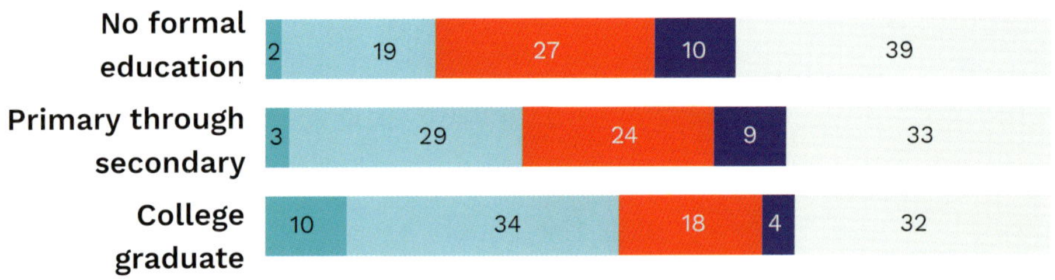

In the 2011 Census, only Hindus, Sikhs, and Buddhists could be enumerated as members of Scheduled Castes, while Scheduled Tribes could include followers of all religions. General category and Other backward classes were not measured in the Census.

Data source: Pew Research Center study conducted between November 2019 and March 2020, among adults in India.

19

Caste and Religion: What the Data Really Shows

They've long been the source of pride, prejudice, politics—and misinformation. Few forces have shaped Indian society as profoundly as caste and religion.

Caste, despite being banned by law and diluted by progress, remains deeply embedded in Indian society. It has defied time (centuries, if not millennia), geography, laws, and even religion—non-Hindus also identify with Hindu caste categories. That means they continue to either practise or face caste identity (if not divisions) even after conversion or being born to other religions. Yet, data on caste is scarce, contested, and politically sensitive. The 2019–20 Pew Research Centre survey found 98% of Buddhists, 74% of Christians, and 50% of Muslims identified as SC/ST/OBC—compared to 71% of Hindus. Caste-based inequality still shows up in access to higher education, with forward castes dominating college graduate numbers.

Religion data is clearer, but just as debated. The Hindu share of population declined from 84% in 1951 to an estimated 79% in 2025. The Muslim share rose from under 10% to about 15%. This sparks concern in some quarters. The real question, however, is not whether the share of Muslims grew, but why? Did it have anything to do with religion? If yes, to what extent?

The population share change is rooted in differences in fertility rates. In 2021, Muslim

KNOW MORE

India abroad: World's most powerful migrants • Page 56

INDIA'S RELIGIOUS COMPOSITION OVER 75 YEARS

Year	**Population** (crore)
1951	**36.1**
1961	**43.9**
1971	**54.8**
1981	**68.3**
1991	**84.6**
2001	**102.9**
2011	**121.1**
2025	**146.4**

Share of religion in population (%)

Data source: Census reports, UN projections and author's estimates done for *The Times of India,* June 2022

fertility (2.3) was higher than Hindu fertility (1.9), but the gap has been narrowing—from 1.1 in 1992 to 0.42 in 2021 and is estimated to converge in 2030. The higher rate isn't religious doctrine, but differences in education, income, and access to family planning. In a less educated, less prosperous Bihar, Muslim fertility in 2021 was 3.6; in richer, more educated Jammu and Kashmir, it was 1.45. According to a study* by the Mumbai-based International Institute for Population Sciences, religion accounts for 15% of fertility preference. Education (35%), and economic status (18%) matter more.

As India grows more literate and prosperous, demographic differences are shrinking. Like so much else in this book, the surprise isn't how divided India is—it's how much it is changing.

	1951	2025
Hinduism	**84.1**	**78.8**
Islam	**9.8**	**15.2**
Christianity	**2.3**	**1.9**
Sikhism	**1.8**	**1.64**
Buddhism	**0.7**	**0.65**
Jainism	**0.5**	**0.35**
Zoroastrianism	**0.1**	**<0.1**
Others/ Religion not specified	**0.4**	**1.45**

FERTILITY RATES, BY RELIGION

Fertility has not only been falling across religions, but it will also continue to slide given the gap between actual and wanted fertility in 2021.

	2005–06	2019–21	WANTED FERTILITY 2019–21
Hindu	**2.65**	**1.94**	**1.6**
Muslim	**3.09**	**2.36**	**1.8**
Christian	**2.35**	**1.88**	**1.7**
Sikh	**1.96**	**1.61**	**1.4**
Buddhist	**1.96**	**1.39**	**1.2**
Jain	**2.02**	**1.60**	**1.5**
Others	**2.65**	**2.15**	**1.7**

Data source: NFHS

FACTORS CONTRIBUTING TO FERTILITY CHANGE 1998–2021

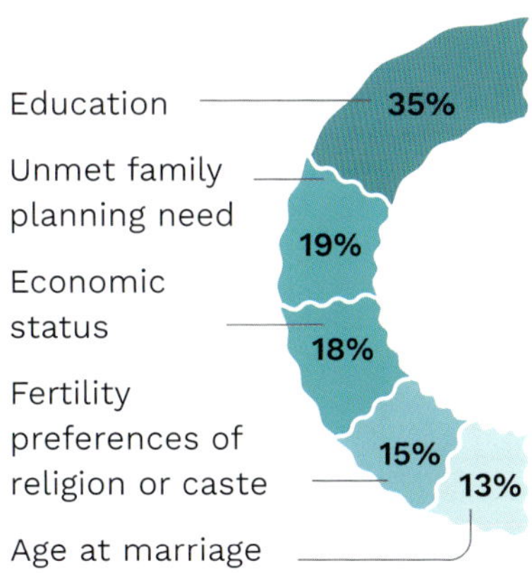

*'Rapid Convergence of Fertility Across all Socio-Religious Groups in India', Srinivas Goli and Shubhra Kriti, International Institute for Population Science, July 2024

INDIA'S MOST OVERBURDENED MINORITY

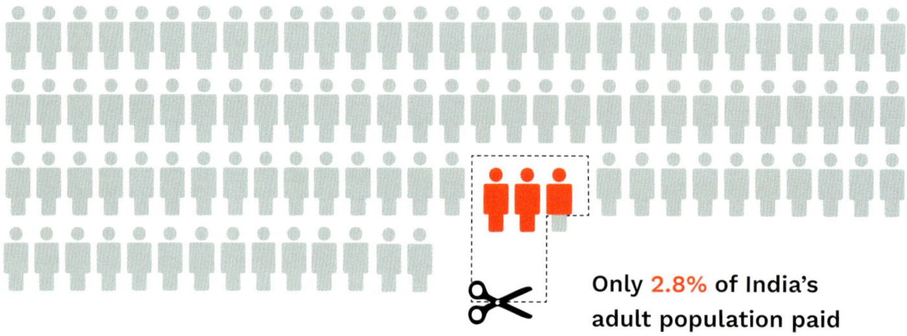

Only 2.8% of India's adult population paid income tax in 2024*

The number is likely to fall in 2025.

In 2020–21, the taxpayer count fell by 47% as 1.7 crore went out of the tax net.

No. of taxpayers could fall steeply because tax-free income was raised from ₹7 lakh to ₹12 lakh a year in the February 2025 budget.

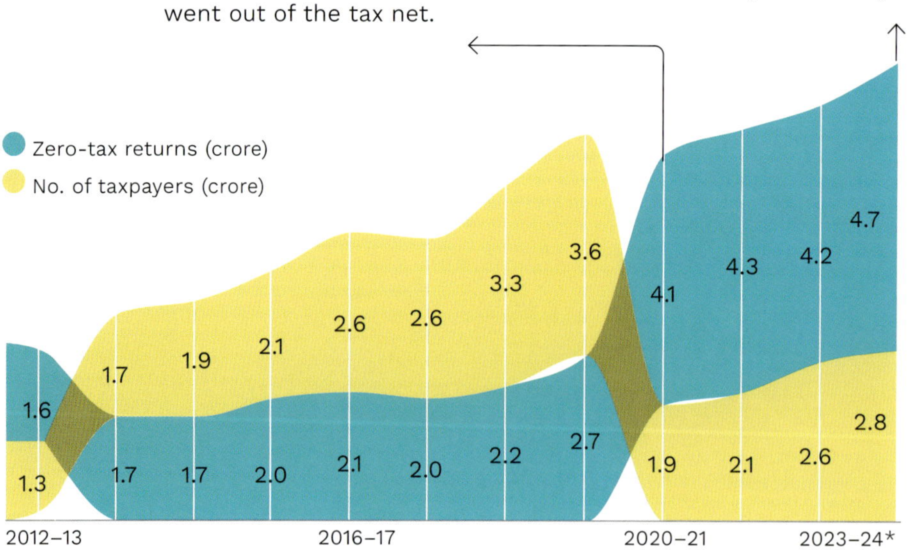

*Assessment year 2023–24 is financial year 2024–25
Data source: incometaxindia.gov.in

1 million=10 lakh; 10 million=1 crore; details on Page xv

20

Why Only 3% Adult Indians Pay Income Tax

In India, paying income tax is a rare distinction—less than 3% adults paid in 2024 and the number will fall in 2025. It is a forced charity, if not a punishment. Public education and healthcare, two fundamental tax-funded services, have vanished from the lives of most urban middle class. They pay twice: once in taxes, and again for private schooling, hospitals, clean water, breathable air, and private security. Most income taxpayers are not government employees and get no pension, unemployment cover, or post-retirement support.

There are countries with higher income tax rates than India. But taxpayers in those countries have access to services that have either never existed or have ceased to exist in India. Then there's the penalty for honesty. Salaried individuals, whose income is fully disclosed and taxed at source, end up paying more than self-employed professionals who can adjust income or expenses. In 2019, the finance minister disclosed that the average salaried taxpayer paid three times more income tax than the average non-salaried taxpayer.

Why is this small group squeezed

WHY INCOME TAXPAYERS HAVE NO POLITICAL VOICE

Share of voters who file tax returns or pay taxes

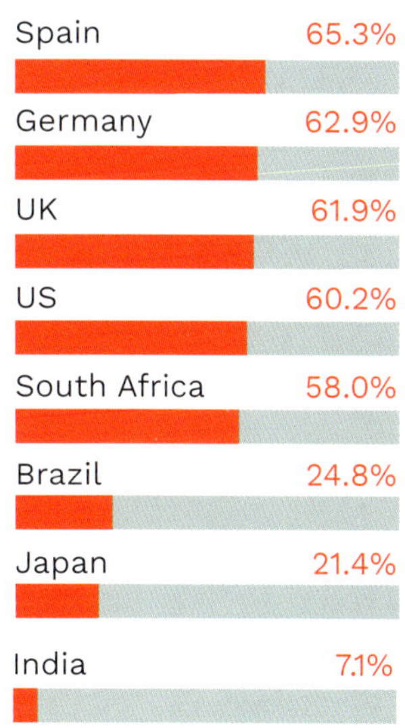

7.1% is the count of tax return filers; tax payers are 2.8%

1.1% OF TAXPAYERS—WHICH IS 0.03% OF ADULT INDIANS—PAID 34% OF TAX

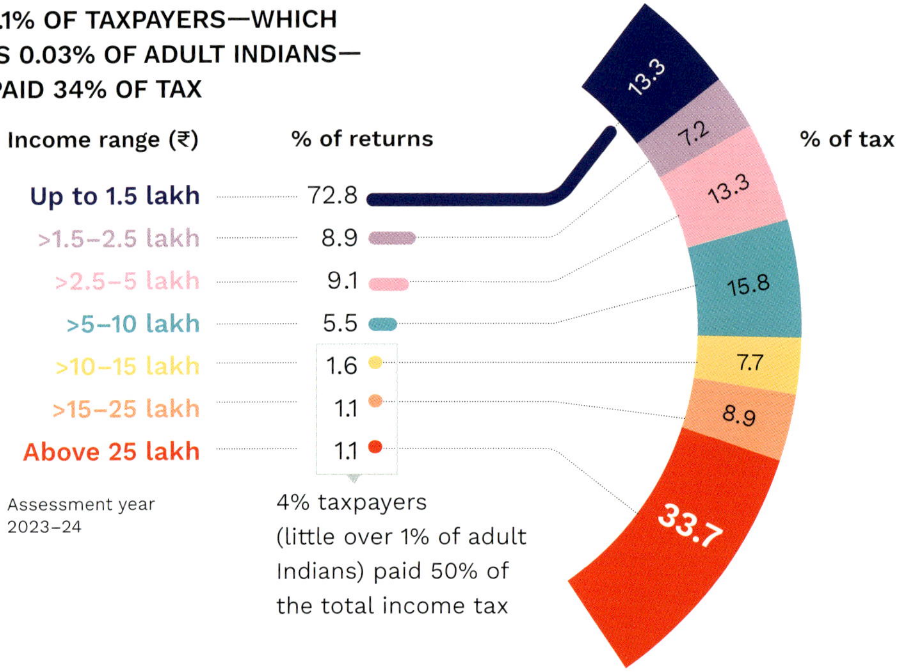

PAID ONCE, PAID TWICE, PAID THRICE...

After paying income tax and cess+surcharge, what a section of taxpayers pays for public goods that should be 100% tax-funded

	Clean air	**Clean water**	**Uninterrupted power**	**Home security**
CUMULATIVE	₹8,000 cr	₹15,000 cr	₹20,000 cr	
ANNUAL RECURRING	₹500 cr	₹1,000 cr	₹1,000 cr	₹10,000 cr
ASSUMPTION	40 lakh purifiers sold at an average price ₹20,000	1.5 crore water purifiers sold at an average price ₹10,000	2 crore back-up units sold at an average price of ₹10,000	2 crore houses paying ₹5,000 a year for security

TOTAL CUMULATIVE: **₹43,000 cr** TOTAL RECURRING: **₹12,500 cr**

Estimates are only for household purchases. Office installations cost not considered so hard? Because too many powerful and profitable groups are exempt. Farmers, even the richest, pay no tax. In 2012, over 8 lakh individuals claimed crores in agricultural income and paid zero tax. In 2014–15, a company claimed ₹215 crore income—all tax-free as 'agriculture' earnings. Professions like law, coaching, and medicine are exempt from GST. MPs enjoy tax-free perks: dozens of flights a year with companion, limitless first-class train travel, free healthcare, rent-free housing, and a ₹20,000 monthly pension. And yes, they also set their own salaries.

Why is this neglect institutionalised? Because income taxpayers form just 2% of voters. They lack political clout. In contrast, rich farmers face no tax and hold major electoral power. This is why, even after nearly ending extreme poverty, 57% of the population (83 crore) gets free food. It's also why states like Karnataka and Maharashtra launch generous cash schemes—only to find many beneficiaries are fake. Income taxpayers can only watch in frustration and see up to 40% of their income (at peak rate) deducted in taxes. Though surcharge on peak rate has recently been cut, the salaried class has to now pay taxes on provident fund contributions and the scope of capital gains tax has been widened.

One last question: if so few pay income tax, is government revenue from it stagnating? The answer on Page 99 may surprise you.

KNOW MORE

A ₹1 lakh crore economy Indians don't know about
• Page 61

BJP RULES PARLIAMENT, BUT WHO RULES THE STATES?

Party position in Lok Sabha and state assembly—
national parties and combined Left

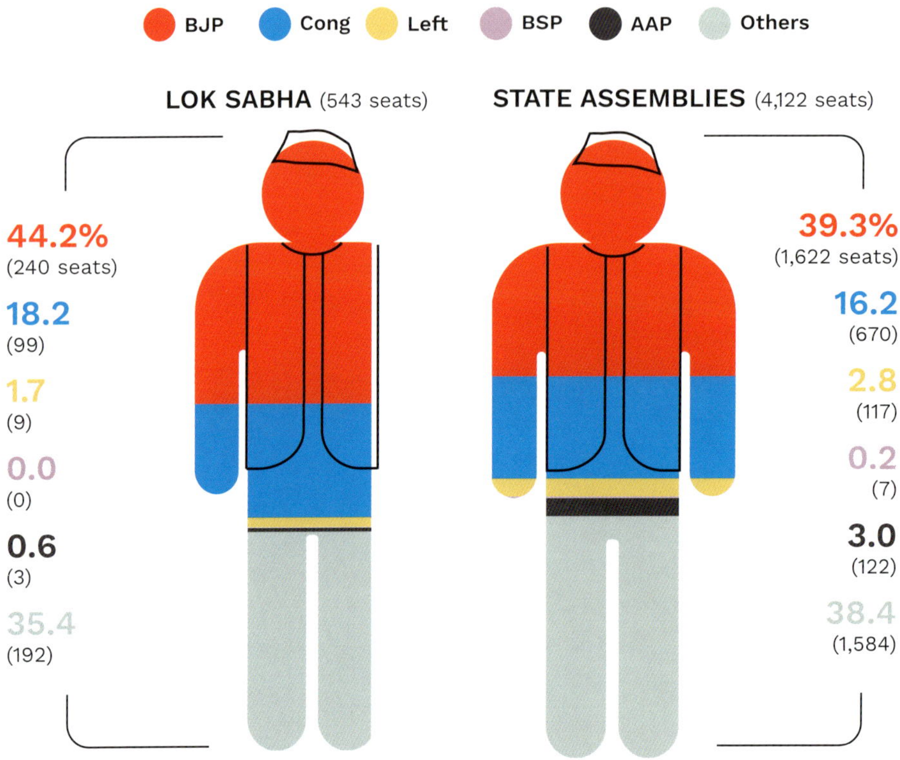

Only national parties—as recognised by the Election Commission—are shown individually.
India has only six national parties. Left includes CPM, CPI, CPI-ML, Forward Bloc, and RSP
Data source: Election Commission (updated till June 2025)

STATE/UTS GOVERNED BY

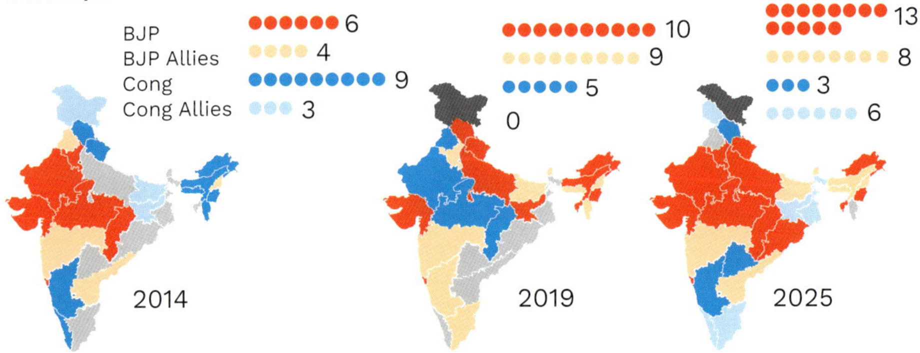

21

What Happens When You Add up Every MLA in India?

You think you know who runs India? Most of us follow who wins Parliament and who runs our own state. But very few stop to ask: which party holds the most power across India's 4,000+ elected MLAs? The answer reveals a deeper political truth. As of June 2025, India had 4,122* elected MLAs spread across 31 full states and 2 half-states (Delhi and Puducherry). When you tally these alongside Lok Sabha MPs, BJP clearly dominates: 44% of MPs and nearly 40% of MLAs are from the party. Since mid-2023, BJP's MLA share has risen by 7 percentage points, while Congress has slipped by 3—BJP has partly made up for the ground it lost in Lok Sabha polls.

But that's only half the story. 'Others'—regional parties and the Left—make up 38.4% of MLAs and continue to wield power in the states. Parties like TMC (215), DMK (133), and AAP (122) have big MLA counts and run governments in states. From Stalin's federalism and language advocacy to Naidu's concern on fertility and tax devolution, it's these parties that are voicing issues national parties often sidestep. Several of India's recent grassroots movements—farm law amendments or the Citizenship (Amendment) Act—were led by regional parties that filled the vacuum left by the Congress's decline.

Why does this broader MLA map matter? Because state legislatures influence not just policies and delivery but also national institutions—Rajya Sabha, Presidential elections, and political discourse itself. In a country where elections at different levels happen every few months, the real political story is not just who wins Parliament, but who's shaping India, state by state.

KNOW MORE

India's silent sacrifice for global peace
• Page 132

*MLA seats keep falling vacant for a variety of reasons and bypolls happen periodically to fill them

22

When Women Lead, Everything Changes

1. FROM BEING WAY BEHIND MEN TO OUTPACING THEM IN SCHOOLS...

Gross enrolment ratio in primary education

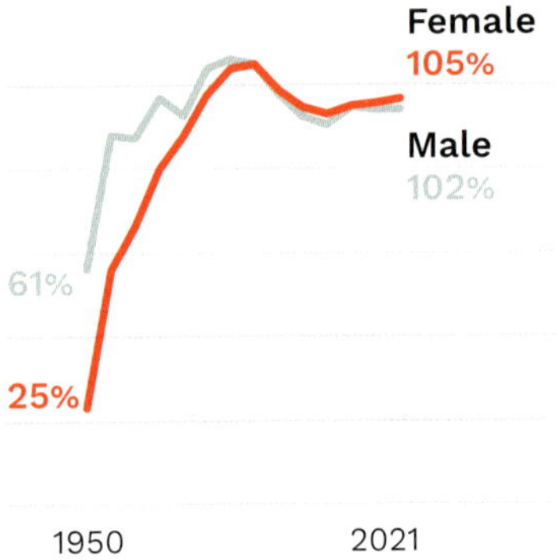

2. AND IN SOME HIGHER EDUCATION STREAMS

Female undergraduate enrolment as % of men

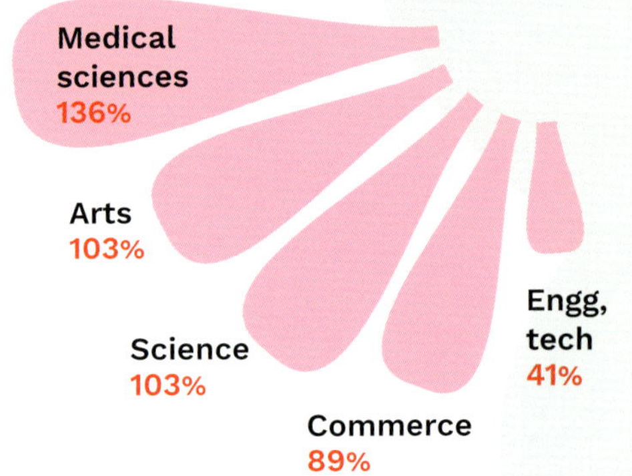

3. WHICH HAS GIVEN AGENCY TO WOMEN OVER DECISIONS LIKE WHETHER TO HAVE A CHILD...

Total fertility rate by level of education of the mother, 2020

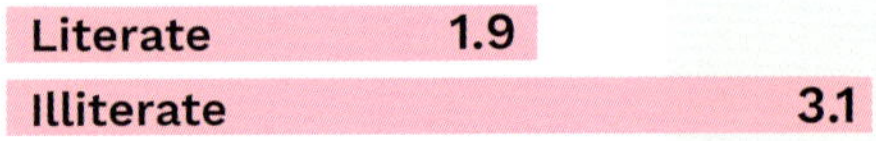

Data source: Women and Men in India, 2024, All India Survey on Higher Education, DataforIndia.com, SRS statistical report, 2022, NFHS3, 4 and 5

Somewhere around 2010, a quiet revolution took place—India's girls began to out-enrol boys in primary school. Not just in cities, but in rural India too. This milestone, decades in the making, is now showing its ripple effects: better child health, smaller families, smarter household decisions.

For too long, India's economic gains—from tech to sports—were disproportionately cornered by men. These charts suggest that is

Amartya Sen, in his book *Development as Freedom*, says the **effect of female literacy on child mortality is much larger than of male literacy or poverty reduction**.

4. AND WHEN TO HAVE A CHILD...

How age-specific fertility rates changed from 2010–12 to 2020–22

Annual fertility rate per 1,000 women in different age groups

5. AND OTHER KEY FAMILY DECISIONS...

Women participation in household decision-making*

*1) Health care for self
2) Major household purchases
3) Visits to her family or relatives

2005–06 data is rough estimate of more than 3 decisions

6. IT HAS ALSO IMPROVED INFANT AND MATERNAL HEALTH AND SURVIVAL

Infant mortality rate
(Deaths of children under the age of 1 for every 1,000 live births)

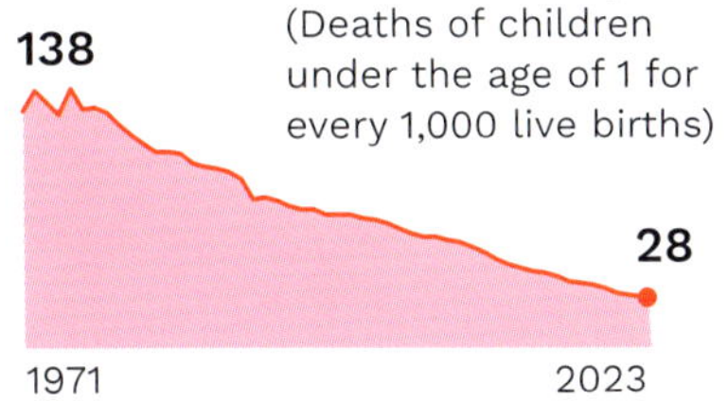

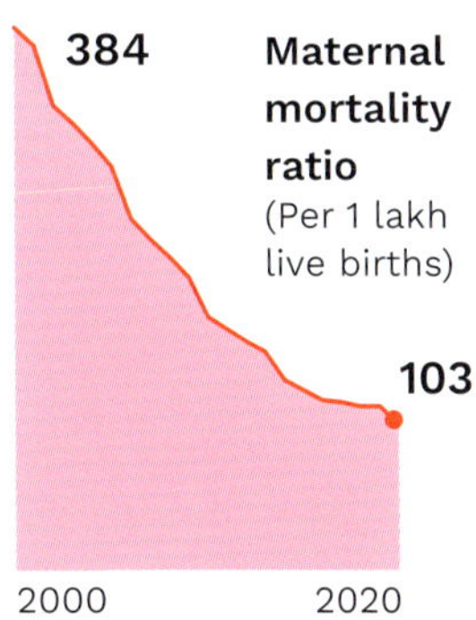

Maternal mortality ratio
(Per 1 lakh live births)

steadily changing. And the shift is showing up not just in homes, but at the ballot box. Election campaigns now revolve around women—with promises, policies, and freebies aimed squarely at them. It's not charity, it's arithmetic: in the 2024 Lok Sabha polls, women voted in greater numbers than men (Page 26). They also live longer (Page 41)—so they are voters for longer.

The rising agency of Indian women is no longer just a hope. It is visible. And it is rewriting India's future.

KNOW MORE

The justice gap in crime against women
● Page 18

23

Are SRK's and Rajini's Future Heroines Even Born Yet?

Shah Rukh Khan

Debut TV: *Fauji*, 1988; Age: 22
At that time some of his heroines were:

Katrina Kaif (*Jab Tak Hai Jaan*)	**5 years old**
Deepika Padukone (*Om Shanti Om*)	**2 years old**
Anushka Sharma (*Rab Ne Bana Di Jodi*)	**Born in May 1988**

Rajinikanth

Debut: *Apoorva Raagangal*, 1975; Age: 24. At that time some of his heroines were:

Aishwarya Rai (*Enthiran/Robot*)	**1 year old**
Deepika Padukone (*Kochadaiiyaan*)	**Born 11 years later**
Sonakshi Sinha (*Lingaa*)	**Born 12 years later**

Films mentioned are first appearance together

In the world of cinema, time stands still—at least for one gender.

Consider the data. When Shah Rukh Khan debuted in Bollywood in 1992 (TV debut 1988), his future co-star Deepika Padukone was six years old. Aamir Khan debuted in 1988, the same year his *PK* heroine Anushka Sharma was born. It's the same story for Rajinikanth, whose heroines have remained in their 20s or 30s while he crossed 70. In Hollywood, Leonardo DiCaprio's dating history famously flatlines, rarely crossing the 25-year mark even as he approaches 50.

This isn't just a celebrity quirk. As research by Christian Rudder* from millions of dating profiles reveals, it's a near-universal pattern. While women prefer partners near their own age, men of all ages—from 20 to 50—rate women in their early 20s as most attractive.

FOREVER YOUNG HEROINES, FOREVER YOUNG MEN'S PREFERENCES

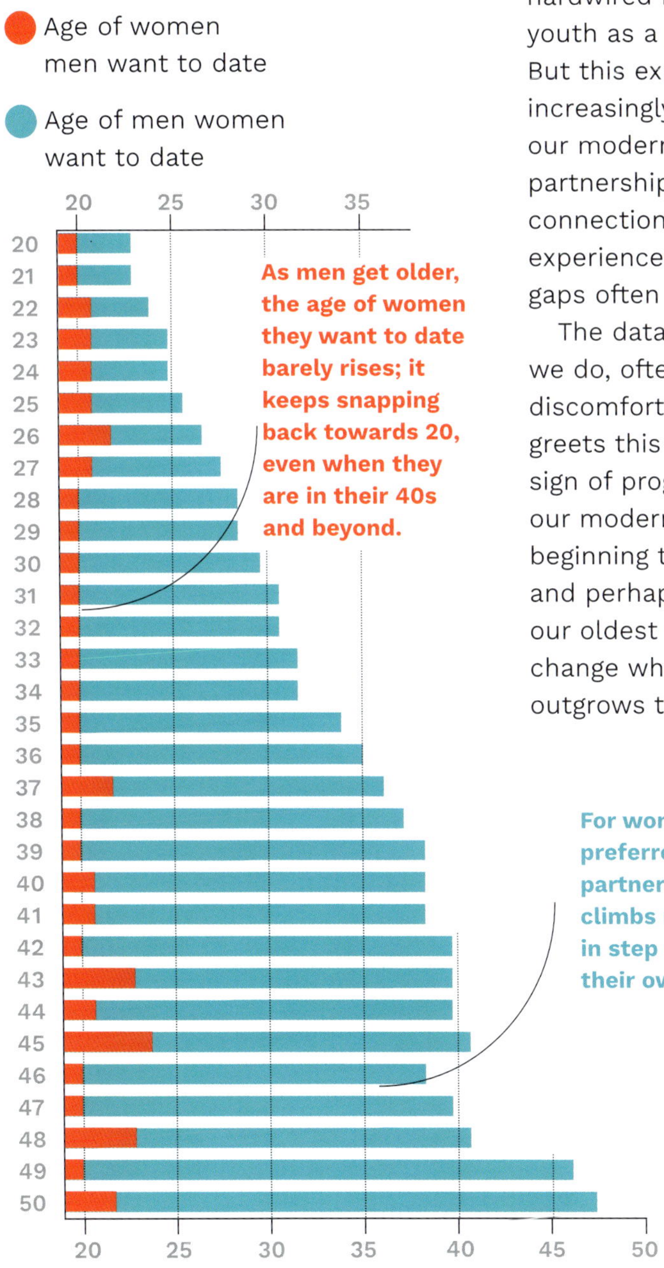

Why? One debatable hypothesis points to evolutionary biology: a hardwired male drive to seek youth as a proxy for fertility. But this explanation feels increasingly at odds with our modern world. We value partnership, intellectual connection, and shared life experiences—things that age gaps often dilute.

The data shows us what we do, often to our own discomfort. The outrage that greets this news is perhaps a sign of progress—a signal that our modern values are finally beginning to wrestle with, and perhaps one day override, our oldest instincts. Norms change when discomfort outgrows tradition.

*Rudder's book *Dataclysm: Who We Are—When We Think No One's Looking* analysed anonymised data of tens of million dating site users.

HOW INDIAN DIASPORA CONQUERED THE WORLD

3.4 crore overseas Indians reside in 200+ countries or territories across the globle

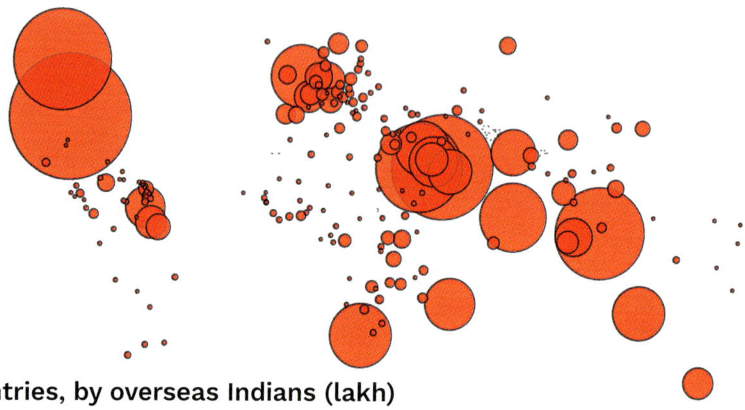

Top 5 countries, by overseas Indians (lakh)

US	56.9
UAE	39.0
Canada	36.1
Malaysia	29.4
Saudi Arabia	27.5

The separate worlds of NRIs and PIOS

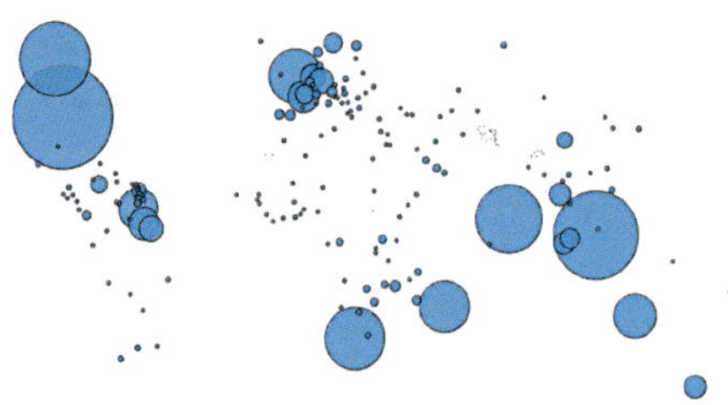

Top 5 countries, by no. of NRIs (lakh)

UAE	38.9
Saudi Arabia	27.5
US	19.2
Canada	17.5
Kuwait	10.1

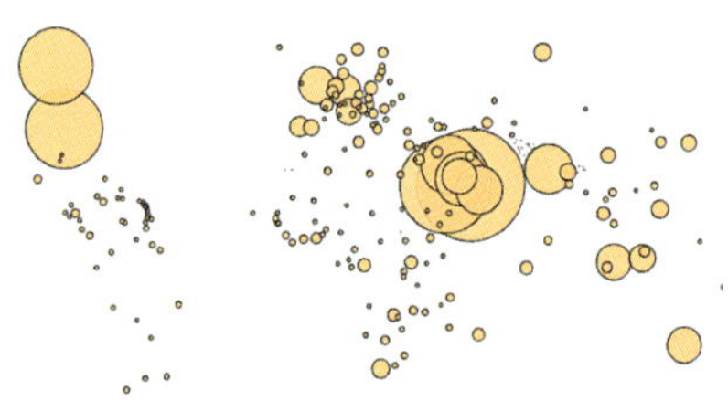

Top 5, by no. of PIOs (lakh)

US	37.8
Malaysia	27.5
Canada	18.6
Sri Lanka	16.0
South Africa	13.2

Data as on January 2025.

Data source: Ministry of External Affairs; reply to a parliament question, 21 August 2025

24

India Abroad: The World's Most Powerful Migrants

'India's diaspora is bigger and more influential than any in history.' This is how *The Economist* headlined its 2023 feature on Indian migrants. As charts in this chapter show, India doesn't just have the largest diaspora—it has several diasporas. Together they tell a story of migration, aspiration, and transformation that spans continents and centuries.

As of January 2025, 3.4 crore people of Indian origin lived in 200+ countries—more than the population of Australia. They were split between non-resident Indians (NRIs) and persons of Indian origin (PIOs) quite widely across countries. While early migrations were linked to indentured labour and colonial ties, recent flows reflect a different force: the global hunger for skilled professionals. Indian-origin professionals now dominate tech, medicine, academia, and entrepreneurship across the West. Their influence runs deep—*The Economist* feature had noted 'Adobe,

THERE WERE 216 INDIAN-ORIGIN ELECTED REPRESENTATIVES IN FOREIGN GOVERNMENTS IN JANUARY 2025

Mauritius	45
Guyana	33
UK	31
France	24
Suriname	21
Trinidad and Tobago	18
Fiji, Malaysia	17
South Africa	12
Singapore	7
US	6
Jamaica, Seychelles	4
Portugal	3
Australia, Kenya, New Zealand, Sri Lanka	2
Argentina, Bahamas, Finland, Madagascar, Mozambique, Papua New Guinea, Russia, Switzerland, Tanzania, Zambia, Zimbabwe	1

LINGUISTIC DIVERSITY IN THE DIASPORA

Indian international diaspora estimates by linguistic group, 2010 (crore)

Malayalam speakers are the dominant diaspora in West Asia; Tamil speakers outnumber them in all other regions. Both are smaller than Hindi speakers

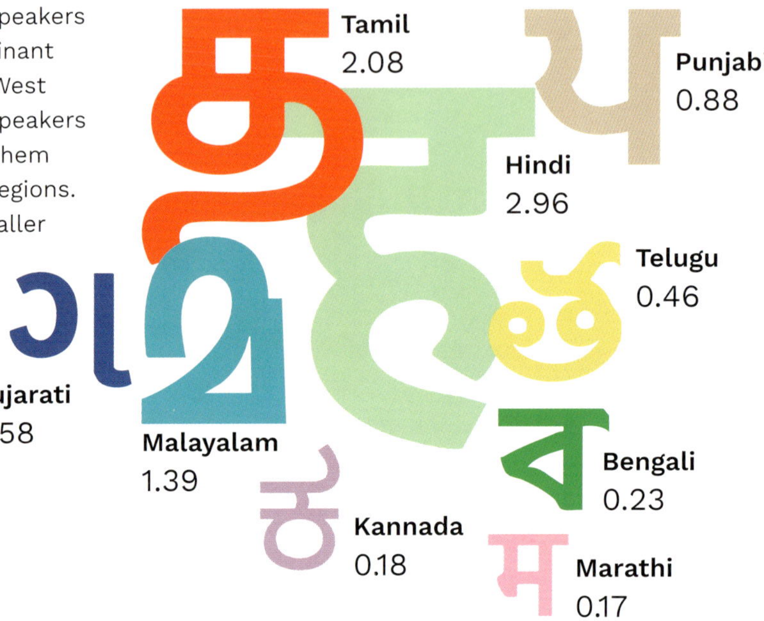

WHAT ABOUT INTERNAL MIGRATION?

(Out of 6.6 crore in 2011)	Internal diaspora (in lakh)	International/ internal ratio	Internal+ external diaspora*
Hindi	335	0.2	7.5%
Telugu	69	0.1	9.7%
Marathi	51	0.1	6.6%
Tamil	39	1.2	11.5%
Gujarati	36	0.3	8.7%
Bengali	31	0.2	3.7%
Punjabi	24	0.8	12.4%
Malayalam	16	1.8	12.2%
Kannada	16	0.2	4.6%

Malayalam and Tamil speakers are the only two diaspora that migrate more globally than internally.

As percentages of their total population, Punjabi and Malayalam speakers form the largest diaspora (internal and external).

*Percentage of speakers of each language that live outside their native-language region, in India or abroad, 2010

Britain and Chanel are all run by people with Indian roots.' From tech giants to top colleges to legislatures in 30-odd countries, people with Indian roots lead or represent some of the most prestigious and influential institutions. In the US, Indians form just 1.5% of the population but account for over 6% of doctors, 10% of tech workers, and 15% of all unicorn founders. They are the richest and most educated ethnic group in several countries, with average incomes and post-graduate degrees far above national averages. Indians abroad also give back—$135 billion in annual remittances in 2024–25 alone, the highest in the world by a wide margin and bigger than annual foreign direct investment. They build temples, fund schools, invest in startups, and support families back home.

There's another Indian diaspora—bigger, poorer, and less visible. According to IIM-Ahmedabad's Chinmay Tumbe**, over 45 crore Indians live outside their home districts. That's one in three Indians. A chunk of it resembles its global counterpart—educated, rich, and influential. But the majority move for survival—drought, discrimination, joblessness, or hopelessness. Many lack voter rights, access to welfare, and housing in their work cities. Their remittances, however, sustain entire villages, and their labour runs everything from construction to service to the delivery economy. Both groups share one thing: the belief that life can be better elsewhere. Whether in New Jersey or Noida, Qatar or Kochi, India's mobile population is reshaping economies—and identities—everywhere it goes.

WANT MORE?

- **For downloadable tables on overseas Indians across 200 countries, scan the QR code on Page 182**

•Internal diaspora is the speakers of a language enumerated outside the core region where the language is spoken.

•Hindi includes Marwari and Bhojpuri.

**Chinmay Tumbe, 'The Internal and International Diasporas of India'.

Data source: Columns 2–4 based on Census 2001 and 2011, Language Files. See Table 1 for international diaspora estimates.

1 million=10 lakh; 10 million=1 crore; details on Page xv

25 | More Married Women than Men—in Every Indian Religion

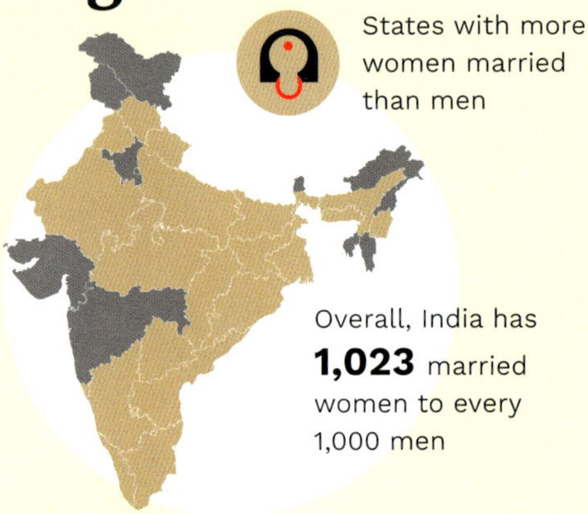

Across every religion, there are more married women than married men. Among Hindus, there are 1,019 married women for every 1,000 married men. The gap is wider for Muslims (1,043) and Christians (1,047), and lower but still present for Sikhs and Jains.

This could partly reflect polygamy or migration—men working abroad while their wives stay behind. But the bigger insight lies in remarriage patterns. It's far harder for widowed, divorced, or separated women to remarry than it is for men. The gap is stark: there are 3,524 widowed women for every 1,000 widowed men. Higher female life expectancy and male mortality contribute to this, but even among separated or divorced individuals, there are over 2,000 women for every 1,000 men. Clearly, men remarry far more often than women—or are more easily accepted if they try.

State-level data shows Kerala has the highest ratio of married women to men (1,131), while Jammu and Kashmir has the lowest. The numbers reflect a broader social reality: for many Indian women, marriage is still a lifelong status—even when the marriage itself isn't.

NO. OF WOMEN PER 1,000 MEN, ACROSS RELIGIONS AND MARITAL STATUS

	Married	Widowed	Separated	Divorced
All religions	1,023	3,524	2,041	2,009
Hindu	1,019	3,439	1,971	1,797
Muslim	1,043	4,383	2,961	3,686
Christian	1,047	4,519	2,180	2,028
Sikh	1,016	2,390	1,021	717
Buddhist	1,023	4,447	2,128	2,295
Jain	1,014	3,451	1,537	1,216
Others	1,041	3,236	1,929	2,561

26 | A ₹1 Lakh Crore Economy You Never Hear About

Every day, over ₹250 crore worth of dung is sold or used in India—mostly in rural areas. In 2023–24, this added up to nearly ₹93,000 crore. Of this, two-thirds was sold as dung manure, the rest as dung fuel. In just 13 years, India's dung economy has tripled in value (not adjusted for inflation). National accounts don't specify whether this is only cow dung—but that's the likely source.

The scale of dung manure use shows how widely organic fertilisers are used. As fuel, dung cakes reflect how deeply recycling is woven into rural life. But this reuse has a dark side: while dung cakes offer free fuel—and sometimes income—they're a major source of indoor pollution for women. Their use is more a sign of poverty than progress, survival rather than conscious recycling. The government now encourages biogas use instead, promoting dung as a renewable energy source rather than a direct burning fuel. NITI Aayog estimates India's cattle produce 3 million tonnes of dung each day. Even if just half of that is processed, it could power rural homes with clean, green energy.

OUTPUT FROM DUNG

(In ₹ crore, at current prices)

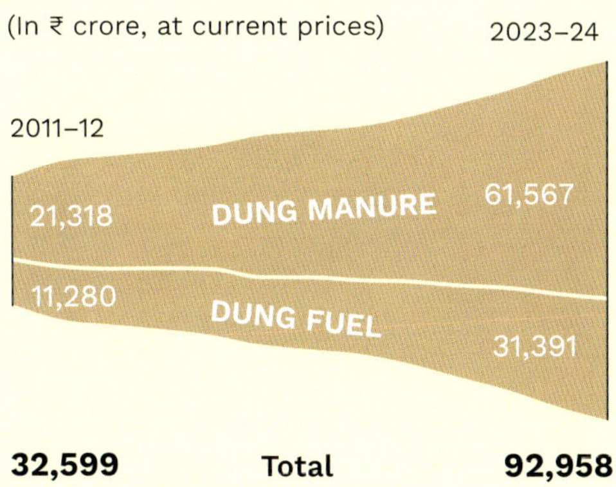

Data source: Census of India, 2011 (left), MoSPI

27

Millions Without Homes; Millions of Homes Without People

An empty house is like an unemployed worker—wasted potential. In 2011, over 11 million urban homes in India were vacant, even as house prices soared and millions lived in slums. That's 12.4% of India's total urban housing stock. With average urban household size at 4.66 people, those homes could shelter nearly 50 million people, or 13% of the urban population.

Vacancies are common in housing markets, but India's rate is too high for a low-income, high-rent country. A key reason is landlord reluctance to rent, driven by pro-tenant rent control laws and slow contract enforcement. Homeowners often fear they'll never get their property back—or spend years in court trying. Rental housing has steadily declined—from 53% in 1971 to 28% in 2011. In slums too, just over a quarter of residents rent. Globally, cities like Vancouver and Washington D.C. now tax vacant homes to bring them back to market. India could do the same. But first, future censuses must ask: why is a house vacant? In a country facing the world's fastest urban growth, that question is far too important to ignore.

2.46 CRORE VACANT HOUSES

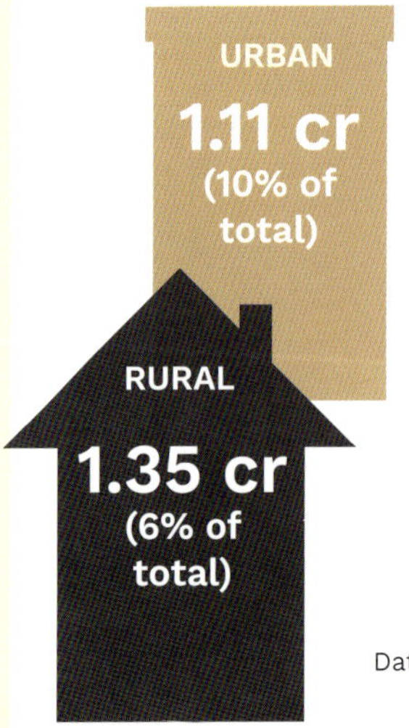

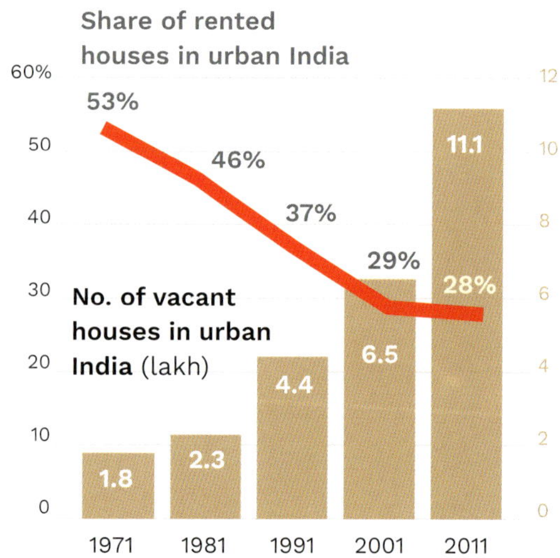

1 million=10 lakh; 10 million=1 crore; details on Page xv
Data source: Census 2011, India's Housing Vacancy Paradox, CSEP, 2021

The First Trillion-Dollar State May Not Be the One You Think

Several Indian states have set the target to grow their economy to $1 trillion. Some analyst reports suggest India could have its first trillion-dollar state by the end of this decade. That's not going to happen. No state has reached even halfway yet. India took 60 years to hit the $1 trillion GDP mark—in 2007.

When a state reaches that number depends on three things: its current economic size, its growth rate, and the rupee's exchange rate. Maharashtra is the biggest by far—worth $439 billion in 2022–23 at an average exchange rate of ₹80.3 to $1. Tamil Nadu, at $294 billion, is next. Then come Uttar Pradesh, Karnataka, and Gujarat, all at the $275–280 billion mark. But size isn't everything. Karnataka and Gujarat are growing faster in dollar terms than Maharashtra. At their current pace, they could cross $1 trillion in 22 years—6 years ahead of Maharashtra. If the rupee strengthens, all could hit the mark sooner. If it weakens, the wait will be longer. Either way, no state is even close yet. The US has 6 trillion dollar states—California's GDP alone was $4.1 trillion in 2024, larger than India's $3.9 trillion.

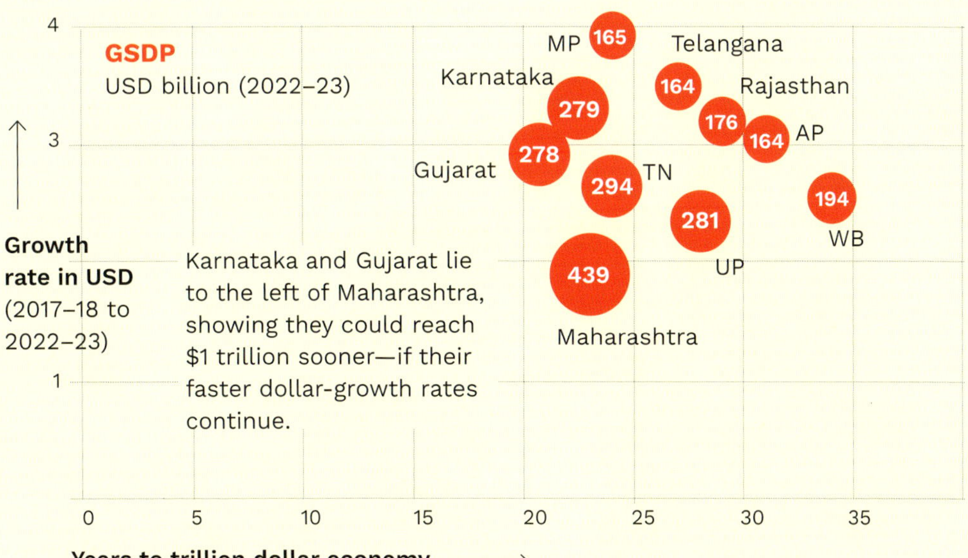

Advance estimates for Maharashtra; quick estimates for Gujarat.
Data source: RBI, state governments of Maharashtra and Gujarat, IMF

29 What Do We Know of Rich Farmers?

Is every Indian farmer poor? No. Is every Indian farmer too poor to pay income tax? Legally, yes. Because all income from farming is tax-exempt—even if it runs into crores. That has made agriculture a giant loophole for tax evasion (see Page 46). But how many Indian farmers actually qualify as rich?

Calculations done for *The Times of India* by Dr Rajesh Shukla of PRICE* offer a framework to answer that. First, they map the income distribution of estimated 7 crore farming households, all of whom are classified as self-employed. Their analysis shows that about 7% of farming families earned more than ₹25 lakh in 2024–25. That's more than double the current income tax exemption threshold. These wealthy farmers don't just earn big—they often own cars and tractors, and still receive multiple government subsidies meant for poor cultivators. About 30% fall in this overlapping category of rich-but-subsidised. According to Dr Rajesh Shukla of PRICE, simply taxing this top layer of farmer households could generate ₹30,000 crore a year in revenue. And end the myth that no farmer is a rich farmer, even in 2025.

51.3% of rural household are self-employed.

78% of self-employed rural household are farmers.

7% (or 50 lakh) farmer households are rich.

Their average annual earning in 2024-25 was **₹25,15,000**.

45% of rich farmers got government benefits and 29% owned a car.

Income tax collected from them could have fetched ₹30,000 crore.

*People Research on India's Consumer Economy

30 Growth Is Getting Less Tangible—and More Powerful

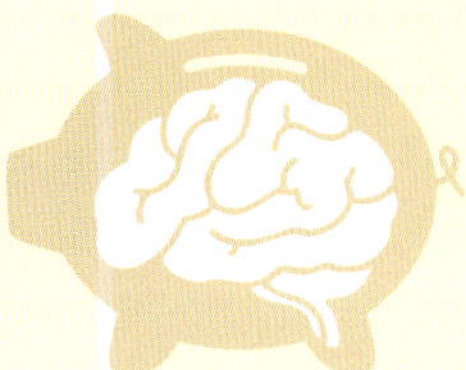

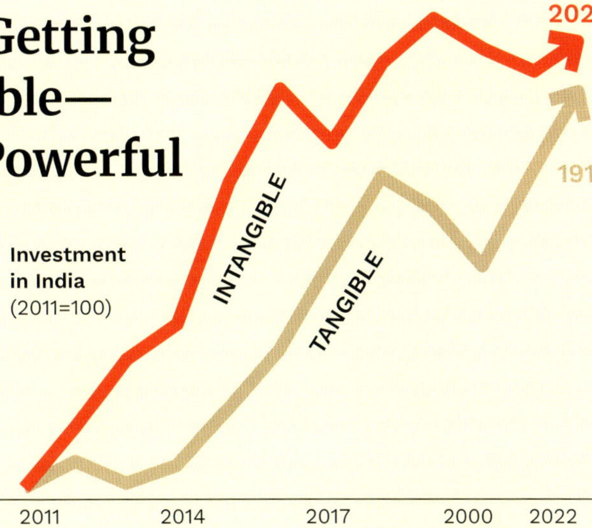

India is racing ahead in an invisible race. Between 2011 and 2022, its investment in intangible assets—software, databases, branding, design, organisational knowledge—grew fastest in the world. Globally too, intangible investments have risen nearly 3.7 times faster than tangible ones.

Modern growth relies not just on factories or roads, but also on knowledge—and often, the two go hand in hand. Today's car isn't just a machine; it's becoming software on wheels. India is attracting both tangible investment in automobile factories (via PLI schemes) and intangible investment in GCCs of global auto giants who are writing the code for tomorrow's mobility. This is India's intangible edge. It powers services, technology, and creativity. And in an age where AI threatens to eat away many service jobs, it's also creating new roles for thousands of skilled youth.

INDIA LEADS WITH FASTEST GROWTH AMONG MAJOR ECONOMIES

Compound annual growth rate in investment (%) 2014–24

	India*	US	France	Germany	UK	Japan*
Intangible	**6.6**	5.3	4.4	3.4	3.2	0.6
Tangible	**6.1**	2.1	1.4	0.1	1.9	0.9

*India data for 2011–2022, and Japan for 2012–23.
Data source: World Intangible Investment Highlights 2025, WIPO

How many new factories were registered in India each day in 2023?

- 5
- 11
- 20

Answer on Page 94

Growth

GDP'S PODIUM FINISH

COUNTRIES RANKED BY SIZE OF GDP IN USD

	1996	1997	2005	2006	2008	2010	2012	2014	2018	2020	2025	2026	2027
1	US	US	US	US	US	US	US	US	US	US	US	US	US
2	Jap	Jap	Jap	Jap	Jap	Chi	Chi	Chi	Chi	Chi	Chi	Chi	Chi
3	Ger	Ger	Ger	Ger	Chi	Jap	Jap	Jap	Jap	Jap	Ger	Ger	India
4	Fra	UK	UK	Chi	Ger	Ger	Ger	Ger	Ger	Ger	Jap	India	Ger
5	UK	Fra	Chi	UK	UK	Fra	UK	UK	UK	UK	India	Jap	Jap
6	Ita	Ita	Fra	Fra	Fra	UK	Fra	Fra	Fra	India	UK	UK	UK
7	Chi	Chi	Ita	Ita	Ita	Bra	Bra	Bra	India	Fra	Fra	Fra	Fra
8	Bra	Bra	Can	Can	Rus	Ita	Rus	Ita	Ita	Ita	Ita	Bra	Bra
9	Spa	Can	Spa	Spa	Bra	India	Ita	Rus	Bra	Can	Can	Can	Can
10	Can	Spa	Kor	Bra	Spa	Rus	Can	India	Kor	Kor	Bra	Ita	Ita
11	Kor	Kor	Mex	Rus	Can	Can	India	Can	Can	Rus	Mex	Mex	Mex
12	Neth	Mex	Bra	Kor	India	Spa	Aus	Kor	Rus	Bra	Rus	Rus	Kor
13	Mex	Rus	India	Mex	Mex	Aus	Spa	Aus	Spa	Aus	Kor	Kor	Rus
14	Aus	Aus	Rus	India	Aus	Kor	Kor	Spa	Aus	Spa	Aus	Aus	Aus
15	Rus	India	Aus	Aus	Kor	Mex	Mex	Mex	Mex	Mex	Spa	Spa	Ind
16	India	Neth	Neth	Neth	Neth	Neth	Ind	Tur	Ind	Ind	Ind	Ind	Spa

Data source: IMF's World Economic Outlook. Years from 2025 onwards are projections. Continuous years data not used to avoid repetition

IT'S A COMEBACK! For much of recorded history—from 1 AD to 1800—India is estimated to have had the world's largest or second-largest economy, driven by its vast population. The Industrial Revolution shifted the balance to Europe and the US. This small chart reminds us: India's rise today isn't an ascent from obscurity, but a return to the world stage after a detour.

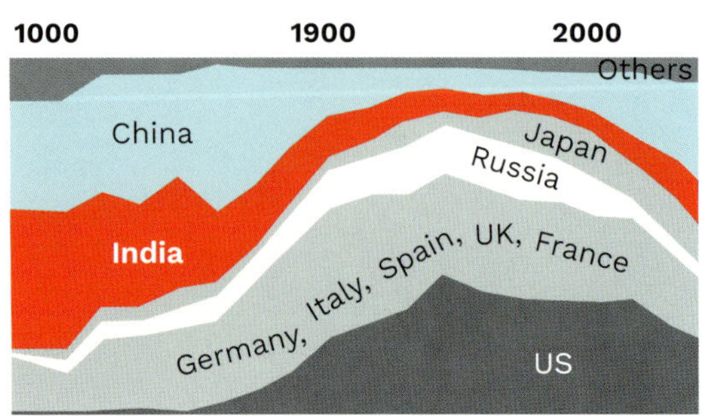

31

From 16th to 5th in 30 Years; Third in Two More?

India joined the world's top 10 economies only in 2015*—but since then, it's been sprinting. In 2021, it overtook its former coloniser, the UK, to become the world's 5th largest economy. By 2026, it's set to overtake Japan and claim the 4th spot. If IMF projections hold, it will be the third-largest by 2027, overtaking Germany. But don't expect another leap soon thereafter. China and the US are far ahead. Here's how stark the gap still is: If India, China, and the US each grew their 2023 GDP by 7%, India would add $261 billion to its economy. China would add nearly five times that—$1.24 trillion—and the US would add $1.89 trillion. Put another way, just a 1.3% increase in the US GDP would generate as much new income as a 50% jump in India's economy. That's the scale India is up against.

Still, India's return to the global leader board has a deeper historical symmetry. For centuries until 1800, India was the world's biggest economy—simply because it had the most people. Back then, output was physical: farming, weaving, building; no machines, no factories. In the pre-industrial world, population was GDP. That's no longer true. Today, the US has just 5% of the world's people but 21% of its income. Productivity and technology, not population, rule the race.

But that balance is shifting again. As China—and now India—combine their demographic scale with modern industrial capacity, the West's edge is narrowing. India is still far behind in per capita income—ranking 142 out of 193 (nominal terms, IMF 2025). But its scale, momentum, and aspirations are starting to align.

*Other than a brief appearance at No. 9 in 2010

KNOW MORE

When engineers and doctors choose political science ● Page 14

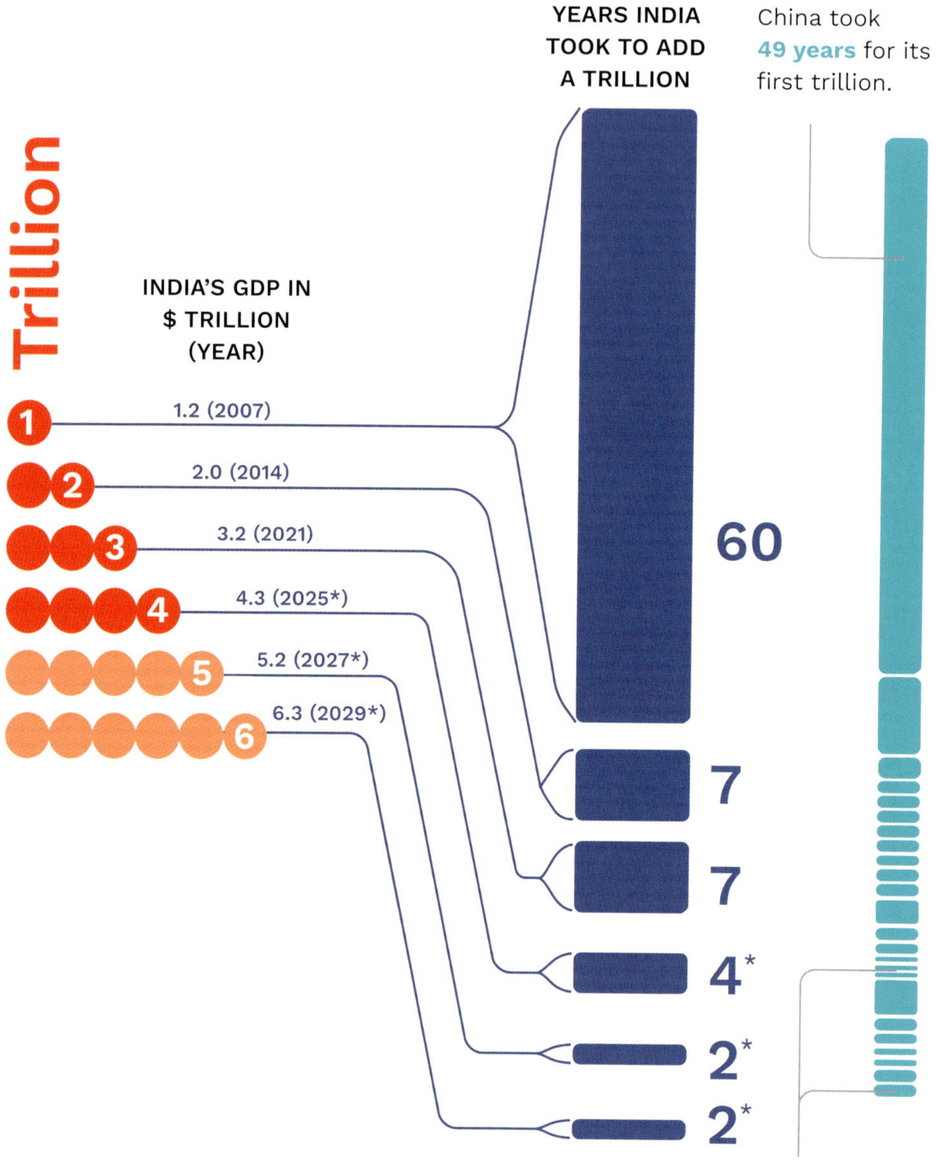

In 2021, China added $3 trillion to its GDP—that's one trillion every four months. It is estimated to be a $24 trillion economy by 2029—four times the size of India.

*Projections
Data source: World Bank, IMF

32

60 Years to the First Trillion—Just 7 to the Next

In 2007, India quietly crossed a major milestone—its economy touched $1 trillion, placing it among the handful of nations with a 13-digit GDP. What took 60 years after Independence to achieve, took just seven more years to double. The story of India's first trillion is a crash course in its economic history. It took 30 years to reach just $100 billion (10% of a trillion), with average annual growth stuck at around 3%. Some economists called it the Hindu rate of growth—to reflect India's apparent comfort with slow progress, even as much of East Asia was racing ahead.

Another 25 years passed before India reached $500 billion. By then, the Chinese economy had crossed the $1 trillion mark. But from there, India accelerated, with the economy growing by nearly 13% a year in dollar terms between 2000 and 2007. That helped the country leap from $500 billion to $1 trillion in just five years. The 'base-effect' (a smaller percentage growth adds the same absolute amount if your starting point—the base—is higher) also helped. The next trillions came quicker—even when growth slowed. By 2014, India hit $2 trillion. If projections hold, we'll hit $5 trillion by 2027 and $6 trillion by 2029. That's six decades for the first trillion, and just two decades for the next five.

KNOW MORE

What does it take to be the richest 10% • Page 110

5 SECTORS THAT MAKE UP THE INDIAN ECONOMY...

Agriculture, forestry and fishing, mining and quarrying

Manufacturing, construction, electricity, gas and water supply

Trade, hotels, transport and communication

Public administration, defence and other services

Financial, real estate and professional services

Figures rounded off. Employment share are rough estimates. Contribution to national income is % share in GVA for 2023–24, revised estimates.
Data source: Economic Survey 2023–24, RBI India Productivity Report

33

Why a Banker Adds 15 Times More to GDP than a Farmer

If India's economy were a company, half its workforce would be stuck in its least productive department. Nearly 46% of Indians work in agriculture, but the sector produces just 17% of national income. At the other end, finance, real estate, and professional services employ just 4% of the workforce but contribute about 23% of the GDP. This mismatch isn't the workers' fault. Much of it is disguised employment—for example, family members are counted as employed on farms, though they don't add to output. Movement of labour from farms to more productive sectors picked up after 2000 but reversed during COVID, when millions of jobless workers returned to villages.

Indian manufacturing in particular, and industry in general, is becoming more capital intensive—not labour absorbing. Like China, factories would need explosive growth to employ a large workforce even as they become less labour intensive. This misfit between where people work and where income gets created is one of the deepest drivers of inequality in the country. At the extreme end of this gap: India's highest-paid CEO earned ₹66 lakh a day in 2023–24. A male casual worker in an Indian city made ₹870 a day. He would have to work every single day for 21 years to earn what the CEO made in one day.

KNOW MORE

India's Inequality Puzzle: Less poor, More Unequal
• Page 118

GDP, POPULATION, AND INCOME DOUBLING TIME

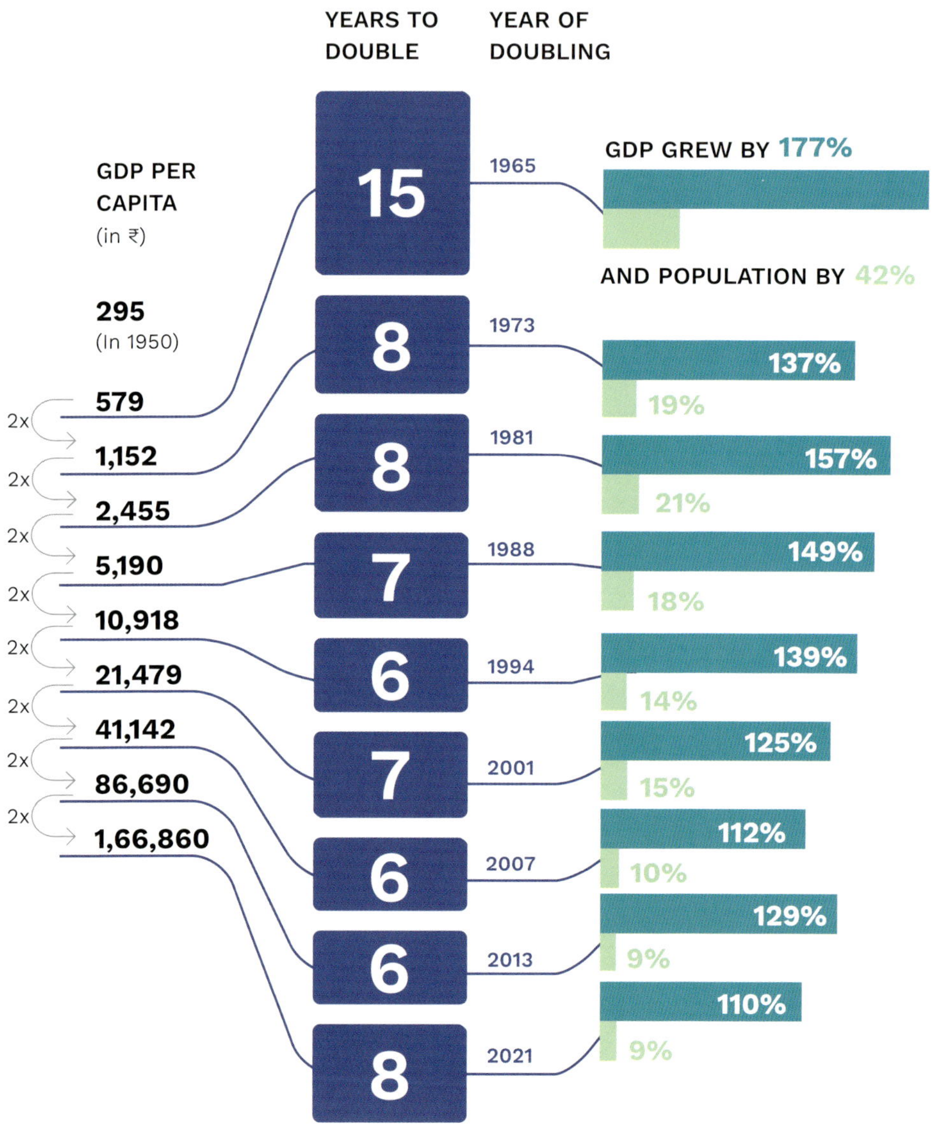

GDP per capita in ₹ nominal terms (not adjusted for inflation).
Data source: IMF and World Bank for per capita income

34

How Fast Does Income Double in India?

A simple way to judge a country's progress is to ask: How long does it take for the average citizen to become twice as rich as before? The answer depends on which era you're looking at. In the first 15 years after Independence, Indians gained the freedom to vote—but not much freedom to grow (i.e., freedom from poverty, destitution, etc.). The economy crawled, and it took the entire period to double the average income of Indians. That was the slowest doubling in independent India's history. Since then, income has doubled every six to eight years—fastest during the early 1990s and 2000s, when it took just six years.

But before you celebrate, remember: a lot of that 'growth' was inflation in disguise. Adjusted for inflation, average income has grown about 10 times over 70 years—not 550 times, as the growth in nominal rupee amount suggests. Also, per capita income isn't what most people earn. It's just national income (GDP) divided by population. When the population grew faster—in the 1950s and 1960s—income growth per person was slower. So where does India stand now? India's GDP ranks 5th in the world. But in per capita income, it ranks 142 out of 193 countries (nominal terms, IMF 2025). That improves a bit when adjusted for cost of living, but the gap between India's economic size and its prosperity ranking remains uncomfortably large.

KNOW MORE
All the wars Pakistan lost to India—without firing a bullet
• Page 124

JOBS, LABOUR FORCE AND UNEMPLOYMENT—AT A GLANCE

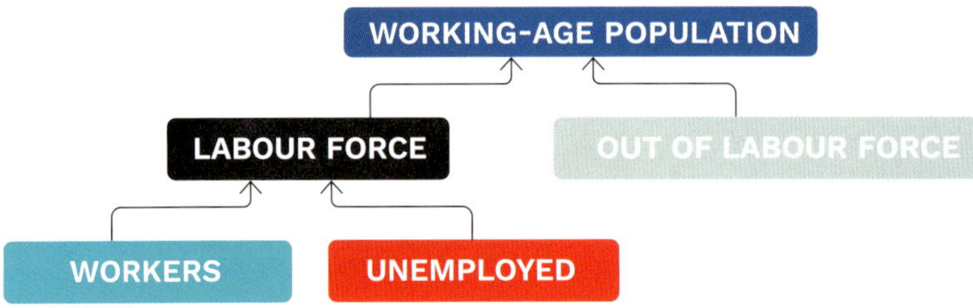

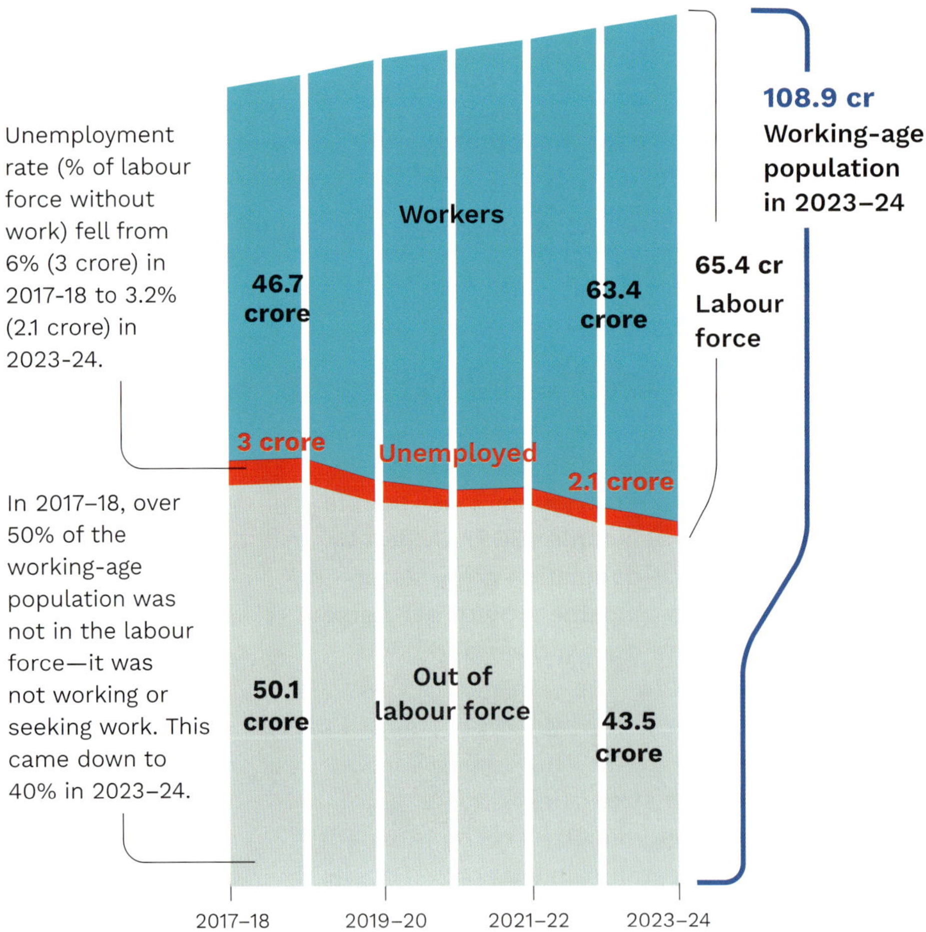

35

Why Everyone Talks about Employment, but Few Understand It

Jobs are the heartbeat of any economy. They drive income, spending, profits, investments, and then back to more jobs. Yet in India, which has the world's largest and youngest population, employment is also one of the most misunderstood topics. Confusion begins with a basic question: What does being employed even mean? As explained on Page 79, the answer is not simple.

Disagreements extend to the number of jobs created—an estimated 3.3 crore (over 90,000 a day) in 2023–24, and 4.1 crore the year before. Sounds hard to believe? Soon, you'll know why that's not necessarily wrong. Even more contested is the quality of jobs. Most working Indians are self-employed, and a chunk of them are 'unpaid helpers'. You can have a job without doing much work (a trend that spiked during COVID), and you can work without getting paid. Quality of job is also affected by length of job: you're considered employed if you worked just one hour in a week or 30 days in a year.

7-YEAR CHANGE IN KEY JOB MARKET DATA
(2017-18 to 2023-24, in crore)

Number of unemployed fell by 90 lakh in 7 years

Here are seven startling truths about India's job market:

1 ● In 2017–18, less than half of working-age Indians were in the labour force (i.e., working or looking for work). That rose to 60% in 2023–24.

2 ● Still, nearly 40% of working-age Indians—21% men and 58% women—neither have a job nor are looking for one.

3 ● Some are still studying (working age starts at 15), while others—especially women—drop out of the workforce due to marriage, mobility, or other constraints.

4 ● You are considered employed if you worked 30 days in a year*, or even just one hour in a week**.

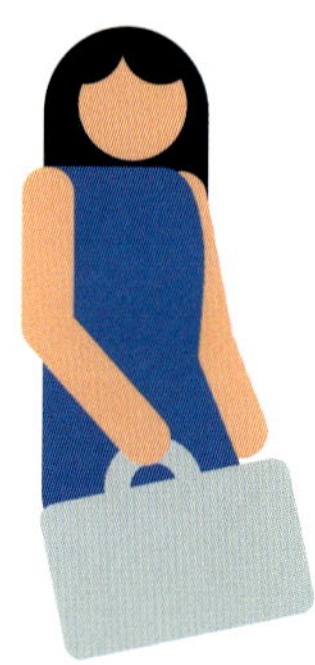

58% of working-age women are not in the labour force—down from 74% in 2017–18

EMPLOYMENT STATUS OF MEN AND WOMEN

● Workers
● Unemployed
● Out of labour force

Figures in crore

Data source: PLFS and UN population.
Working age is 15 and above. Total of male and female data is marginally higher or lower than total labour force or number of workers because absolute figures are derived from UN projection of population for different years. The Government of India only releases percentages.

For use of currency and units in the book, see Page xv

5 ● You can be working for free and still be counted as employed. In 2023–24, 10% of employed men and 37% of employed women were unpaid helpers.

7 ● Just 3.2% of adults were unemployed in 2023–24. The figure for April 2025 was 4.5%.*

6 ● Though only 3-4% of adults are unemployed, 58% Indians (80 crore) get daily free food from government—suggesting around 20 crore adults have a job but not enough income to feed themselves or their families.

***Employed in Usual Status:** Includes both Principal Status and Subsidiary Status. A person is employed under Principal Status if they worked for a significant part of the year (a 'relatively long part' of 365 days). Those who worked at least 30 days in the year but not long enough to qualify for Principal Status are counted under Subsidiary Status. People may hold multiple jobs.

****Current Weekly Status (CWS)**: Captures whether a person worked at least one hour in any day of the previous seven days. This is the basis for the monthly employment estimates (started January 2025), while the annual Periodic Labour Force Survey (PLFS)—released every October/November—uses data from the July–June period. As of the writing of this book, the latest available data are the 2023–24 annual report, while the April 2025 monthly report includes only CWS.

KNOW MORE

Are companies getting bigger than countries?
● Page 104

THE DISAPPEARING ACT OF INDIAN UNEMPLOYMENT

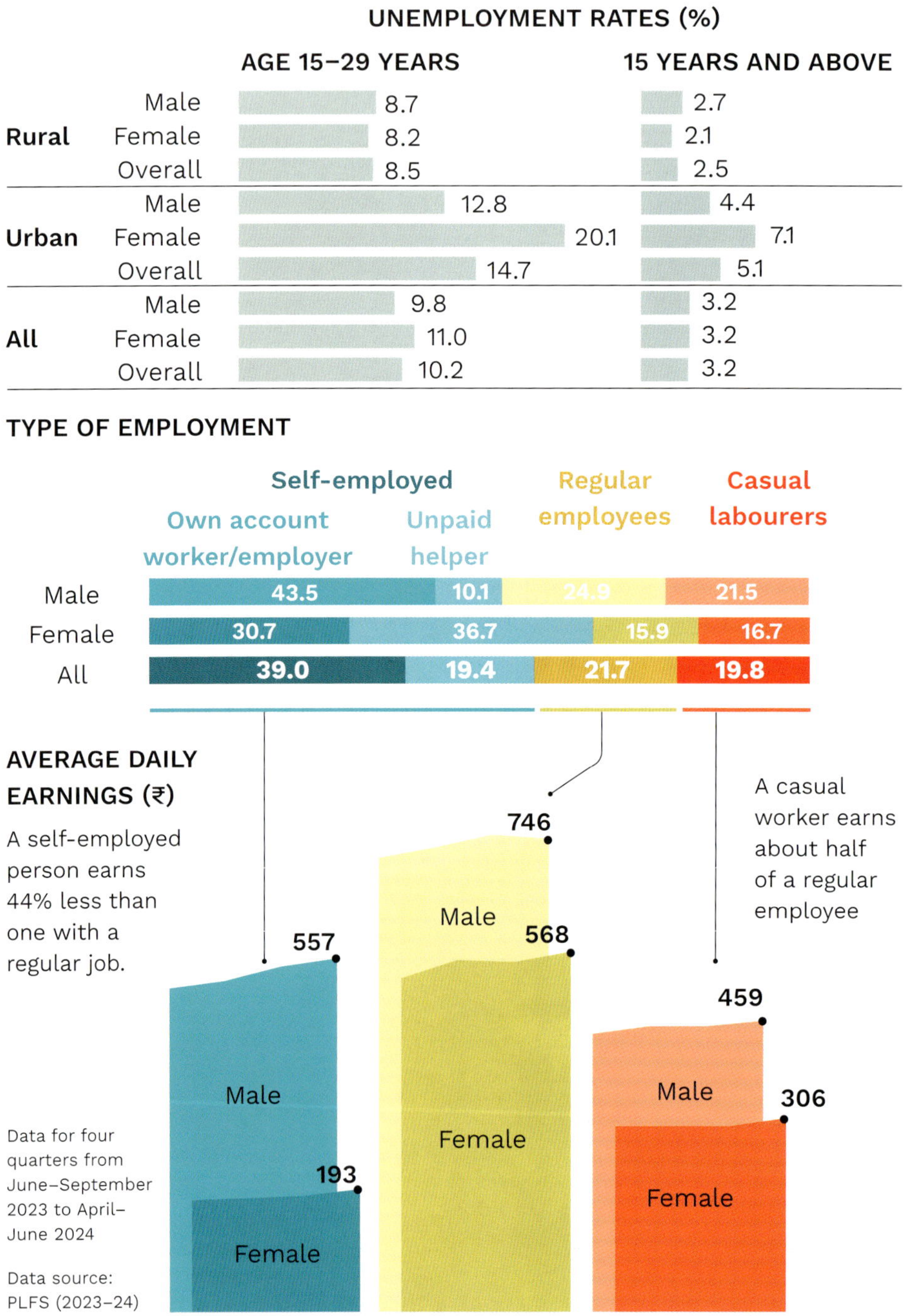

Data for four quarters from June–September 2023 to April–June 2024

Data source: PLFS (2023–24)

36

Why Nobody in India Is Jobless after 30

No matter the gender or location (urban or rural), Indian youth face far higher unemployment than the national average—up to 4 times higher. Urban young women (age 15–29) are the worst off—over 20% can't find jobs. Nearly 13% urban young men too are unemployed. But here's the twist: once people cross age 29, unemployment starts vanishing. Why? Because they stop looking for jobs and become self-employed, which is counted as being in employment. Nearly 60% of employment in India is self-employment. Among women, it is 67%. And a third of these are unpaid helpers, often family members working for no wages. That's where many youth unable to find jobs end up—technically employed, but often unpaid and invisible.

The job most people aspire to—'regular salary'—is held by just 22% of the employed. Some good news: the share of casual labour (the lowest paid category) has shrunk slightly in recent years, while salaried roles have grown. A welcome shift is more women entering the workforce. But that progress is blurred if large shares are unpaid helpers. It's a form of disguised unemployment and under-employment—a key reason so many Indians with jobs need daily free food (see Page 79).

'People are not waiting for that Brahminical job to fall into their lap. Once they get into their thirties, all men are working.

—Abhijeet Banerjee, Nobel Laureate, in his interview to *The Times of India*, October 2019

KNOW MORE

Districts of India: Count them if you can • Page 152

EDUCATED, ASPIRING, AND UNEMPLOYED

YOUTH UNEMPLOYMENT RATE (15-29 YEARS)

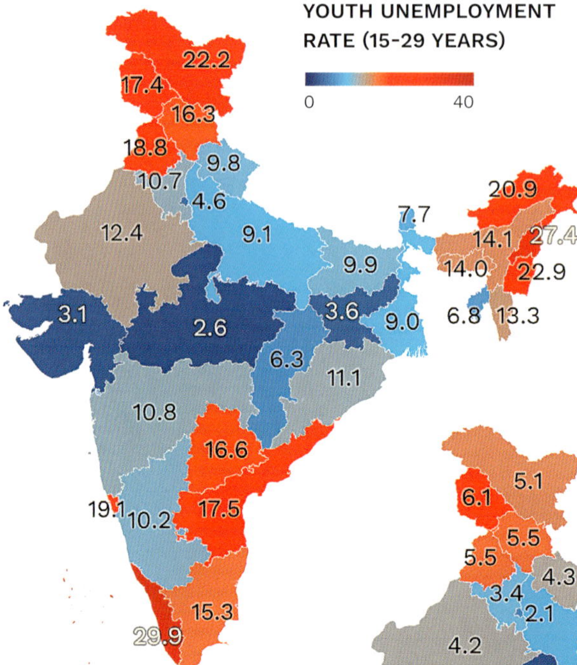

In Kerala and J&K youth unemployment is 3 to 4 times higher than overall unemployment.

OVERALL UNEMPLOYMENT RATE (15 YEARS AND ABOVE)

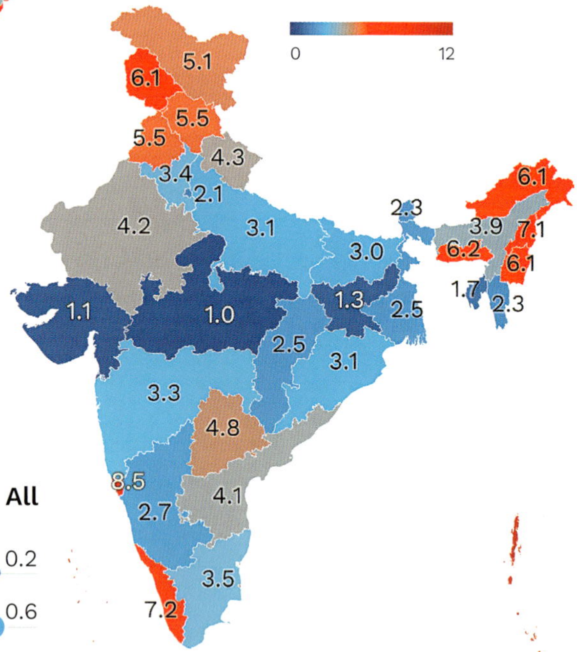

UNEMPLOYMENT RATE BY EDUCATION LEVEL

(2023–24)

	Male	Female	All
Not literate	0.4	0.1	0.2
Primary	0.8	0.2	0.6
Middle	1.8	0.9	1.6
Secondary and above	5.9	10.6	7.1

A woman with a secondary or higher education is 12 times more likely to be unemployed than a middle-schooler. For men, the difference is 3 times.

Figures in %
Data source: PLFS

37

Why Jobs Shrink as Education and Prosperity Rise

Some of India's richest and most socially developed states have the highest youth unemployment. In 2023–24, 30% of youth in Kerala and 19% in Goa were jobless. Andhra Pradesh, Punjab, and Telangana weren't far behind—despite lower overall unemployment. What's going on?

Part of it is caused by education and aspirations. In more literate and prosperous states, young people aim higher. They delay or reject low-quality jobs that youth in less affluent states like Bihar, Chhattisgarh, Jharkhand, or Uttar Pradesh might accept. It's not a population problem—these poorer states have far more youth, but still report lower youth unemployment.

This pattern isn't unique to India. China, with a larger workforce, is grappling with 15–20% youth joblessness. Across the world, economic growth is becoming less employment-intensive. Every 1% rise in GDP created 0.40% growth in employment in 1983–93. By 1993–2004 that had fallen to 0.29%, according to a Cambridge University study*, and the trend has worsened since. With AI accelerating automation, job creation is being further squeezed.

Fortunately, India is also emerging as a global talent hub. Its young population is filling workforce gaps worldwide—at every level. From CEOs of American tech firms to caregivers, drivers and plumbers in Europe, India is exporting its labour far beyond the traditional Gulf region. But global demand is still too small to absorb the flood of aspirants at home.

INDIA HAS THE SECOND LARGEST WORKFORCE

Population aged 15–64 as % of total

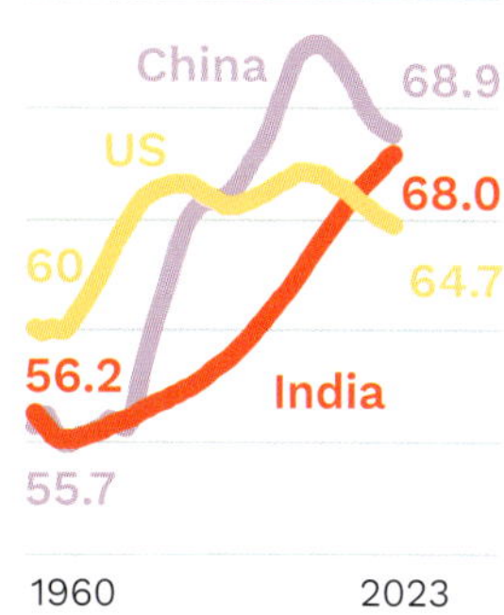

*Labour Intensity in Indian Manufacturing, Cambridge University Press, June 2015

KNOW MORE

Who is really unemployed in India? ● Page 76

WHEN SAVING MORE LOOKS LIKE SAVING LESS

% SHARE IN HOUSEHOLD SAVINGS

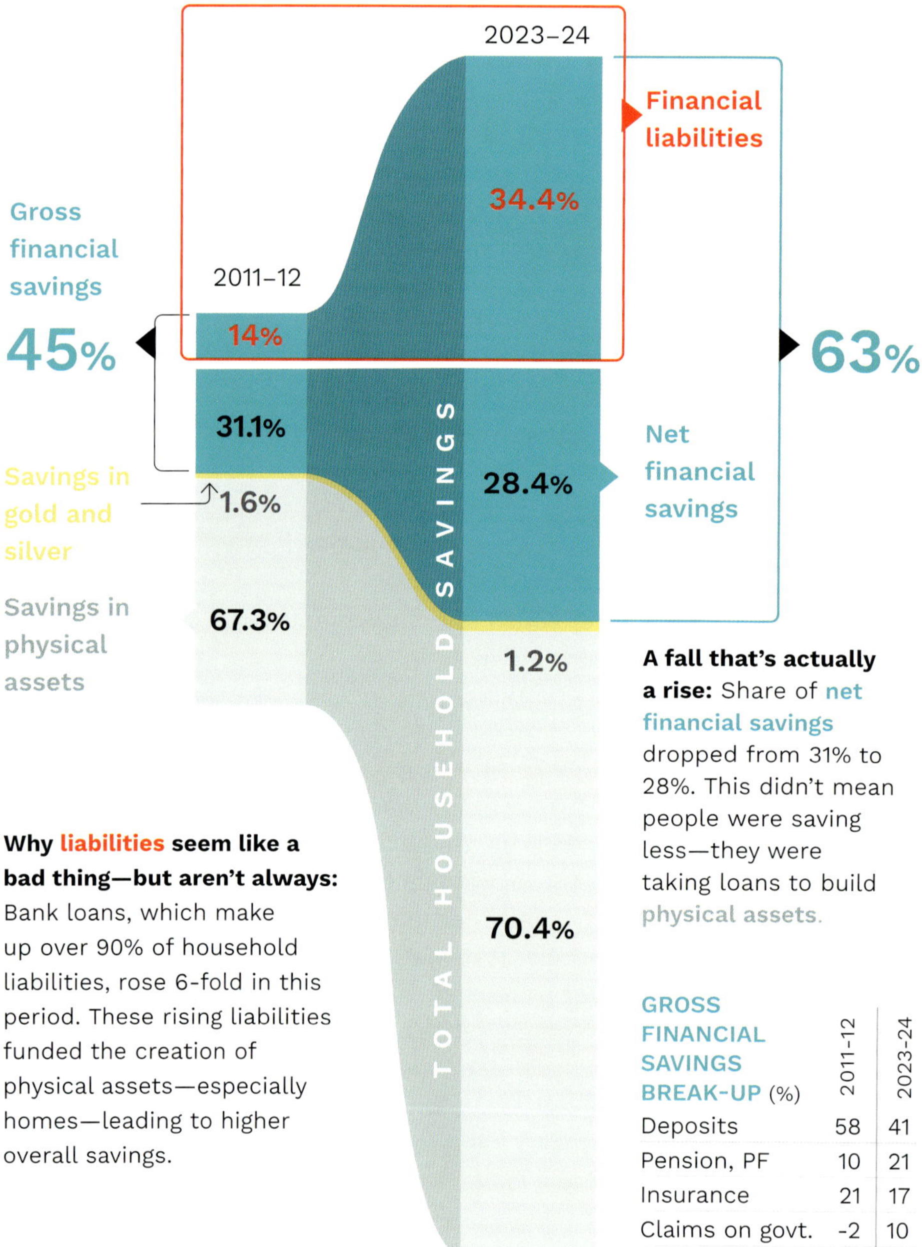

A fall that's actually a rise: Share of net financial savings dropped from 31% to 28%. This didn't mean people were saving less—they were taking loans to build physical assets.

Why liabilities seem like a bad thing—but aren't always: Bank loans, which make up over 90% of household liabilities, rose 6-fold in this period. These rising liabilities funded the creation of physical assets—especially homes—leading to higher overall savings.

GROSS FINANCIAL SAVINGS BREAK-UP (%)	2011-12	2023-24
Deposits	58	41
Pension, PF	10	21
Insurance	21	17
Claims on govt.	-2	10
Shares, debs.	2	8
Currency	11	3

Data source: MoSPI-Financial Assets and Liabilities of Households, May 2025

38

From Caution to Confidence: India's Great Savings Shift

In 2023–24, Indians saved over ₹15,000 crore every day—more than double the amount a decade ago and nearly triple compared to 2011–12. But beyond the sheer growth in savings lies a deeper shift in how and where they save—one that reflects not just rising income surplus but also growing financial confidence and ability to secure the future.

The share of financial savings has risen by 18 percentage points in 12 years, but traditional forms like bank deposits and cash are slowly losing ground. Riskier but high-return options like stocks and mutual funds (mostly equity funds) are drawing more savers—many investing through disciplined SIPs rather than speculation, although there is a set of investors who indulge in wild speculation (see Page 90). Alongside equities, provident and pension schemes like EPF and PPF are gaining traction—understandably so, given the near absence of public safety nets for job loss, retirement or healthcare unless one is officially classified as 'poor'.

But while gross financial savings have soared, net financial savings have fallen. Why? Because Indians—especially the middle class—are borrowing more. Not just because they can (higher income=higher creditworthiness), but also because they've embraced a credit culture that prioritises present consumption. In just over a decade, household liabilities rose from 14% to 34% of total savings.

What about physical assets? Their share remains high because of booming home prices. The urban middle class in big cities now mostly lives in crore-plus houses. But for most, that's also their only home—making them asset-rich, but cash-poor.

KNOW MORE

Fools and their money are still parting • Page 90

HOW COVID TURNED MILLIONS INTO INVESTORS

1. RETAIL INVESTOR BASE TRIPLED IN JUST 5 YEARS

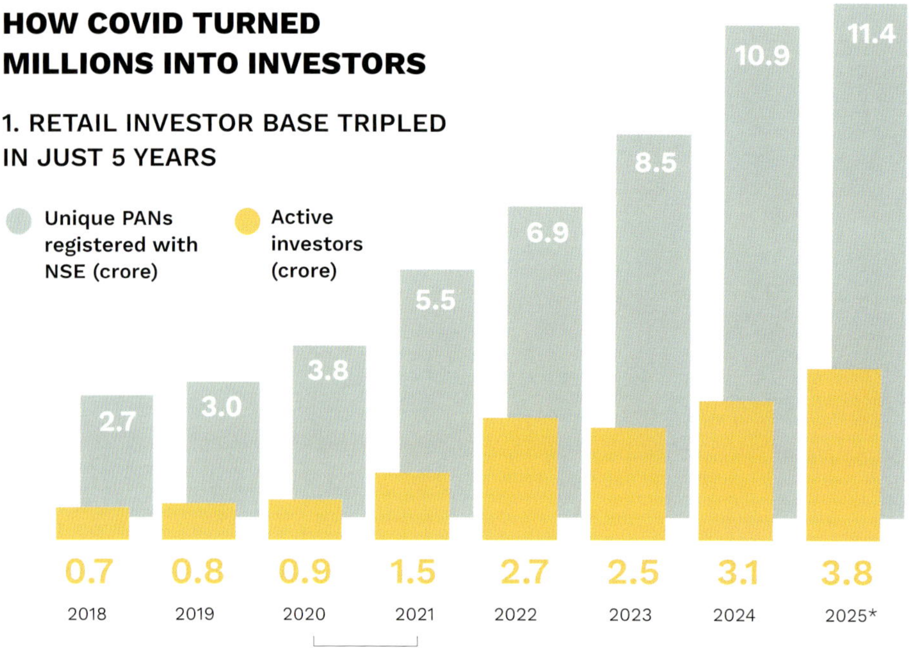

No. of investors rose 70% during peak pandemic year

In 8 years, the investor count jumped by over 5 times

*Till 31 May.
Data source: NSE India Ownership Tracker, March 2025

---

2. THEIR HOLDINGS NOW RIVAL FOREIGN INVESTORS

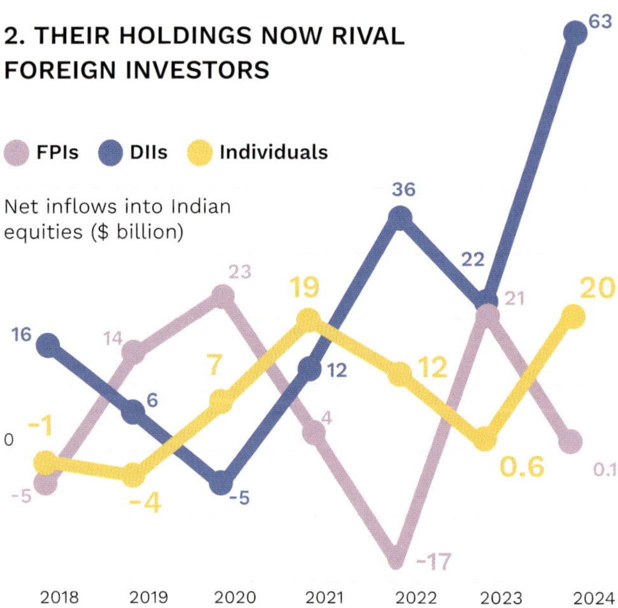

Directly and indirectly (via mutual funds) individual investors owned a record 18.2% of NSE market cap in March 2025, outpacing share of foreign portfolio investors. In 2014, FPI's share was 11 percentage points higher than that of individuals.

1 million=10 lakh; 10 million= 1 crore; details on Page xv
Data source: NSE Market Pulse, May 2025

39

From Savers to Shareholders: India's New Wealth Story

The dread-filled stillness of the COVID years may have done something remarkable—it nudged Indians to think harder about their financial future. And many acted by turning to the stock markets, not as gamblers but as wealth builders. The National Stock Exchange now has over 11 crore unique registered investors—3x higher than the COVID year 2020. Active investors on the exchange reached nearly 4 crore in March 2025, more than 4 times the number 5 years ago. Over 62% of recent new investors came from districts beyond India's top 50. From Jorhat to Jaisalmer, retail investors now trust markets like never before.

Their trust has paid off—so far. Indian stock markets have delivered positive returns for nine straight years, and the market cap of NSE-listed firms has grown 6-fold since 2014—from ₹73 lakh crore to over ₹425 lakh crore. An estimated ₹46 lakh crore in household wealth has been created since FY21, ₹25 lakh crore in just the last two years. The investor profile, too, is transforming. The median age has

KNOW MORE

How our differences became our divisions • Page 166

dropped from 38 to 32, with 40% now under 30. Every 1 in 4 investors is a woman. And monthly SIP inflows—₹8,000 crore in January 2020—have surged past ₹28,000 crore by mid-2025. An AMFI-Crisil study found the share of SIP assets held for over three years rose from 13% in March 2020 to 52% in March 2025, showing disciplined long-term bets by middle class investors.

The post-pandemic surge in investing has proved to be more than a fad. It is a quiet financial revolution—millions of Indians, young and old, rich and modest, investing their way into something even upper-middle class Indians struggled to create: wealth.

3. THEY'RE INVESTING ACROSS A WIDER SET OF COMPANIES

Decile-wise portfolio share of three types of investors

	FPIs	DMFs	Retail investors	Total M-cap
1	89.1	82.6	65.9	79.6
2	7.3	11.2	14.4	11.1
3	2.4	4.1	8.5	4.6
4	0.8	1.5	4.7	2.3
5	0.2	0.5	3.0	1.2
6	0.1	0.1	1.6	0.6
7	0	0	1.0	0.3
8	0	0	0.6	0.2
9	0	0	0.3	0.1
10	0	0	0.1	0

Retail investors vs institutions: Unlike mutual funds (DMFs) and foreign investors (FPIs) who invest heavily in India's top companies, individual investors spread their money across all sizes of companies (Decile 1 to 10 in the table). This wider spread may reflect limited access to research—or it could be a sign of retail investors hunting undervalued or high-growth bets.

4. RETAIL PARTICIPATION SHOWS MORE COMMITMENT

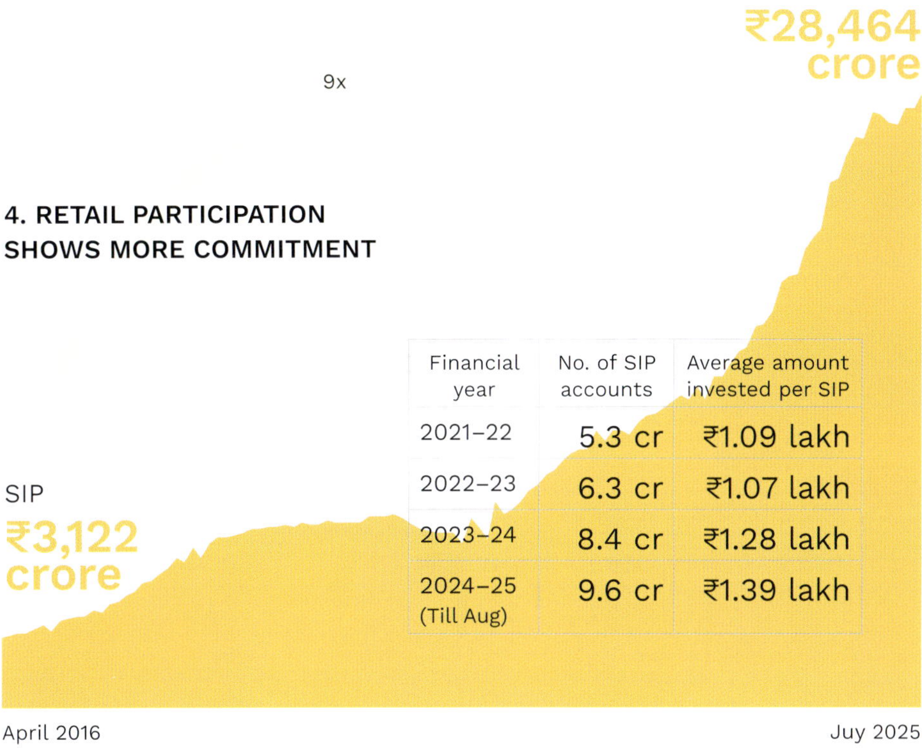

Financial year	No. of SIP accounts	Average amount invested per SIP
2021–22	5.3 cr	₹1.09 lakh
2022–23	6.3 cr	₹1.07 lakh
2023–24	8.4 cr	₹1.28 lakh
2024–25 (Till Aug)	9.6 cr	₹1.39 lakh

5. AND THEY'RE STAYING INVESTED LONGER

Change in share of SIP AUM across holding period (%)

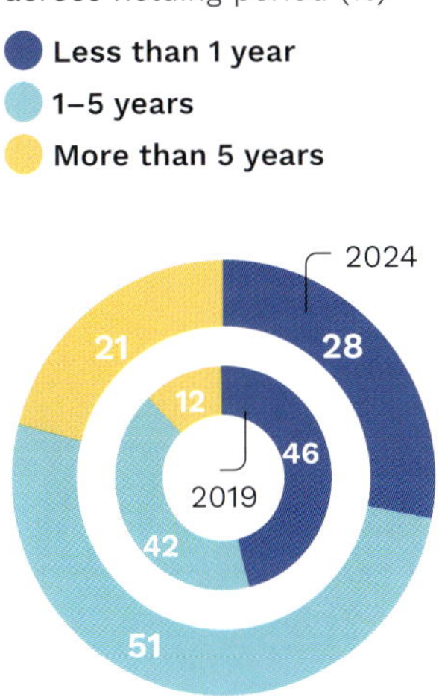

6. THIS PATIENCE HAS BEEN REWARDED—SO FAR

Household wealth accretion in Indian equities (₹ lakh crore)

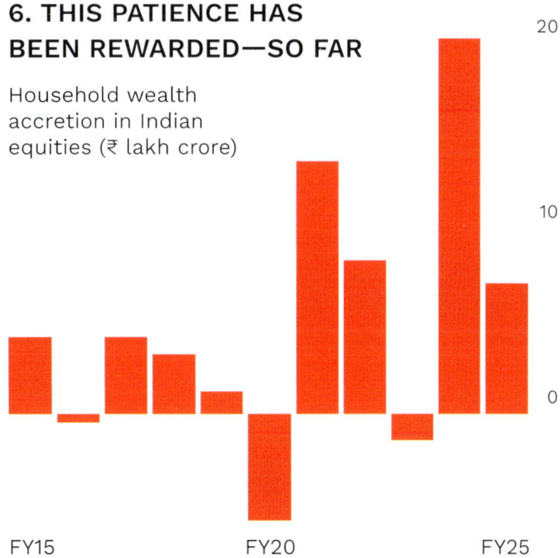

Data source: CMIE Prowess, AMFI, NSE EPR calculations

HOW THE POOR LEGALLY PAY THE RICH

43% of the investors were under 30 years old, and 93% of them reported losses →

Age of F&O investors	Share of total investors	% of investors who lost
<30yrs	43%	**93%** lost money
30–40	35%	**91%** lost money
40–50	15%	**89%** lost money
50–60	4%	**85%** lost money
>60	3%	**79%** lost money

92% of those earning less than ₹5 lakh annually incurred investment losses →

Income of F&O investors	Share of total investors	% of investors who lost
<5 lakh	76%	**92%** lost money
5–10 L	18%	**90%** lost money
10–25 L	5%	**84%** lost money
25–50 L		**75%** lost money
50–100 L	1%	**75%** lost money
>100 L		**85%** lost money

F&O INVESTORS AND LOSSES BY STATE

	F&O traders	Loss/ person
Telangana	2.1 L	₹2.0 L
Andhra Pradesh	2.1 L	₹1.5 L
Maharashtra	18.1 L	₹0.7 L
Gujarat	10.1 L	₹0.9 L

A TRAGIC WEALTH TRANSFER

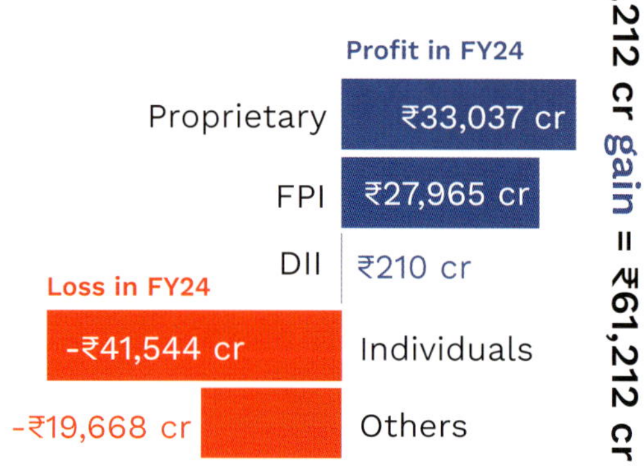

Data source: *Analysis of Profits and Losses in Equity Derivatives Segment (2022–2024)*, SEBI

40

Why Fools and Their Money Are Still Being Parted

It's one of the world's largest income transfer schemes—with a twist: the poor give money to the rich. In 2023–24 alone, nearly 1 crore Indians lost over ₹61,000 crore in futures and options (F&O) trading—₹5,000 crore a month, lost legally, voluntarily, and often repeatedly. Futures and options are trades that bet on future stock prices.

These aren't scam victims duped in a single click. Many lose slowly, week after week, over months and years. In Jharkhand—India's second-poorest state—1.4 lakh people lost an average of ₹78,000 each in a year. The poorest, youngest, and those from smaller towns are trading the most—and losing the most.

Why this obsession with financial self-destruction?

Because the pain comes in tiny doses—losing ₹500 every week for 10 weeks hurts less than losing ₹5,000 in one go. Social media 'experts' promise big gains just around the corner. Algorithms keep people hooked. Trading apps make entry effortless. It feels thrilling, private, even empowering—until it isn't.

And when the dust settles, it's the institutions who walk away with the money: in 2023–24, proprietary traders and foreign investors booked a combined profit of ₹60,000 crore. The rich didn't beat the market—they just waited while the poor fed it.

F&O is not just risky. It's a technical instrument that demands deep knowledge and institutional muscle. It is, simply put, the wrong tool in the wrong hands. But try telling that to a 25-year-old from a Tier-3 town with a smartphone, a ₹10,000 windfall—and a dream.

KNOW MORE
First image of an emptying planet
• Page 148

INDIA'S WORST INFLATION YEARS ARE BEHIND IT

2013 was the last year of double-digit inflation

No. of years of double-digit inflation in each decade

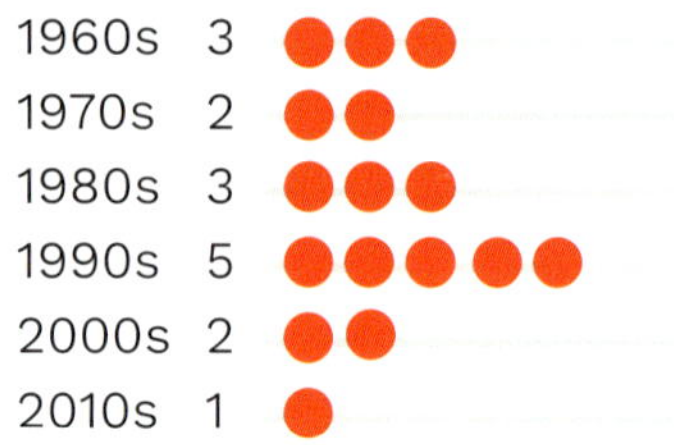

BUT KEY PRODUCT/SERVICE PRICES DOUBLED IN THE LAST DECADE

Charts are plotted with index values between 2012 (base year=100) and 2024; % change is between first and last years

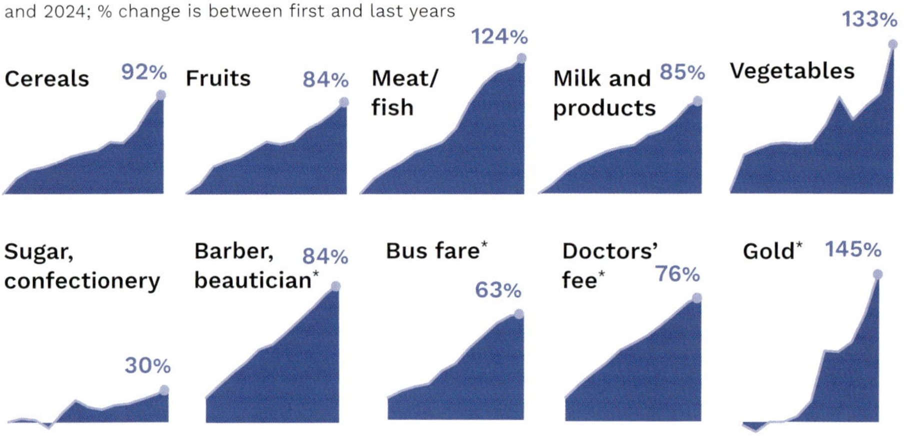

The overall point-to-point inflation between 2012–13 and 2024–25 was 88%.

*From 2014 to 2024

WHY INFLATION IS CALLED THE INVISIBLE TAX

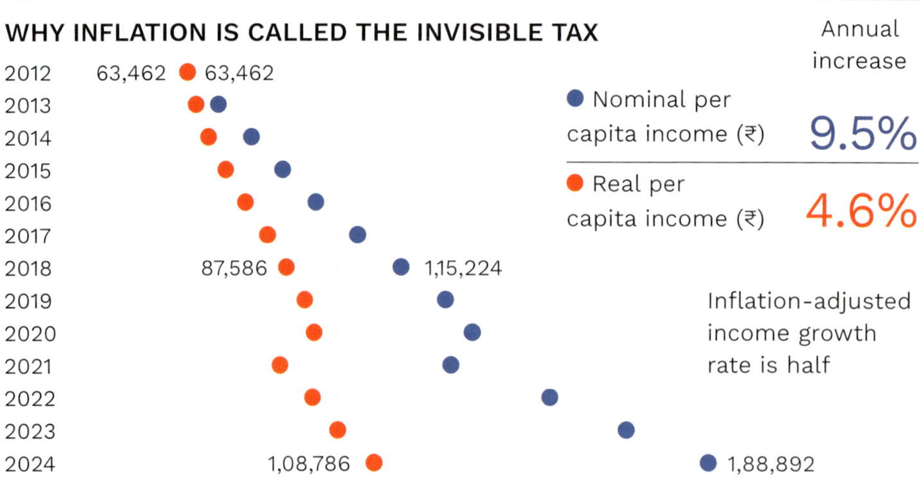

Data source: Dataforindia.com, National Accounts Statistics, Ministry of Statistics and Programme Implementation

41

How India Half-Won Its War on Inflation

In every decade since Independence, India saw at least two years of double-digit inflation. But not since 2013. This drop isn't all luck. In 2015, the government and RBI signed a landmark agreement to formally target inflation—setting a 4% goal, with an upper tolerance of 6%. It has worked, so far. Price stability has powered a long spell of prosperity.

But there is a story that overall inflation hides. Look at how the prices of milk, fruit, meat, and even gold moved differently between 2012 and 2022. The southern states saw higher inflation than the rest of India—but they also had higher incomes. That's the key: inflation isn't just about prices, it's about what it does to your income as an invisible tax on it. That's why the RBI has to fight harder to lower this 'tax' over time—long-term inflation rates in richer countries are still lower than India's.

To understand how national inflation differs from personal inflation, turn to Page 146. Because raising a child in India is a perfect case study in how the real cost of living is different for every family.

SAME COUNTRY, DIFFERENT INFLATIONS

State-wise inflation during 2014–2024

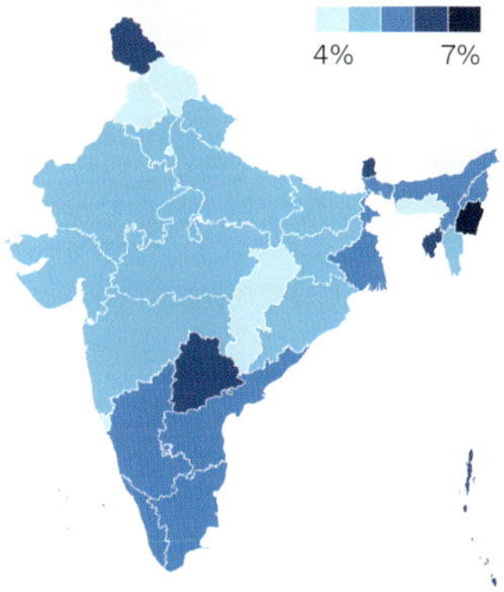

Over time, variation in inflation across states has narrowed.

KNOW MORE

How savers turned shareholders, and created wealth
• Page 86

WORKFORCE MORE THAN DOUBLED, LED LARGELY BY CONTRACT JOBS

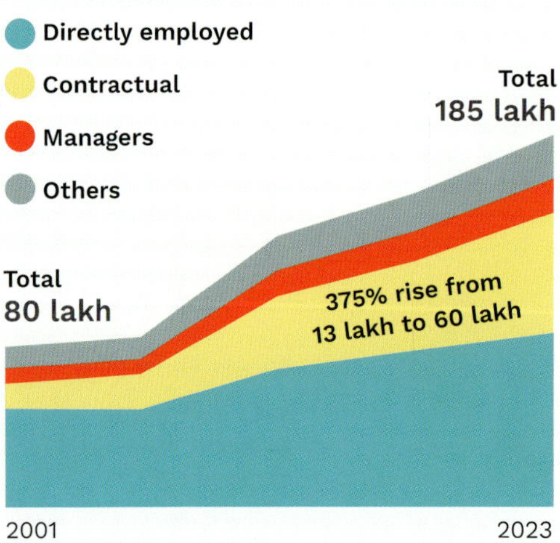

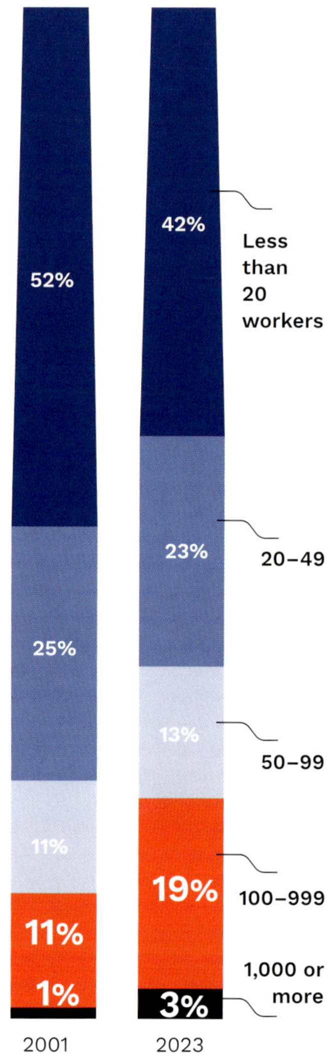

Share of factories by employment size

FACTORIES WITH 100+ WORKERS HAVE NEARLY DOUBLED

42

11 New Factories a Day: Hope for Manufacturing Revival?

India's growth story often carries a lament: we skipped the stage where factories drive mass employment and incomes. While China and South Korea rode manufacturing to prosperity—with over 25% of their GDP from it—India's share peaked at 18% and now sits at just 13%. The reasons are well-known: labour laws that punished formalisation, inspector raj, and policies that protected small over scalable. But the story may not be over—it may just be unfinished.

New data from the Annual Survey of Industries 2023 shows a quiet transformation. In the past two decades, India has added nearly a lakh (83,000) new factories. Not only are they more numerous—they're bigger. Average output and jobs per factory are rising. Maharashtra, Tamil Nadu, and Gujarat remain hubs, but new clusters are sprouting in central and northern states too. Factory employment has nearly tripled—but contract workers grew 5-fold,

KNOW MORE

India just got out of one poverty, and got into another

• Page 117

reflecting India's still-rigid labour rules. The wage gap between managers and floor workers continues to widen, even as overall wages rise.

Yet there's real hope. India now exports billions in smartphones, cars, and electronics. Giants like Apple, Samsung, and Hyundai are producing here. Smaller units are quietly assembling global brands. The future depends on sustained policy support—PLI schemes, real ease of doing business, and smart state-level reforms. Automation will raise productivity but shrink job intensity. Even so, India's massive wage advantage offers a toehold. This isn't just about GDP. It's about jobs, dignity, and whether the factory floor can again be a ladder to the middle class.

SALARIES HAVE RISEN BY 4X TO 8X, MANAGERS GAINING THE MOST AND DIRECTLY EMPLOYED THE LEAST

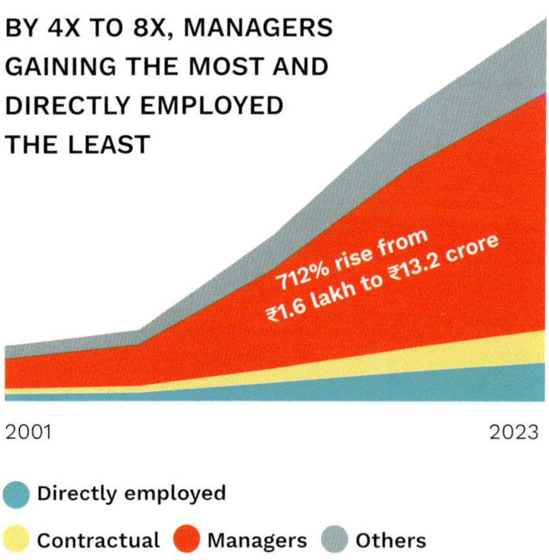

TOP 10 INDUSTRIES, BY FACTORY EMPLOYMENT

Apparel
7.6 lakh

Auto parts
7.5 lakh

Medicines
5.1 lakh

Cotton yarn
4.2 lakh

Steel
4.1 lakh

Bidis
3.8 lakh

Rice
3.4 lakh

Vehicle repair
3.2 lakh

Pharma ingredients
2.9 lakh

Brick
2.8 lakh

TAMIL NADU HAS THE MOST FACTORIES AND JOBS, GUJARAT AND UTTAR PRADESH HAVE GROWN FASTER

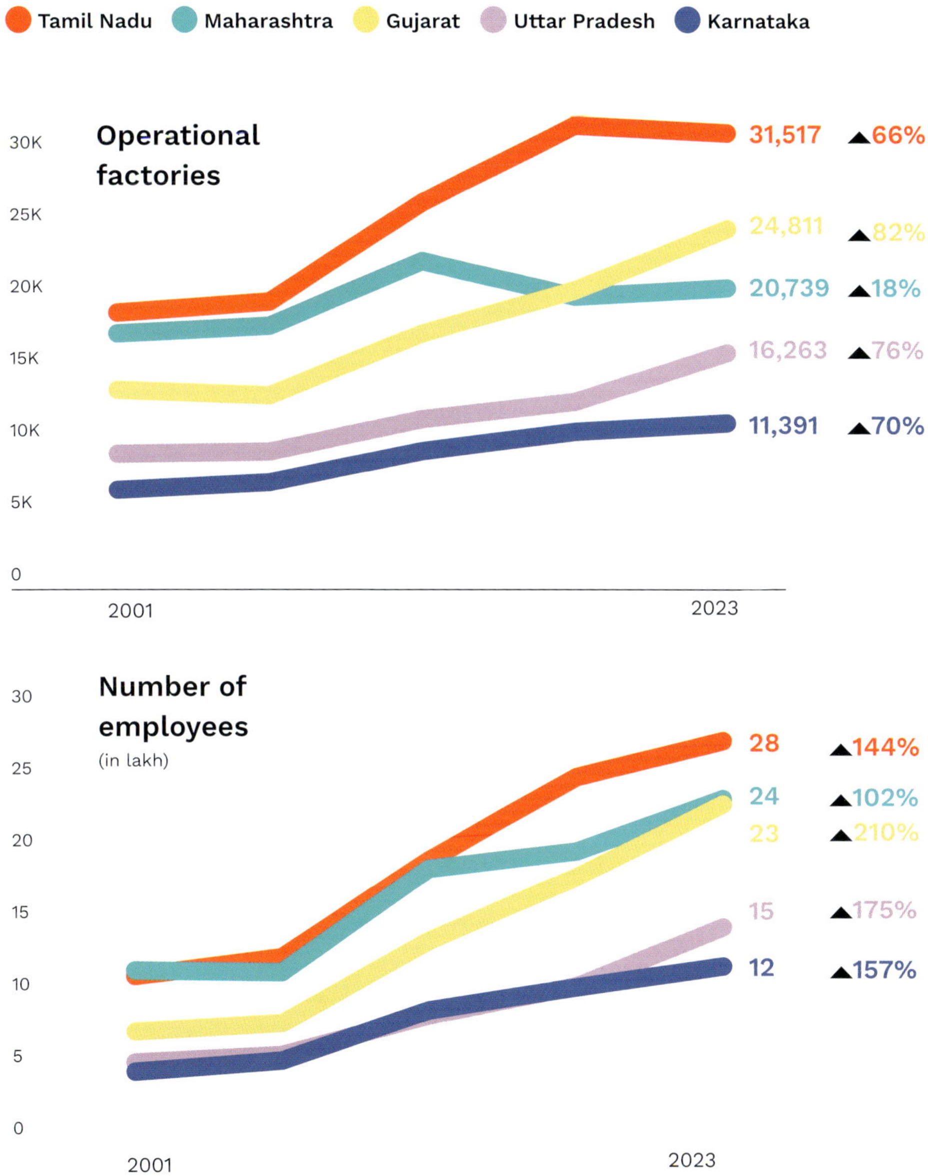

Data source: Dataforindia.com, Annual Survey of Industries (2001, 2005, 2012, 2018, 2023), Ministry of Statistics and Programme Implementation

WHEN INCOME TAX TOOK OVER THE GOVT'S COFFERS

₹3.5 lakh crore
Revenue from income tax, 2016–17

4x in 9 years

₹14.4 lakh crore
2025–26*

SHARE IN TAX REVENUES

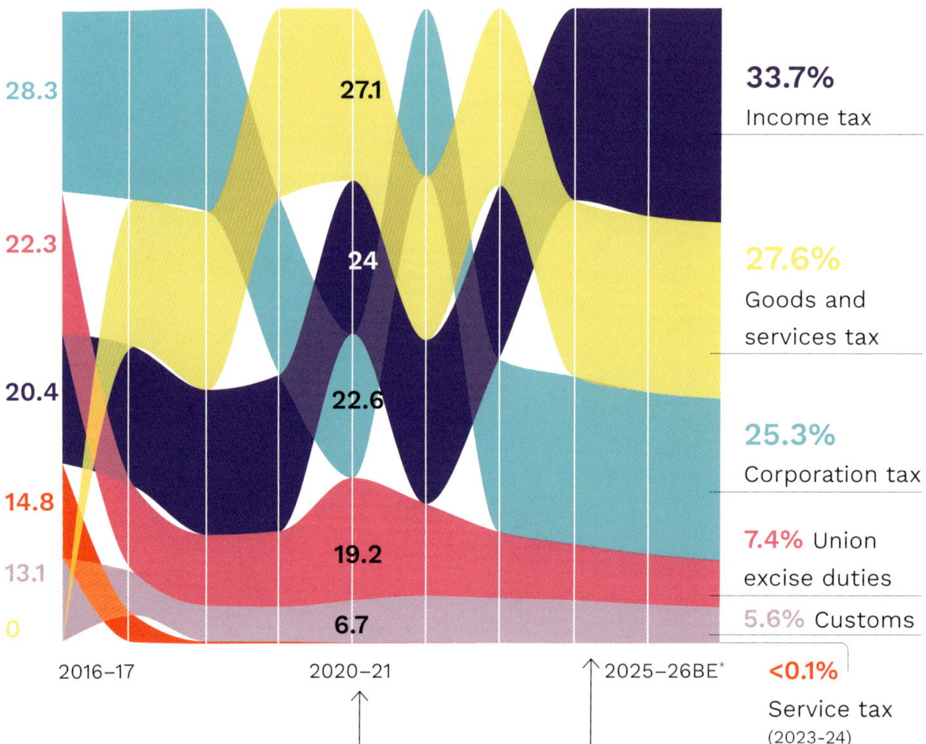

In 2020–21, income tax collections had overtaken corporate income tax but only for a year. GST was the top grossing tax that year.

Income tax revenues overtook GST in 2023–24 and the gap has widened to over 6 percentage points in 2025–26 estimates.

In 2020–21, revenues from all taxes—except customs and excise—fell due to the pandemic.

1 million=10 lakh; 10 million=1 crore; details on Page xv

*Budget Estimates

Data source: Receipt Budget, 2025–26

43

How a Tax Paid by Just 3% Became India's Biggest Revenue Source

What if your salary doubled twice in 10 years? And if this 4x growth in income came despite a bad year in between? And if all this helped you build some real wealth?

Sounds like a dream? The Government of India will tell you it's not. Between 2016–17 and 2025–26, the Centre's income tax revenues rose over 4-fold. Since income tax is a share of Indians' earnings, this surge is a signal: either Indians earned more, or more Indians entered the tax net, or tax rates went up. Tax rates didn't rise, and on Page 46 you will find how the number of Indians paying income tax remains minuscule. What changed was the nature of income and how well the government captured it—especially capital gains from a booming stock market. The government also got better at tracking income.

The result: in 2023–24, income tax became the single largest source of revenue for the Indian government—overtaking corporate tax and even GST. It may be a global first: a country where just 3% of adults pay income tax, and yet it's the largest source of government earnings. It is a sign of rising inequality. But it also marks a structural shift: the tax system is becoming more progressive. For decades, most tax came from what people bought or produced, not what they earned. That burdened the poor as much as the rich. Now, with direct taxes dominating, the weight is shifting upward. A tax once seen as elite is now central to India's economic story. The next question: can a few keep carrying the many?

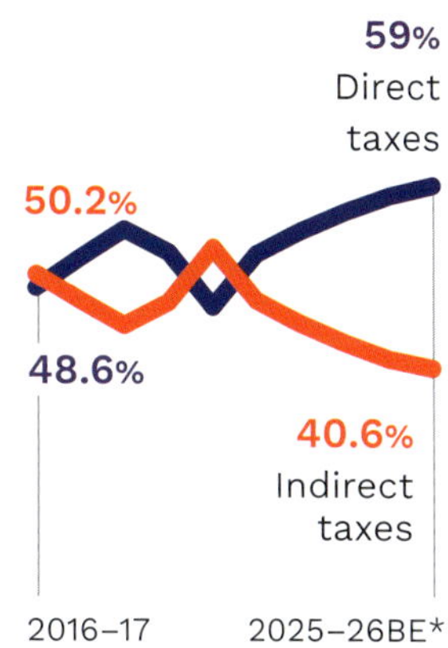

Few minor taxes like estate duty and wealth tax were not taken into account.

44

The Four Faces of Indian Income

How rich is the average Indian? That depends on which of the four income lenses you use. There are at least four ways economists measure a country's per capita income, each offering a different insight into prosperity. Per capita income in current rupees is the rawest form: national income divided by population, without adjusting for inflation (yellow chart). This number has grown 109 times between 1980 and 2024—but that includes the effects of rising prices.

Per capita income in constant rupees adjusts for inflation. This is a better measure of real purchasing power over time. Using this, India's average income grew by six times from 1980 to 2024. Dollar-denominated income (current US dollar) helps compare India with other economies globally. But it is vulnerable to exchange rate swings. The 1991 rupee devaluation caused per capita income in dollars to fall by 18% even though real income in rupees fell only by 1% and in current rupee terms it rose 13%—all in the same year.

Finally, purchasing power parity (PPP) income adjusts for cost of living between countries. It tells you how far your money goes in India versus, say, the US. By this measure, India's per capita income in 2024 looks nearly four times higher than its dollar income.

Each measure has its place. Want to know how much richer India is than in the past? Use constant rupees. Want to know how India compares with others? Use dollars or PPP. And if you want to know India's rising share in global prosperity?

That's the PPP share of global GDP—up from 2.7% in 1980 to over 7% today.

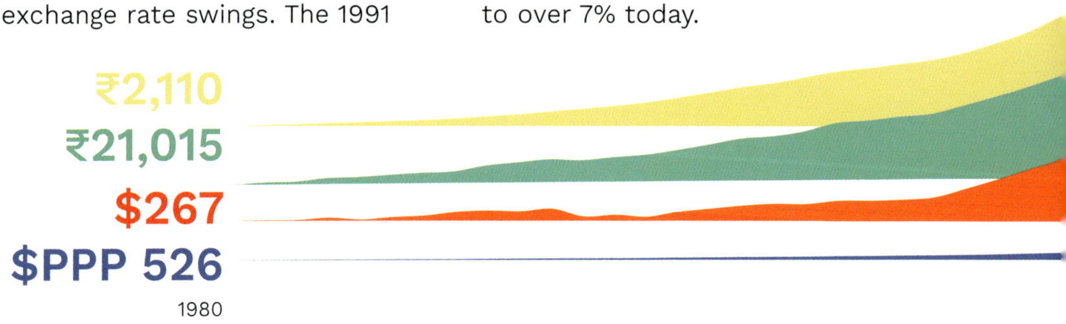

KNOW MORE

- Different income measurements matter even more for GDP comparisons. For example, India is the fifth largest economy in US dollar terms, but it is the third largest in PPP dollar terms.

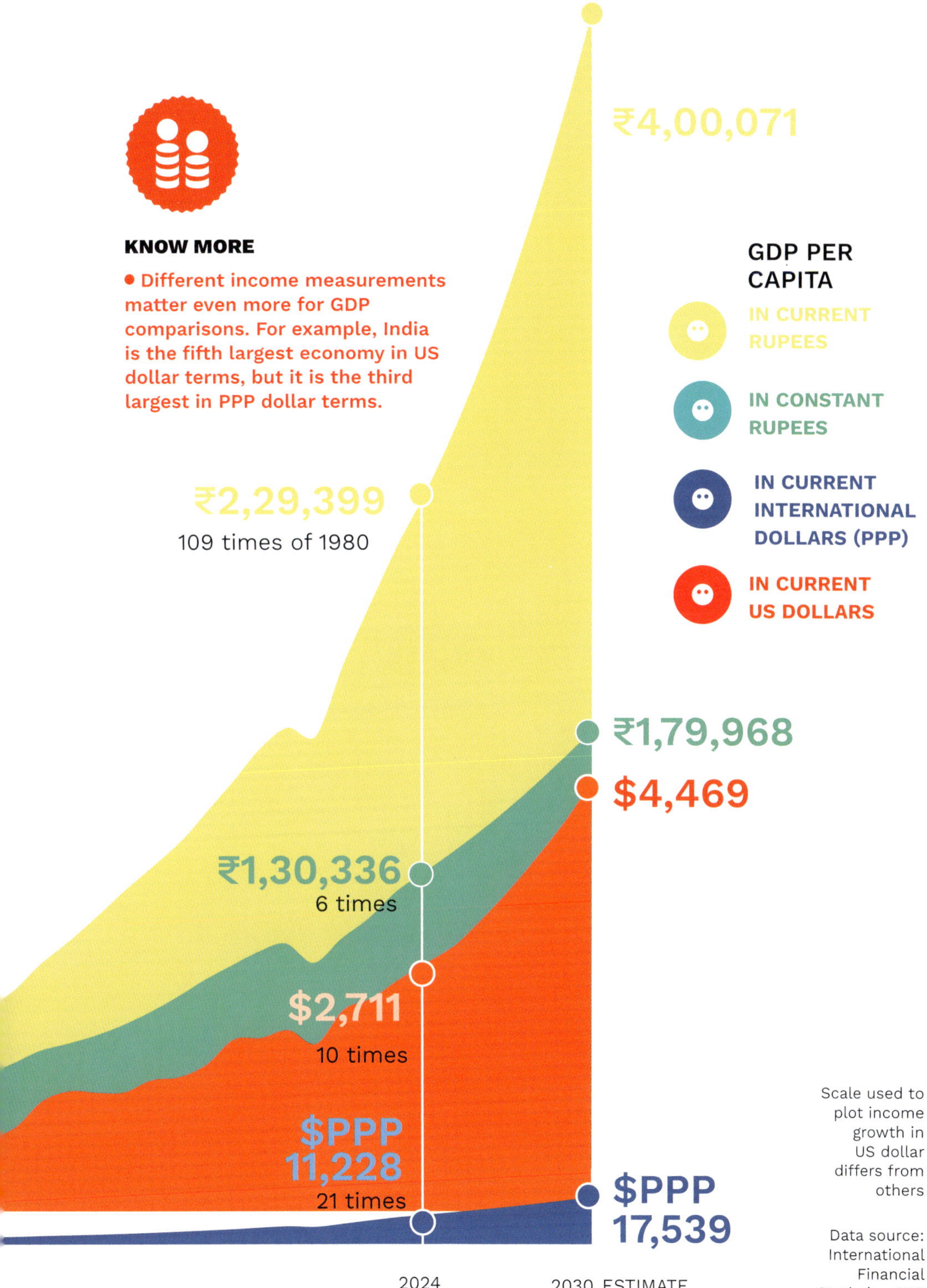

Scale used to plot income growth in US dollar differs from others

Data source: International Financial Statistics, IMF

HOW 1 GB OF DATA BECAME CHEAPER THAN A SAMOSA

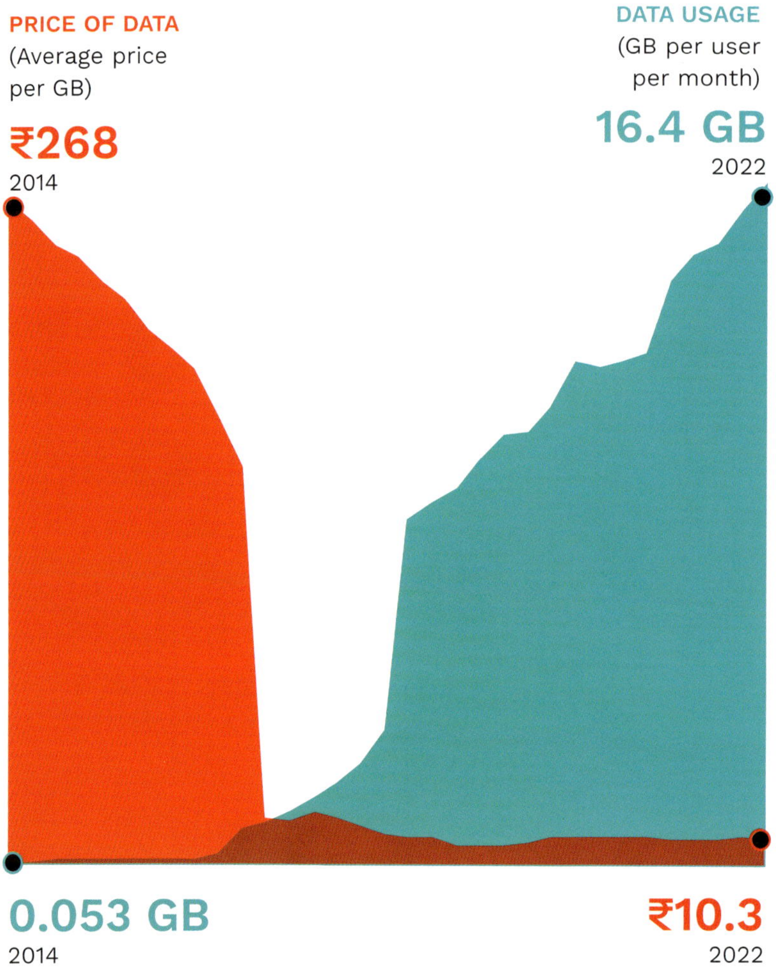

Data source: Telecom Regulatory Authority of India, statsofindia.in

45

The 2016 Revolution That's Still Changing India

The last column of the table below is a textbook definition of what economists call the law of demand and supply.

	Mar 2016	Mar 2017	Change
Price of 1 GB data (₹)	208	19.1	-91% ↓
Data consumption (MB)	133	1006	656% ↑

In one year, the cost of mobile data fell by over 90%—and data use jumped more than seven-fold. That pricing collapse didn't just make internet access cheaper. It rewired India's relationship with information, entertainment, education, and money. Suddenly, every Indian had almost unlimited access to the world—in the palm of their hand.

The price of 1 GB data has since halved again, while monthly data usage per user has surged to 16 GB. India is now among the world's top data consumers. And this wasn't funded by a government subsidy or a global tech push or competition—it was mostly triggered by Jio's 2016 mobile service launch, which forced the industry to slash prices. That same year, another digital milestone passed quietly: India issued its one-billionth Aadhaar number. The country's digital identity and digital consumption revolutions began together—and continue to shape how India lives, learns, works, and buys.

KNOW MORE

60 years to the first trillion. Just 7 to the next ● Page 70

110% OF ECONOMY, OR 4% OF IT?

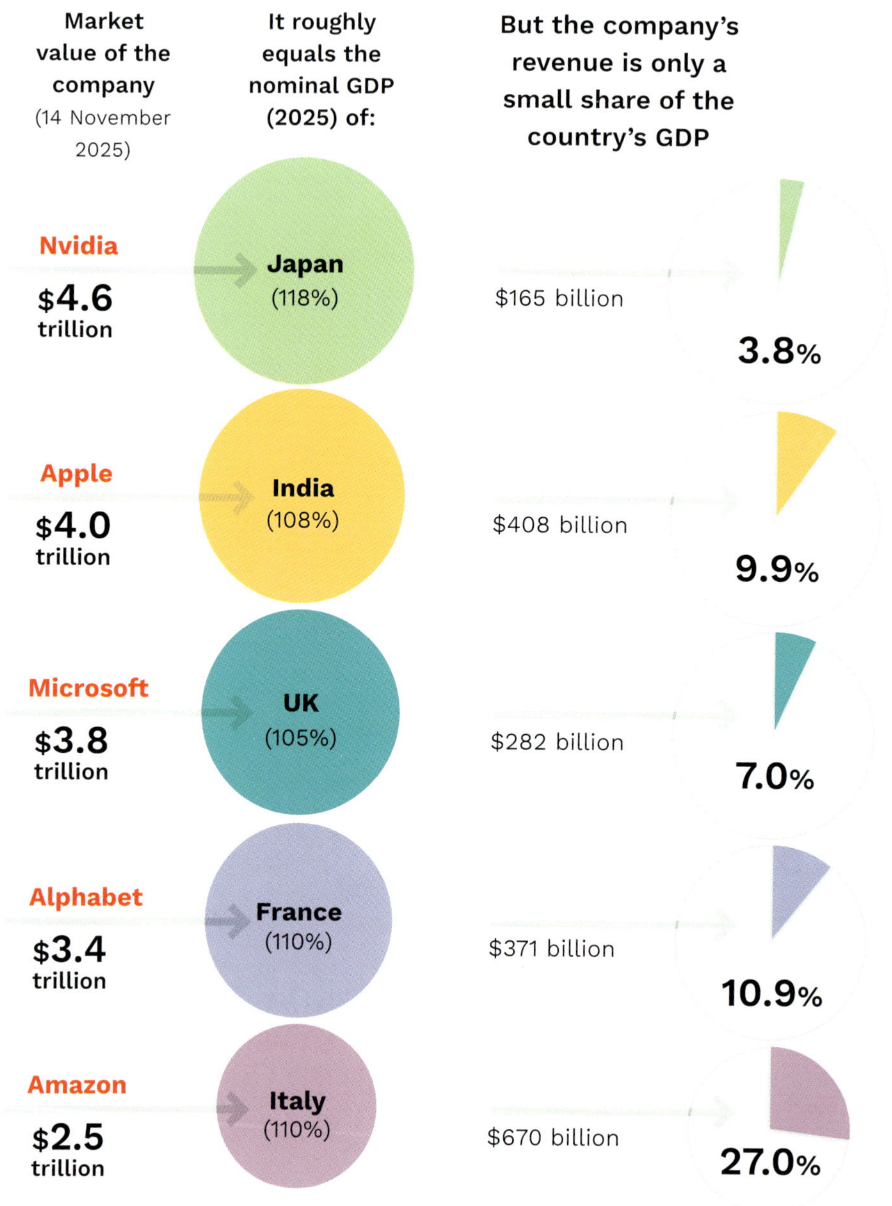

Five most valuable companies on 14 November 2025 compared with countries with similar annual GDP; revenue data is for 4 latest quarters.
Data source: companiesmarketcap.com, IMF's 2025 GDP projections

46

Are Companies Getting Bigger than Countries?

When Nvidia briefly crossed a market value of $5 trillion in October 2025, a few headlines announced that the chipmaker was now 'worth more than India'. A week later, the comparison shifted to Japan. The message was the same: a single American firm had overtaken entire economies. The claim is numerically correct and economically meaningless.

It's not just comparing apples and oranges; it's comparing an apple's price tag to an orchard's entire annual harvest. A company's market cap is its 'price tag'—a stock of value, decided by the market, based on what investors believe it will be worth in the future. If a few large shareholders tried to sell, the valuation would collapse. A country's GDP is its 'annual harvest'—a flow of value, measuring everything it actually produced in a year.

A harvest to harvest comparison would be comparing sales of a company with GDP of a country. Doing this makes the same companies look tiny. Even comparing revenue to GDP has its own distortions. Corporate revenue counts the full value of inputs bought from other firms. GDP does not: it nets out intermediate purchases to avoid double-counting. This is why a retailer such as Walmart can generate sales larger than the GDP of Norway while producing only a fraction of the value, jobs, or innovation that a country generates. The only sensible comparisons match companies to sectors, not nations: Nvidia to global semiconductor output, Apple to electronics and smartphones, Amazon to retail and logistics.

'Company X is larger than country Y' survives because it sounds arresting. It is better read as a statistical curiosity, not a statement about economic power. Countries are not listed on stock exchanges—and their value cannot evaporate at the opening bell.

FROM TEXTILES TO TECH, HOW INDIA'S EXPORT BASKET HAS TRANSFORMED

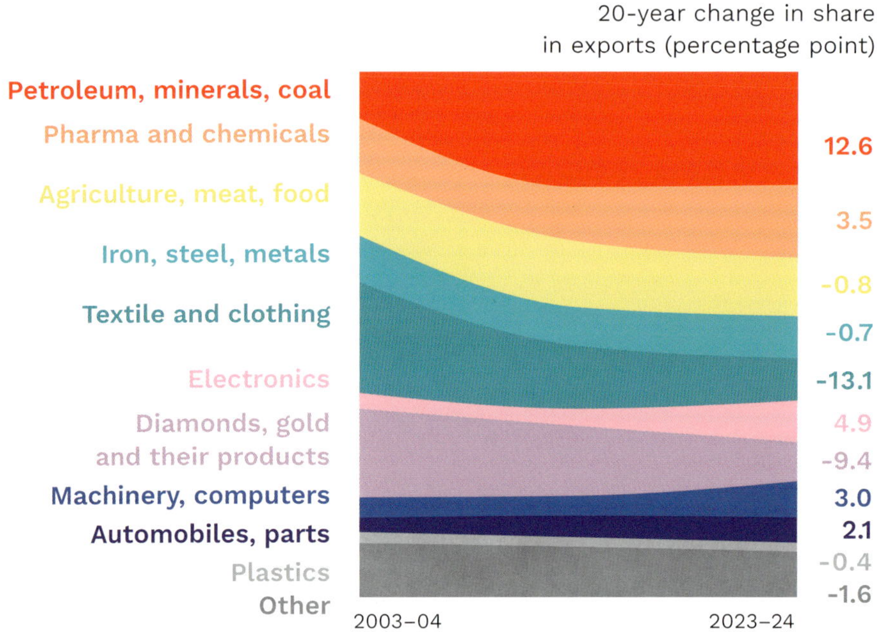

Data source: GTRI

FEW NEW BIG-TICKET EXPORTS

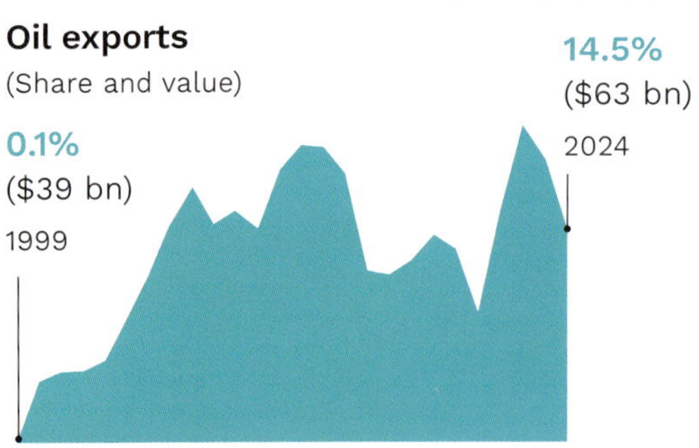

Data source: RBI handbook of statistics, Department of Defence Production

8x jump in export of electronic goods (₹0.38 lakh crore to ₹3.27 lakh crore)

127x growth in mobile phone exports (₹0.01 lakh crore to ₹2 lakh crore)

16x in defence exports (₹1,522 crore to ₹23,622 crore

47

How India Rewrote Its Trade Story in 20 Years

India's trade basket today would be unrecognisable to a planner from the 1990s. In just two decades, the country has seen a foundational shift in what it exports, and imports, and how much of its economy leans on trade. From petroleum products to mobile phones, cars to defence equipment, India's new export champions are a far cry from the textiles, tea, and software story of the past. Petroleum-related products made up nearly a fifth of all exports in 2023–24—up from a negligible 0.1% in 2000. Electronics, machinery, and automobiles have all gained ground.

But many of these new exports are import-intensive: exporters import crude oil, chips,

TOTAL EXPORTS, IMPORTS, AND DEFICIT SINCE 1948

Data source: Unctad

1 billion=100 crore; details on Page xv

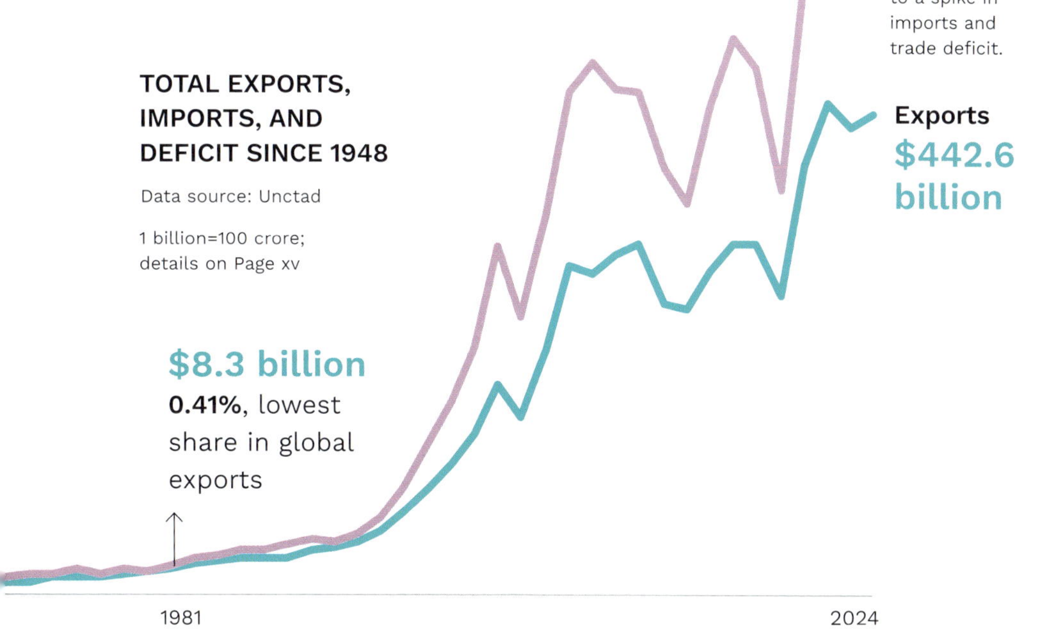

THE SILENT RISE OF SERVICES EXPORTS

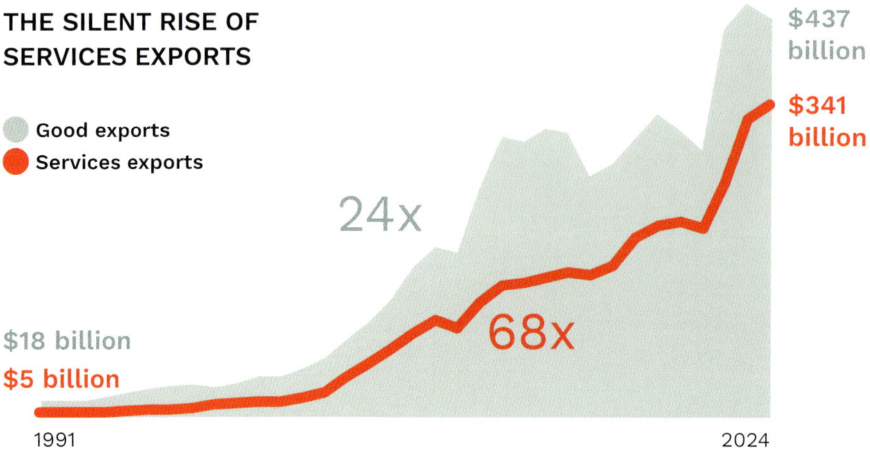

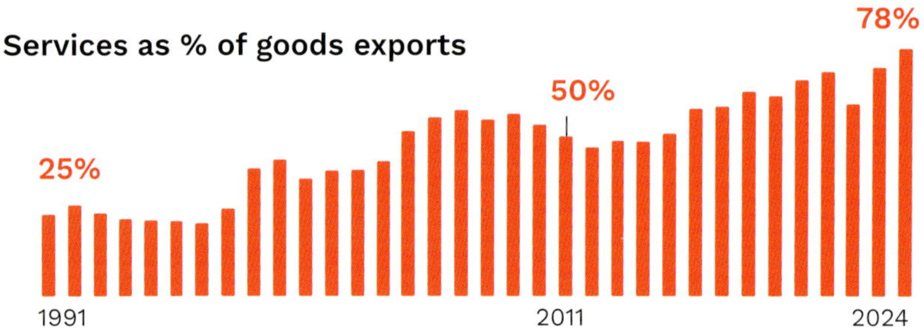

SOFTWARE MAKES UP HALF OF SERVICES EXPORTS

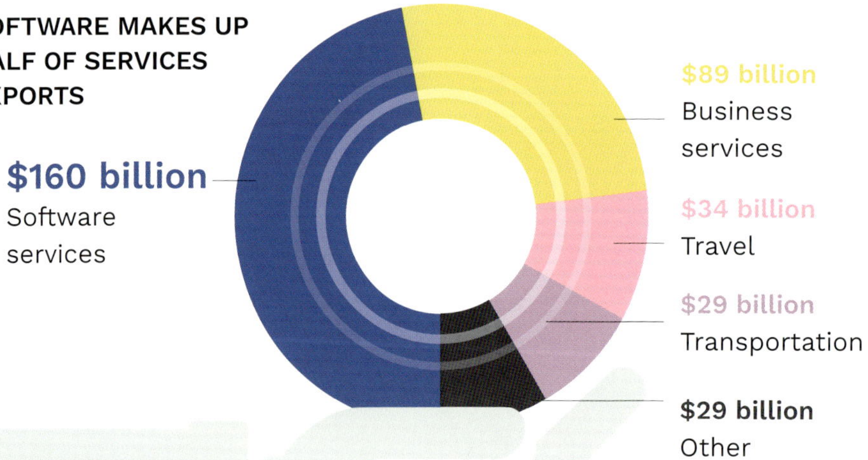

Data for 2024.
Data source: RBI

components, and metals to export petrol, mobiles, and automobiles. That's why in the five years since the COVID-low of 2020 while exports grew by an impressive 60%, imports outpaced it with a 90% rise. Unlike China, which set a record with a $1 trillion trade surplus in 2024, India's trade deficit is high and rising. But there's a silver lining. Many of India's new exports are in manufacturing, a long-neglected area. The benefits of such exports go beyond trade—foreign direct investment, large-scale and stable employment and technology transfer. Schemes like PLI (production linked incentive) ensure that domestic manufacturing grows over time.

Then there are services exports—often ignored in trade debates—that India is quietly becoming a big power in. From just 25% of goods exports in 1991, services now account for nearly 80%. Within that, apart from large and storied software services, is the growing share of 'business services'—often linked to India's booming Global Capability Centres (GCCs). These GCCs are home to some of the most cutting-edge research and application work across industries. They numbered 1,700 at the end of 2024 and employed 1.9 million people generating $65 billion revenues.

India is also far more globalised than it's ever been. In fact, trade (goods+services) now makes up 47% of GDP—more than China or the US. That's a staggering turn from the early decades of independence when self-reliance was doctrine, and global trade was seen as a necessary evil. The biggest takeaway? India has embraced globalisation—not ideologically, but practically.

TRADE-WISE, INDIA IS MORE GLOBALISED THAN CHINA OR THE US

Trade as % of GDP

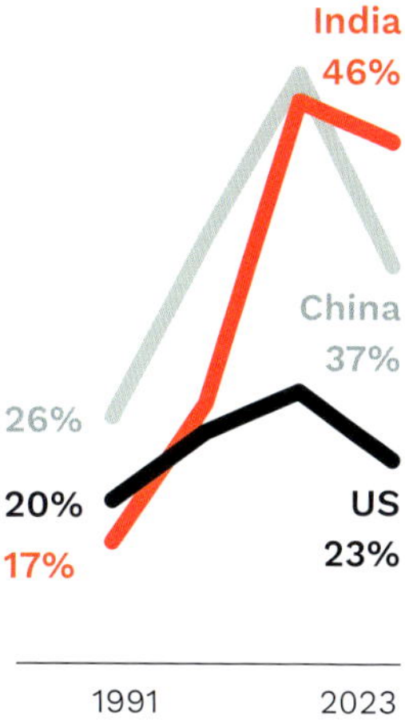

KNOW MORE

The 3% nation: India's most overburdened minority • Page 46

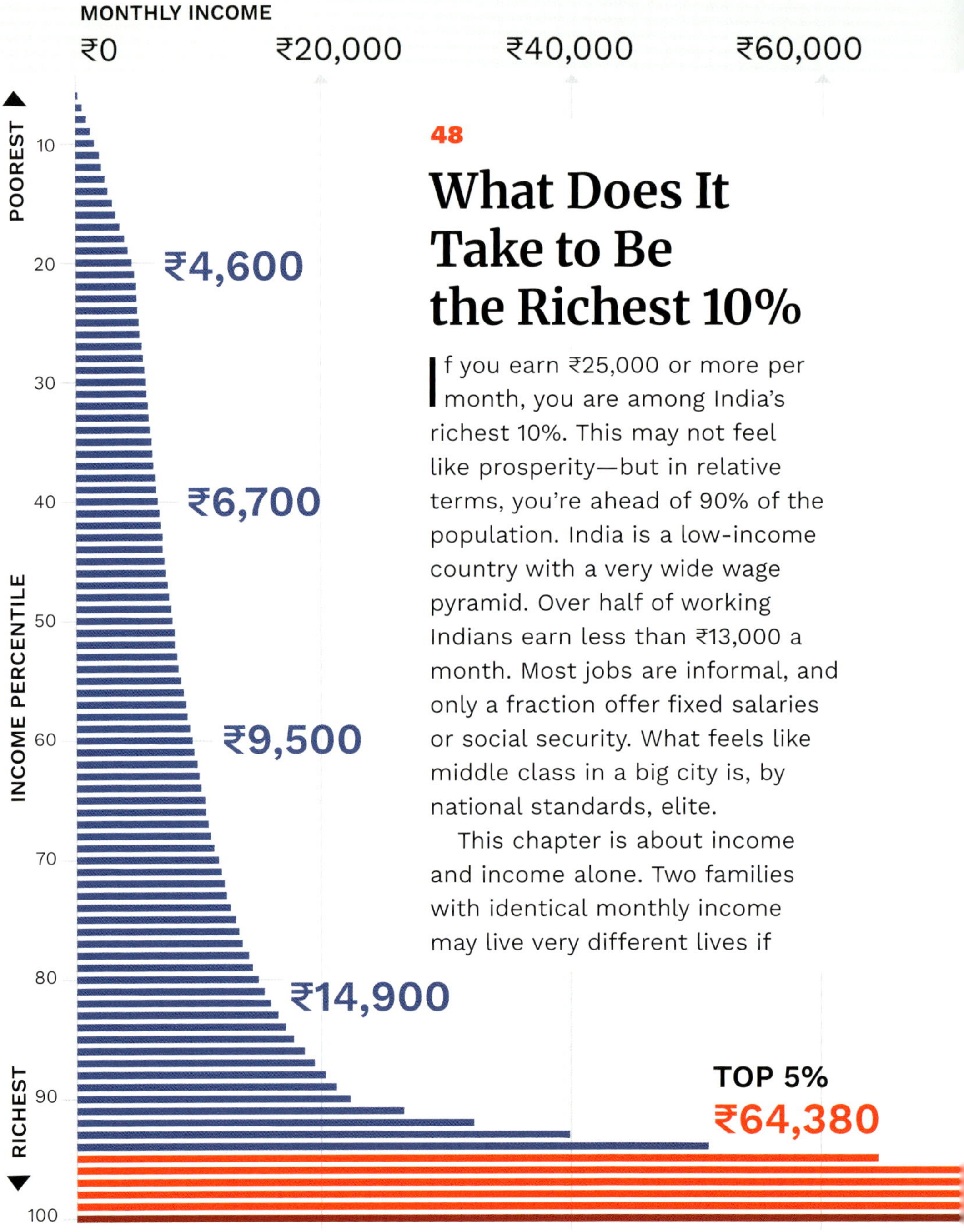

48

What Does It Take to Be the Richest 10%

If you earn ₹25,000 or more per month, you are among India's richest 10%. This may not feel like prosperity—but in relative terms, you're ahead of 90% of the population. India is a low-income country with a very wide wage pyramid. Over half of working Indians earn less than ₹13,000 a month. Most jobs are informal, and only a fraction offer fixed salaries or social security. What feels like middle class in a big city is, by national standards, elite.

This chapter is about income and income alone. Two families with identical monthly income may live very different lives if

MONTHLY INCOME

₹1,00,000 ₹1,20,000 ₹1,40,000

one owns a house and the other rents. That's the difference between income and wealth—and it matters. Wealth provides security, buffers against shocks, and opens future opportunities. And India doesn't yet measure wealth as rigorously as it does income.

So, if you're in the top 10% income bracket, what does it mean? Not that you're set for life—but that you're better off than most, and your choices matter. Much of India's political and social debate revolves around helping 'the poor'. But we often underestimate where we stand—and how much of India looks up to us, economically and aspirationally.

Understanding your place in the pyramid, not just by what you earn, but also by what you own, is key to making sense of India's inequality—and why getting to the top takes more than just hard work.

KNOW MORE
India's inequality puzzle: less poor, more unequal
● Page 118

Data source: World Inequality Database, 2021, statsofindia.in, State of Inequality in India, IFC

TOP 3%
>₹1,00,000

TOP 1%
₹3,70,000

HOW BUDGET DESTINATION INDIA BEATS EXOTIC EUROPE IN TOURISM RECEIPTS

	TOP 10 IN TOURISTS' ARRIVALS (million)	RECEIPTS (USD billion)	RECEIPTS PER ARRIVAL (USD)
France	79.4	59.7	752
Spain	71.7	72.9	1,017
US	50.9	135.2	2,656
Turkey	50.5	41.4	820
Italy	49.8	46.6	936
Mexico	38.3	28	731
UK	30.7	67.6	2,202
Germany	28.5	31.5	1,105
Greece	32.7	22.3	681
Austria	26.2	19.7	752
India	14.3	21.4	1,493

Data for 2022. Greece data for 2023

International tourists stay over three times longer in India than in France

Unlike France, over 50% of India's tourists are long-haul travellers

Where France and India get their tourists from

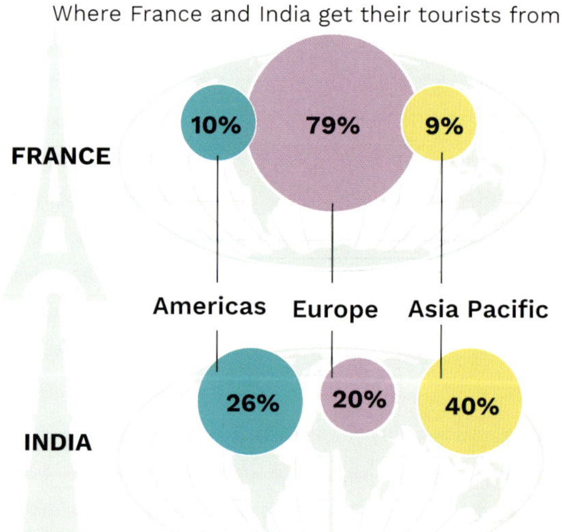

1 million=10 lakh; 10 million=1 crore

Data source: Ministry of Tourism, UN Tourism, Statista.com

49

Why Do Tourists Spend More in India than in Europe?

It might sound counterintuitive, but the average international tourist spends more in India than in France, Spain, Turkey, or Italy—four of the world's most-visited countries. In 2022, France hosted 79.4 million foreign tourists—five times more than India. But each tourist in India spent nearly twice as much as a tourist in France. Greece did even worse. Only Germany, Spain, and the UK came close to India's 'per tourist' revenue—and these are all far more expensive destinations.

So what explains this paradox? One big reason: distance. Over 50% of India's tourists come from North America, Western Europe, and Australia. In contrast, nearly 80% of Europe's tourists are Europeans. Long-haul travellers stay longer—and spend more. In France, the average stay is under a week. In India, it's often 3 to 4 weeks. While daily spend in France is double that in India, it evens out—or even reverses—over time.

Given India's size, diversity, and value proposition, it attracts fewer tourists than it should. The case is strong for the country to bring in many more tourists, and get more out of each.

KNOW MORE
Monsoon makes roads dangerous—and driving safer!
• Page 130

RICHER PLATES, SMARTER HOMES, A PACKAGED FUTURE

Change in percentage share of spending on different heads of consumption (2014–15 to 2023–24)

Increase · Decrease · No change

Figures are in constant prices, meaning they've been adjusted for inflation. This helps isolate actual shifts in consumption patterns from changes merely driven by price increases.

	FY15	FY24
Food	**29.0**	**26.4**
Bread, cereals, pulses	7.0	5.6
Meat	0.9	1.1
Fish, seafood	1.5	1.7
Milk, dairy products	6.1	5.7
Eggs	0.2	0.3
Oils and fats	1.5	1.3
Fruit	4.3	3.5
Vegetables	3.3	2.7
Sugar, jam, chocolate	1.4	1.1
Food products n.e.c.*	2.2	2.9
Coffee, tea, cocoa	0.2	0.2
Mineral water, soft drinks, juices	0.3	0.3
Alcoholic beverages	**0.7**	**0.6**
Tobacco	1.3	0.7
Narcotics	0.4	0.5
Clothing, footwear	**6.5**	**4.6**
Housing rentals	16.0	12.9
Water supply	0.9	0.9
Electricity	1.3	1.4
Gas	0.8	0.8
Liquid fuels	0.3	<0.1
Solid fuels	1.1	0.7

	FY15	FY24
Household furnishing	**3.3**	**3.6**
House appliances	0.1	0.2
House maintenance	1.5	1.5
Health	**4.2**	**5.2**
Transport	**14.4**	**18.9**
Vehicle purchase	1.6	2.5
Use of transport	5.0	7.2
Transport services	7.8	9.3
Communication	**2.6**	**2.9**
Recreation, culture	**1.0**	**0.8**
Audio, visual, photography	0.2	0.3
Other recreational items, gardens, pets	0.3	0.3
Recreational and cultural services	0.1	0.1
Newspapers, books, stationery	0.3	0.2
Education	**3.7**	**4.4**
Restaurants, hotels	**14.7**	**15.9**
Personal care	1.3	1.2
Insurance	1.4	0.9
Financial services other than insurance	4.2	4.3

*Includes packaged food. Some items in same categories were merged
Data source: National Accounts Statistics, 2025, MoSPI

For a complete list of value of consumption expenditure, percentage change and percentage share, scan the QR code on Page 184

50

From Richer Plates to Smarter Homes: What New Spending Habits Reveal

India's consumption story is now unmistakably one of rising prosperity—but whether it's making us healthier or just more aspirational is less clear.

Spending on food has halved in share—from over 50% of the total consumption budget 4 decades ago to just over 25% today. But within that, the mix has changed sharply. Spending on meat, fish, and eggs has surged, while cereals, vegetables, and fruits have grown much more slowly. This may surprise those who mistakenly think India is a country of vegetarians. On Page 10 you will find nearly 80% of Indians are non-vegetarian, and that share is rising. A standout category is the obscurely named 'Food Products n.e.c.'—essentially, packaged and processed foods. Its share has exploded. So has spending on restaurants and hotels, which tripled in nominal terms and doubled in real terms. Is that healthy? We don't yet know.

Besides food, spending on household appliances and private vehicles has soared. Within housing, it's utilities—electricity, water, gas—that rose the most, suggesting people now pay for basic amenities instead of depending on unreliable free access. Spending on health and education has doubled too. That shows Indians value them. But it also underlines the state's continued failure to deliver quality public services for which it collects taxes.

The upshot? The data reflects rising prosperity, more protein, and smarter kitchens. But it also reveals cracks in public infrastructure—and the fast rise of ultra-processed consumption.

KNOW MORE

Who eats meat in India and how much • Page 10

How Indian savers became investors and wealth creators • Page 86

HOW INDIANS MOVED ACROSS 9 INCOME LEVELS IN 45 YEARS

Of the nine income levels shown below, the percentage of Indians living in the bottom two fell sharply—they moved into one of the seven higher levels.

CHANGE IN % OF INDIANS LIVING IN EACH INCOME LEVEL, 1977 AND 2022

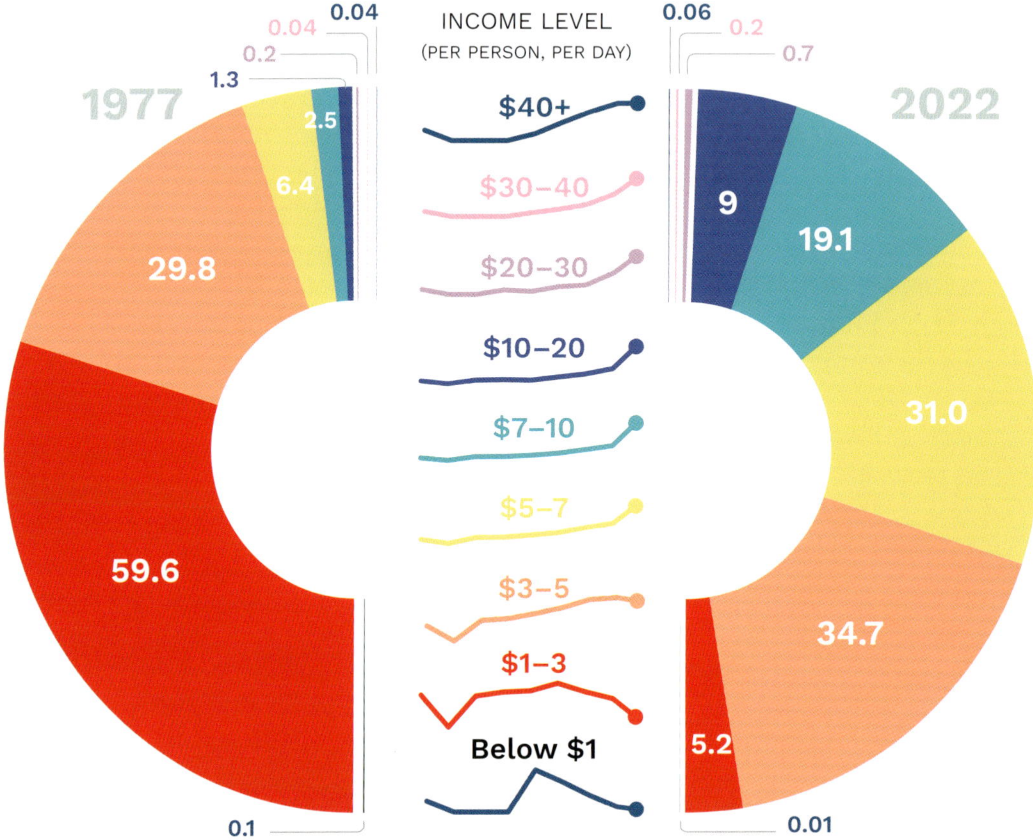

CHOOSE YOUR POVERTY LINE

$PPP2.15/day

International poverty line until June 2025; **2.3%** Indians below it in 2022–23 (down from 16.2% in 2011–12)

$PPP3/day

Applies after June 2025; **5.3%** Indians below it in 2022-23 (down from 27.1% in 2011–12)

$PPP3.65/day

For low-middle income countries; **28%** Indians were below it in 2022–23*

$PPP4.20/day

New line for low-middle income countries; **24%** Indians were below it in 2022–23

Income in international dollars ($PPP) per day per person; One $PPP=₹23 in 2024.
*India is now a low-middle income country.

51

India Just Got Out of One Poverty, and Got into Another

In June 2025, India nearly pulled off a historic feat: eliminating extreme poverty. But just as it reached the finish line, the line moved. As the country moved up the income ladder—from a low-income to a lower-middle-income country—the international poverty threshold shifted from $PPP2.15 to $PPP3.65 per day. By the older standard, just 2% of Indians are now poor. By the new one, it's 28%.

Yet, there's much to celebrate: 378 million Indians exited this upgraded poverty line in just over a decade. Even rural poverty fell sharply, narrowing the rural–urban gap from 7.7 to 1.7 percentage points. People above the poverty line attained new levels of relative prosperity. Back in 1993, just 9.7% of Indians earned $PPP5–$PPP7 a day. Today, 31% do.

But poverty isn't just about money. A 2022 World Bank report showed that 15.5% of Indians are 'multidimensionally poor', deprived of basics like education, healthcare, or sanitation. And among those below the poverty line, the intensity of deprivation remains high. Though Bangladesh has more people living below the poverty line than India, the intensity of poverty is identical, i.e., the average poor person suffers equally, in both countries.

The fight against poverty is one of India's biggest achievements. But the war isn't over. In a country where 58% still rely on free food, it's worth remembering that being barely above the line isn't the same as being out of poverty.

50% of mean income

Used in some developed countries; **25%** Indians were below it in 2023–24**

60% of median income

Another developed country benchmark; **16%** Indians were below it in 2023–24**

Multidimensional poverty (2022)

17% urban and **32%** rural Indians were poor by this measure

Data source: ourworldindata.org, World Bank's Poverty and Equity brief for India, April 2025.
**'Four Facts on Inclusive Growth in India', Surjit S. Bhalla and Karan Bhasin, The Economic and Political Weekly, 1 March 2025.

CONSUMPTION INEQUALITY IS FALLING BETWEEN THE RICHEST AND THE POOREST

Richest–poorest consumption spending difference

Urban

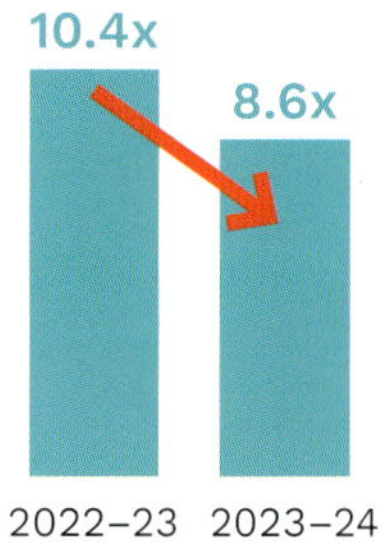

Rural

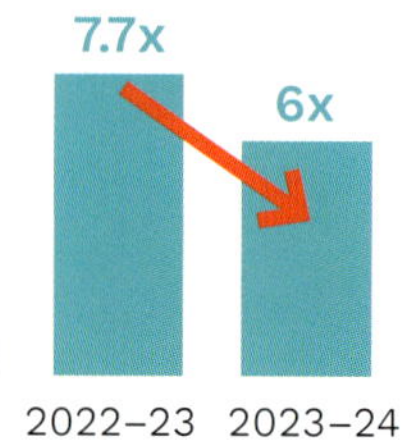

AND BETWEEN RURAL AND URBAN CONSUMERS

1.8x (2011–12) ↘ **1.7x** (2023–24)

Urban–rural consumption spending difference

INCOME INEQUALITY WIDENED BEFORE NARROWING A BIT AFTER 2021

Share in pre-tax income

- Top 10%
- Bottom 50%

Share of top 1% (not shown in chart) has gone up from 6% in the early 1980s to 22% in 2023

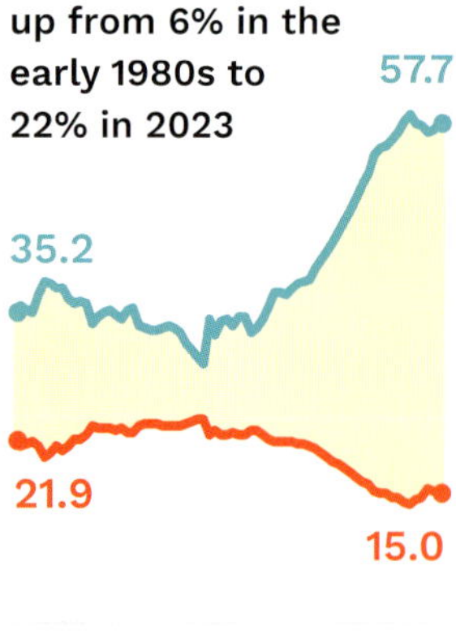

WEALTH INEQUALITY CONTINUES TO WIDEN

Personal wealth

- Share of top 10%
- Share of bottom 50%

Share of top 1% (not shown in chart) has gone up from 12% in the early 1980s to 40% in 2023

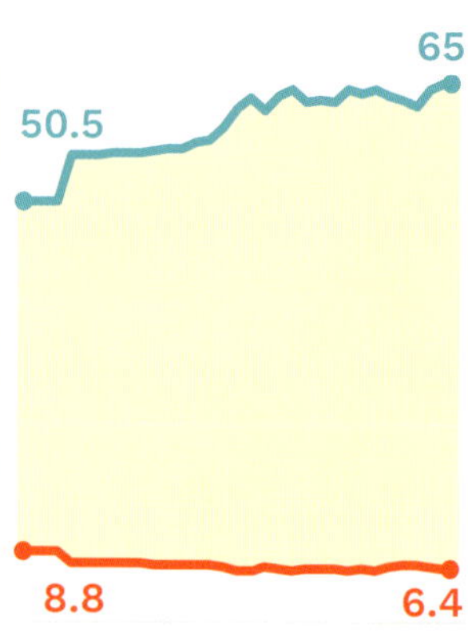

AVERAGE INCOME

Per capita GDP in PPP $ (constant, 2024)

The period of fastest rise in inequality was also the period of fastest growth in average income

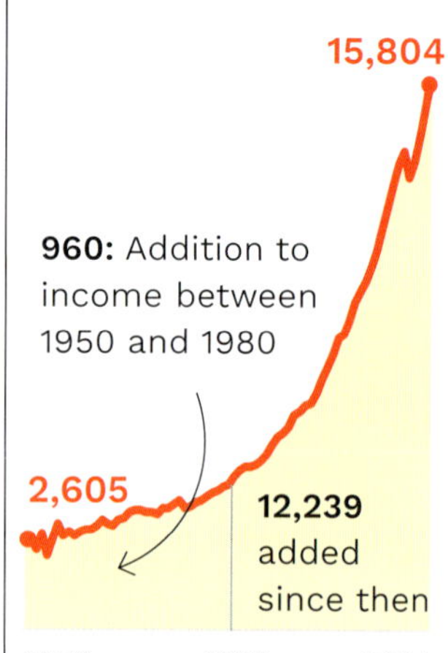

Data source: Household Consumption Expenditure Survey, 2023–24 MoSPI, World Inequality Database

52

India's Inequality Puzzle: Less Poor, More Unequal

India's richest 5% in cities spent an average of ₹20,000 per person per month on consumption in 2023–24, that is ₹80,000 for a family of four. The poorest 5% spent just ₹2,400. But there's a silver lining: the gap is narrowing. A year ago, the rich were spending 10.4 times more than the poor; now it is 8.5. The rural–urban consumption divide, too, has shrunk modestly—thanks largely to free daily ration for 83 crore people, which isn't fully captured in official consumption surveys.

When it comes to income inequality, the picture is mixed. The World Inequality Database (WID) says India's top 10% earners now take home nearly 58% of all income—up from just 16% in the 1950s. The bottom 50% have seen their share fall from 21% to 15%. However, the income gap peaked in 2017 and has since narrowed slightly. India's Gini index, the most widely quoted global measure of inequality, confirms this marginal improvement. One caveat: WID's numbers use pre-tax income, ignoring nearly 40% income tax paid by top earners. That likely overstates inequality, as does probable exclusion of subsidies.

The wealth gap, though, is soaring. India's richest 10% hold 65% of the nation's wealth. The top 1% now control 40%—up from 25% in 2000. And yet, this was also the period when India saw the fastest rise in average wealth and the steepest fall in poverty. Wealth creation is a relatively new phenomenon for most Indians—accelerated only recently by SIPs in the stock market and growing home ownership through EMIs (Page 89).

The one inequality to target is inequality of opportunity. As economist Neeraj Kaushal wrote in *TOI* in August 2025: 'Why do people leave equal Bihar for unequal Mumbai or Delhi? For opportunity.' Their lives may worsen in the short term, but hope improves. The real inequality India must confront isn't of income or assets—it is of access and opportunity.

WHEN DEMAGOGUERY LEADS TO EMPOWERMENT

In just 5 years, women-only cash schemes have gone from one state's experiment to a 15-state welfare model.

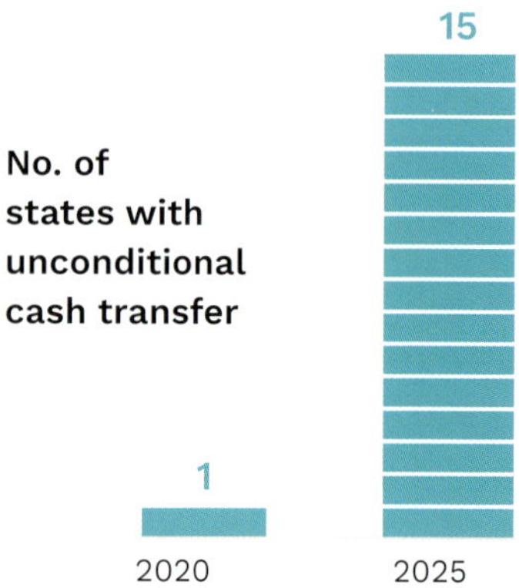

From 0.01% to 0.69% of GDP in 6 years—among the sharpest spending jumps in India's welfare history

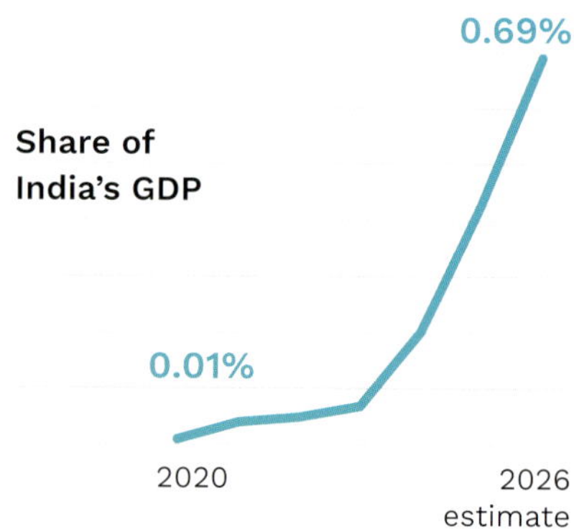

15 crore

women beneficiaries*

About 1 in 5 Indian women now receives money directly from these schemes.

5 states

spending over 1% of their GDP and more than 5% of expenditure on these schemes

₹2.5 lakh crore

estimated spending in 2025–26, up from ₹1,600 crore in 2020–21

*Higher if one-time payments (for example, Bihar in November 2025) are included.

Data source: RBI, PRS Legislative Research, Axis Bank

53

The Invoice for Female Democracy

It could be generosity or politics. Or India's newest development experiment—testing whether dignity and empowerment can begin with a bank transfer. In 2020, only one state offered unconditional cash transfers exclusively for women. By 2025, that number had jumped to 15. Spending has shot up too.

The fiscal impact is real. In Andhra Pradesh and Maharashtra, these payouts now exceed 100% of their traditional social-welfare budgets. Karnataka and Himachal Pradesh would run surpluses without these schemes; with them, they slip into deficit. The RBI has warned that this crowds out money for roads, schools, and power. Seen this way, it looks like the price of political competition—mostly financed by the 3% of adults who pay income tax.

But another lens is more illuminating: look at the outcome, not the intent. The outcome is the empowerment of nearly half of India. Women now vote at higher rates than men in many states. They live longer too—which means they vote for longer. As their political weight has grown, parties have shifted from viewing women as dependents within households to recognising them as independent economic and electoral agents. Consider it a long-overdue salary for their unpaid labour—and a pathway to the economic agency we explore in chapter 22 (page 53).

In today's India, the line between 'dole' and 'development' is being redrawn—by the female voter.

KNOW MORE
When women lead, everything changes ● Page 52

WHEN CHINA PULLED AHEAD

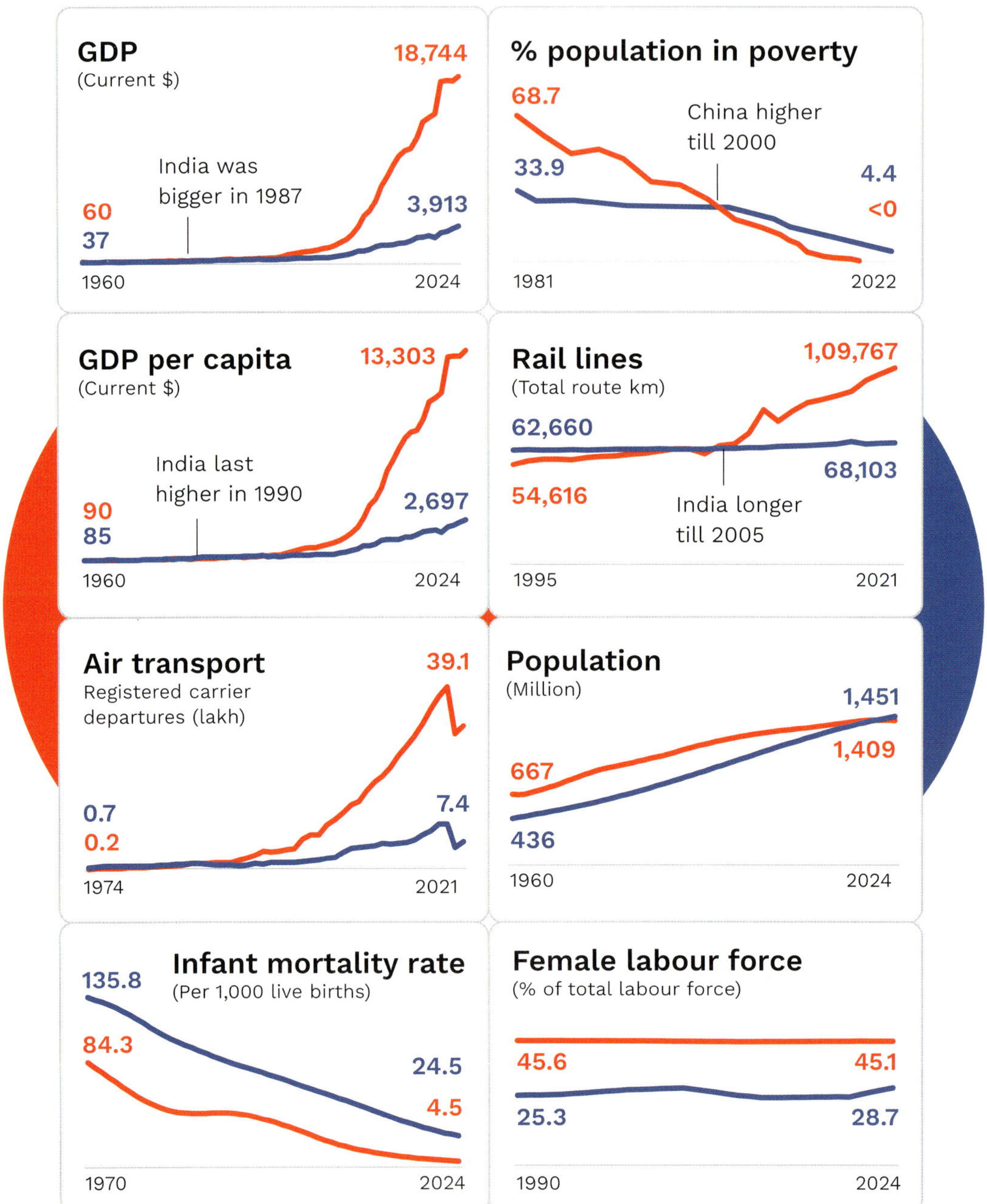

Figures are from common source for both countries, and may differ elsewhere in the book.
Data source: World Bank

54

Two Countries, One Start Line

The interesting thing about the eight charts here isn't how they look at the end, but where they begin—India and China at the same starting line in many development races. Until 1981, the two economies were roughly the same size. Through much of the 1980s, the average Chinese was poorer than the average Indian. In 2000, China had fewer railway tracks than India. Today, China's GDP is 5 times larger, its people 7 times richer, and its train tracks 60% longer.

A key reason for this takeoff lies in what China built before opening its economy: a strong foundation of public health and education. By the 1980s, it already had higher life expectancy and lower infant mortality than India—signs of a healthier, more skilled population. So when China embraced markets, its human capital was ready. India, by contrast, entered the liberalisation era with weaker basics, and its after-effects still show—in high stunting and wasting among children and low female workforce participation, to count just two.

Democracy is what China lacks—and it has paid a steep price for it: the silent deaths of 30 million (3 crore) in the 1958 famine were never acknowledged. The now-reversed one-child policy has triggered a looming population collapse. India's democracy avoided such disasters—but also made urgent reforms harder to push through.

Today, as the world's most populous nation, India can script its own China moment—on its terms. As Amartya Sen wrote in his book *Development as Freedom*, the true measure of progress is the expansion of human freedoms—economic, political and social. India has delivered more political freedom than China, but China offers a model for expanding economic and social freedoms as well.

KNOW MORE

11 new factories a day—hope for manufacturing revival • Page 95

1 An average Pakistani was once richer...

GDP PER CAPITA
(constant 2015 USD)

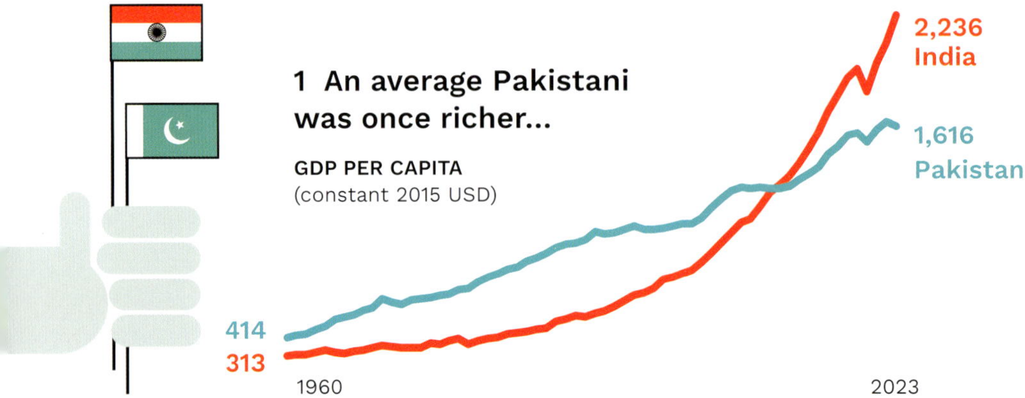

2 ...lived longer too...

LIFE EXPECTANCY AT BIRTH
(Figures in years)

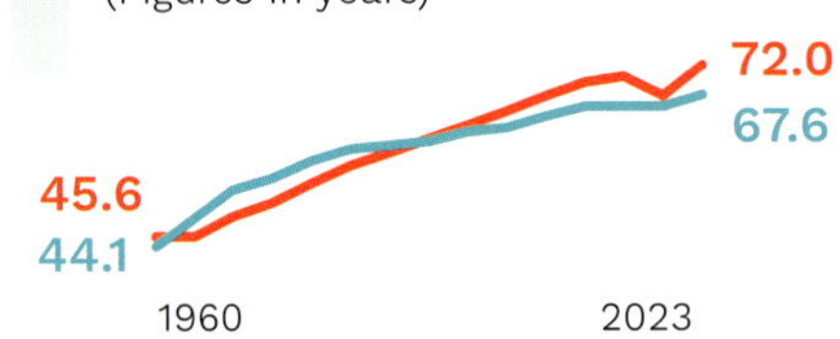

3 ...had a safer childhood...

INFANT MORTALITY RATE
(Per 1,000 live births)

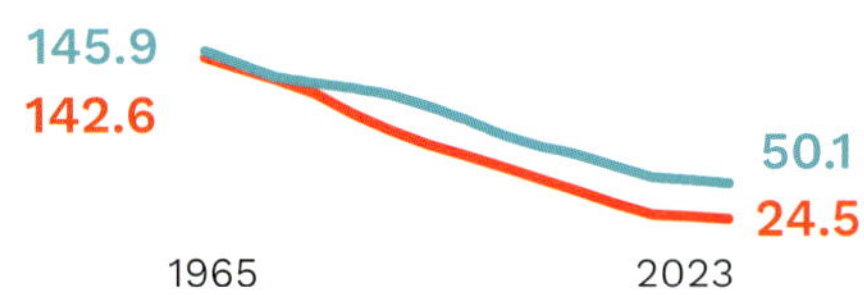

4 ...had fewer kids...

ADOLESCENT FERTILITY RATE
(Births per 1,000 women aged 15–19)

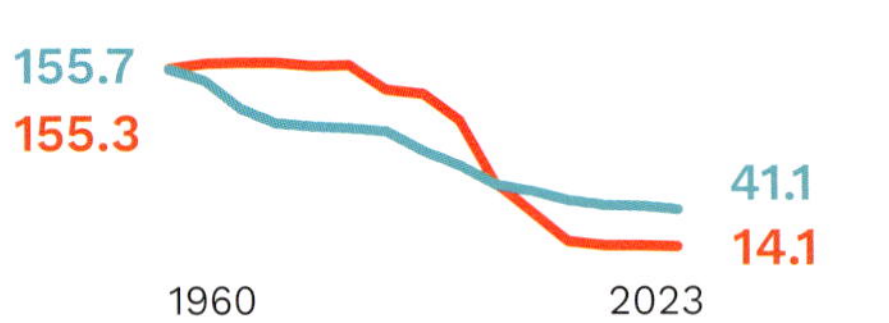

5 ...and similar living standards...

ELECTRIC POWER CONSUMPTION
(kWh per capita)

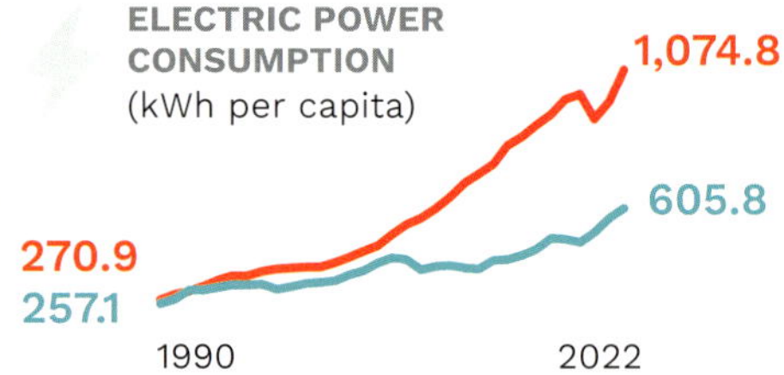

6 ...economy gap with India wasn't so wide...

INDIA'S GDP AS A MULTIPLE OF PAKISTAN'S
(constant 2015 USD)

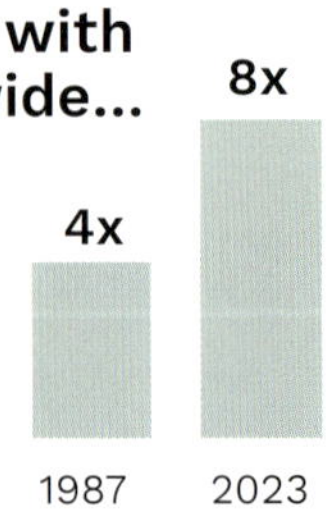

7 ...and inflation was low

CONSUMER PRICE INFLATION
(Annual %)

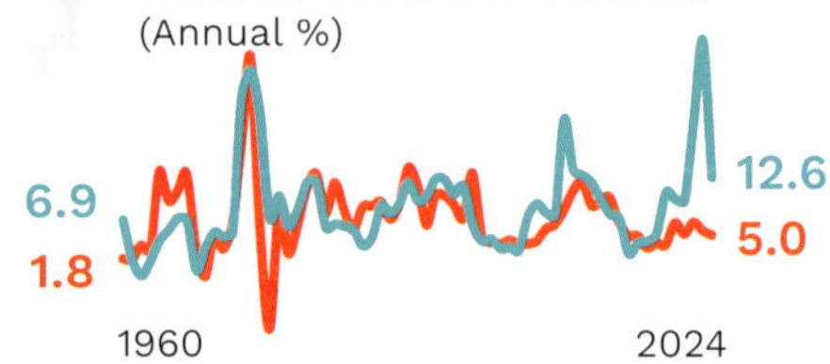

Data source: World Development Indicators. Uses comparable data for both countries from the most recent year available. GDP and PCI are in constant 2015 US dollars. Change in base year can change numbers significantly

55

The Wars Pakistan Lost to India—Without Any Bullets Being Fired

It may have looked 'moth-eaten' to its founder Mohammad Ali Jinnah, but Pakistan was anything but that at the time of Independence. A Pakistani child had a better chance of surviving infancy and a Pakistani adult lived longer and earned more than their Indian counterpart. But as India got down to the task of strengthening its democracy and alleviating poverty, Pakistan slipped into self-sabotage. Its leaders poured money into military arsenals, while schools, hospitals, and power grids stood neglected. Over time, it went nuclear, but lost the real war—for better human development.

The result? Today, Pakistanis live shorter lives, earn less, and study less than Indians. Until as recently as 2005, Pakistan's per capita income was the same as India's—today it's nearly half. The only thing the state of Pakistan outspends India on is its military, which hasn't won a single war. A bigger contrast between the reality and the illusion of security will be difficult to find. A tragic consequence for India, as it too needs to spend much more on its defence than it would have to if it had a less hostile neighbour on the western border. Keeping that handicap in mind, the charts here tell the story of the wars India won without firing a bullet—not against a people, but against a state that chose guns over growth.

8 Pakistan lost these 'development wars' (see left page) largely due to its army's stranglehold

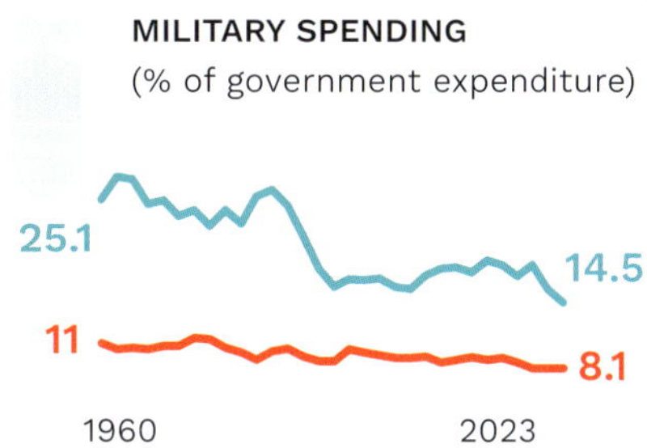

KNOW MORE
How India's coastline increased by 50% • Page 128

FROM BEHIND THE WORLD TO AHEAD OF IT

Share of population with access to electricity

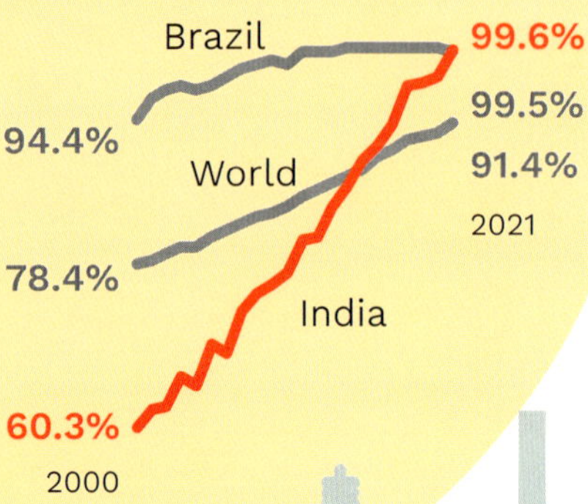

LAGGARDS BIHAR AND ASSAM CATCHING UP WITH LEADER KERALA

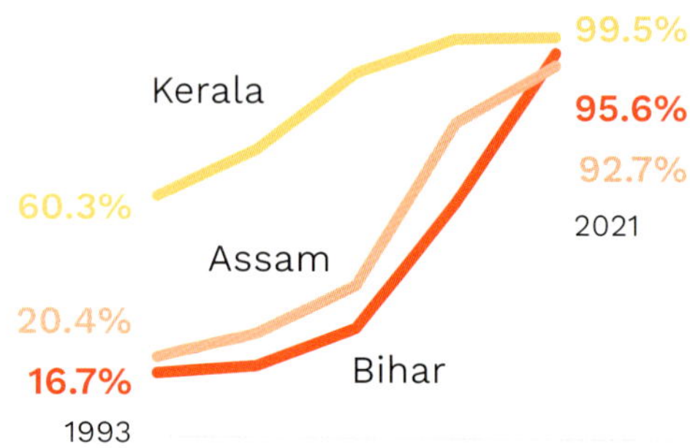

ELECTRICITY IS ACTUALLY FLOWING INTO THE POWER LINES

Share of lighting source

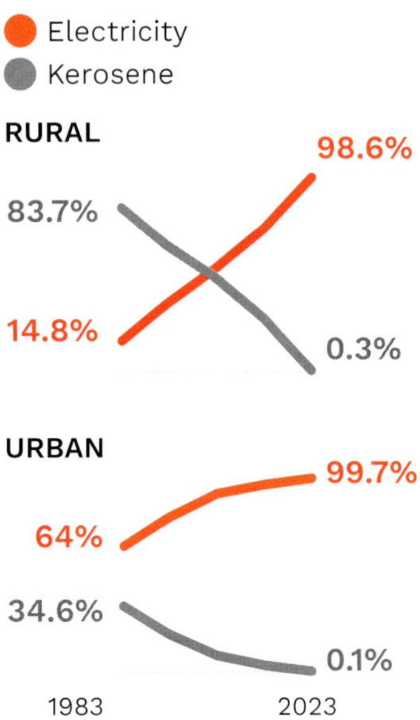

POWER SUPPLY HAS NOT ONLY KEPT UP BUT TURNED GREEN TOO

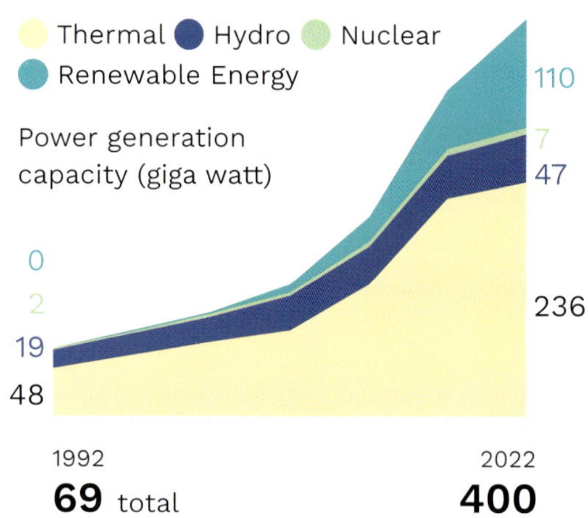

Share of renewables jumped 14x from 2% in 2002 to 28% in 2022.

Data source: DataforIndia, Council on Energy, Environment and Water (CEEW)

56

Power to the People — and the Planet

On 27 April 2018, Leisang village in Manipur made history as the last Indian village to be electrified. That day, all of India's 600,000+ villages were finally on the power map. Four years later, in 2022, the government closed the Saubhagya scheme after powering 2.9 crore unelectrified homes, taking household electrification from below the global average in 2000 to 10 points above it in 2022. Progress was broad-based. Bihar, where only 1 in 4 homes had electricity in 2000, hit 96% coverage by 2022. Unlike earlier, electrification now meant actual power flow, not just wires on poles. One indirect but definitive proof: near-zero kerosene use for lighting.

Even more remarkable, this electrification surge came alongside India's greenest-ever power expansion. In just a decade, total electricity generation doubled. And the share of renewables jumped 14x—from 2% in 2002 to 28% in 2022. Programs like Surya Ghar, which aims to provide subsidised rooftop solar for 1 crore homes, show the transition is far from over. This chapter of India's development proves that equitable growth and sustainability can go hand in hand. As the country races toward its 2070 net-zero target (Page 159), the power grid tells a powerful story—not just of access, but of aspiration. It also proves that sustainable development at scale can be a reality.

KNOW MORE

Who really owns India Inc • Page 135

A LONGER COAST

CHANGE IN COASTLINE BETWEEN 1970 AND 2025 (km)

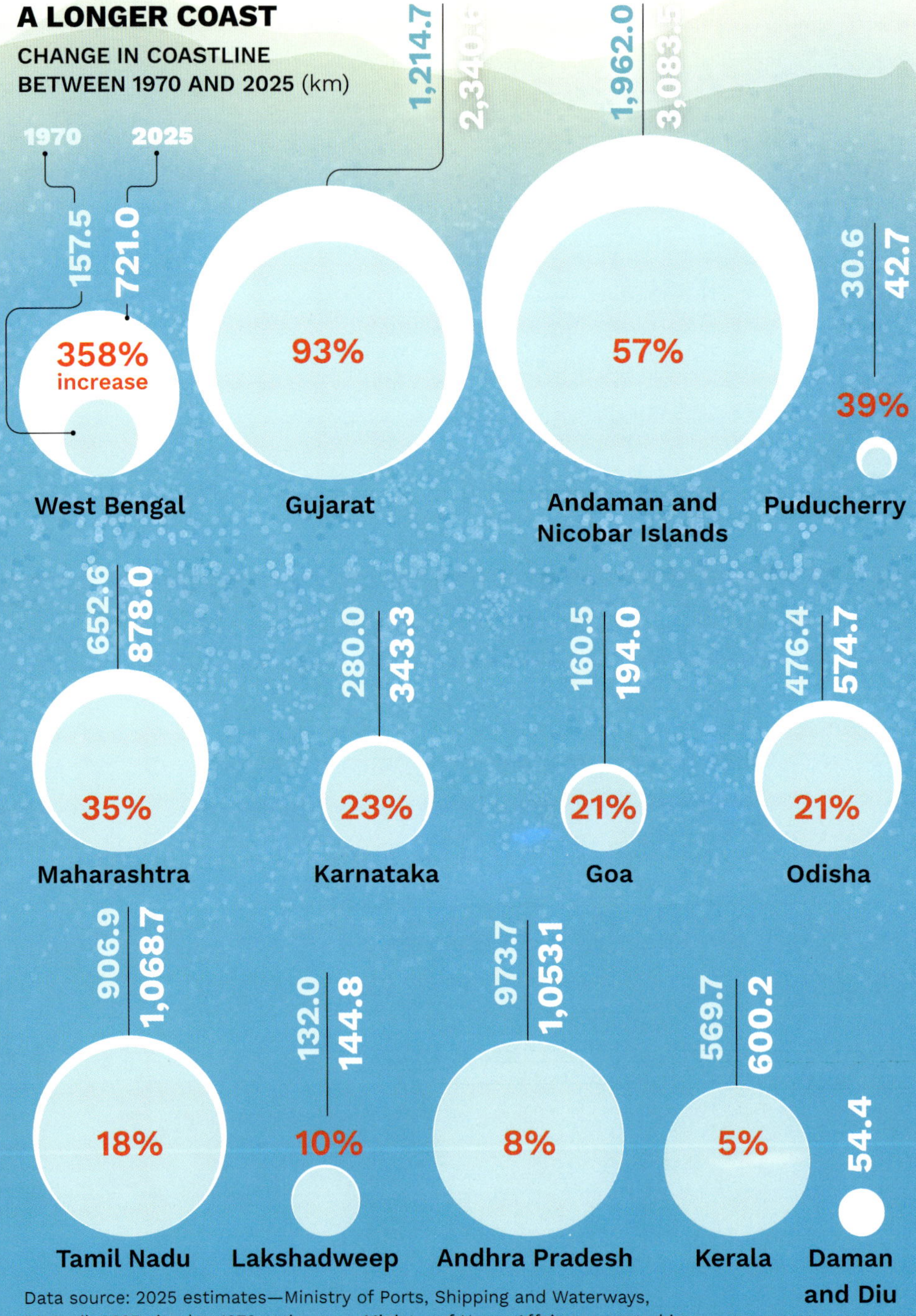

Data source: 2025 estimates—Ministry of Ports, Shipping and Waterways, 29 April, 2025 circular. 1970 estimates—Ministry of Home Affairs as quoted in EnviStats India 2024, pg 80. 1970 estimates for Goa includes coastline of Daman and Diu

57

How India's Coastline Went Up by 50% Almost Overnight

On 29 April 2025, India's coastline grew by nearly 50%. No war was won, no disputed land recovered. The expansion—an addition of 3,582 km—came via a quiet circular from the Ministry of Ports, Shipping and Waterways. It included a table that revised the total length of India's coastline from the long-used 7,517 km to 11,099 km.

The key reason? A change in how the coastline is measured. The earlier figure, in use since the 1970s, came from maps drawn at a small scale (1:4,500,000 or smaller), which missed many details. The new number, compiled after a multi-agency effort across five ministries starting in 2010, used modern GIS software at a much larger scale (1:250,000). This captured every tiny inlet, curve, bay, and island fringe—each one adding a little more length.

Imagine drawing a map of a city on a small sheet. You can only fit in the major roads. But on a giant canvas, you can sketch every alley, garden, and gutter. The same principle applies here. The revised number also includes the peripheral coastline of 1,298 offshore islands—comprising 1,059 islands and 239 islets—that may have been missed in earlier counts. There are islets that are visible only during low tide. What's the big deal about such small pieces of land? Because they're part of India's sovereign territory. Remember: China and Japan once came close to conflict over the uninhabited Diaoyu/Senkaku Islands in the East China Sea.

State-wise, Gujarat and Andaman and Nicobar Islands together make up nearly half of this new coastline. Goa, often at the top of the mind for sea-loving Indians, contributes only a small slice. Sometimes, what you see is not always what you measure—or what you count as official.

KNOW MORE

Spirits, shame, and statistics: India's alcohol puzzle • Page 30

58 | The Monsoon Makes Roads Dangerous—and Driving Safer!

For most Indians, the monsoon is the most awaited season. It brings relief from the scorching summer and triggers the kharif sowing season. But in cities, it also brings chaos—waterlogged roads, overflowing drains, flooded underpasses, and stalled traffic. Yet amid all this mess lies a surprising silver lining: the monsoon makes India's roads safer.

An analysis of accident data from the National Crime Records Bureau over the past 20 years shows that the three peak monsoon months—July, August, and September—consistently record fewer road accidents than other months. August, which is deep into the monsoon in most of India, sees 13% fewer accidents than May and 12% fewer than January. The pattern is clear: accidents peak in May, when the skies are clear, visibility is good, and average vehicle speeds are higher. They fall during the monsoon, when poor road conditions force caution.

AVERAGE NUMBER OF ACCIDENTS BY MONTH, AND THEIR SHARE IN TOTAL (2003–2022)

Data source: NCRB

JAN	8.9%	37,348
FEB	8.4%	35,187
MAR	8.7%	36,712
APR	8.2%	34,619
MAY	8.9%	37,406
JUN	8.3%	35,080
JUL	7.8%	32,985
AUG	7.8%	32,902
SEP	7.8%	32,616
OCT	8.2%	34,677
NOV	8.3%	35,019
DEC	8.6%	36,176

12% fewer accidents in August, peak of monsoon, compared to January, peak of winter

59 Welcome to Delhi, Bihar's Second-Largest City!

Since the 1990s, Delhi has been India's biggest migrant magnet—even without counting its booming satellite cities. In the 2011 Census, of the 1.7 crore people living in Delhi, over 64 lakh (38%) were born in other Indian states. That share is estimated to have crossed 50% today, over a much larger base of nearly 2.8 crore. That's almost 1.4 crore migrants in a single city.

One striking outcome: Delhi ranks as the second- or third-largest urban base for residents of many Indian states. In 2011, 29 lakh Delhiites were born in Uttar Pradesh—more than Lucknow's urban population at the time—making Delhi the second-largest 'UP city' after Kanpur. The same holds true for Bihar and Haryana, and even for Punjab and Uttarakhand. For Punjab and Uttarakhand, Delhi ranks as their third- and fourth-largest city, respectively. It's not just the north. An estimated 10 lakh Malayalis live in Delhi, most of them born elsewhere. This confluence of communities gives the city a unique identity. Delhi is nobody's hometown—and everybody's.

URBAN AGGLOMERATION (in lakh)

The Delhi data is the number of people living in the National Capital Region who were born in the respective states.

Uttar Pradesh	
Kanpur	29.20
Delhi	**29.05**
Lucknow	29.03

Bihar	
Patna	20.49
Delhi	**11.48**
Gaya	4.76

Uttarakhand	
Dehradun	7.06
Hardwar	3.11
Delhi	**3.10**

Haryana	
Gurgaon	9.02
Delhi	**6.59**
Panipat	4.45

Punjab	
Amritsar	11.80
Jalandhar	8.70
Patiala	4.50
Delhi	**2.50**

1 million=10 lakh; 10 million=1 crore; details on Page xv
Data source: Census 2011

WHO FUNDS UN PEACEKEEPING?
10 COUNTRIES CONTRIBUTED 81% OF THE $5.6 BILLION FUNDING FOR 2024–25

	% share in total funding
United States	27.0
China	18.7
Japan	8.0
Germany	6.1
United Kingdom	5.4
France	5.3
Italy	3.2
Canada	2.6
South Korea	2.6
Russia	2.3

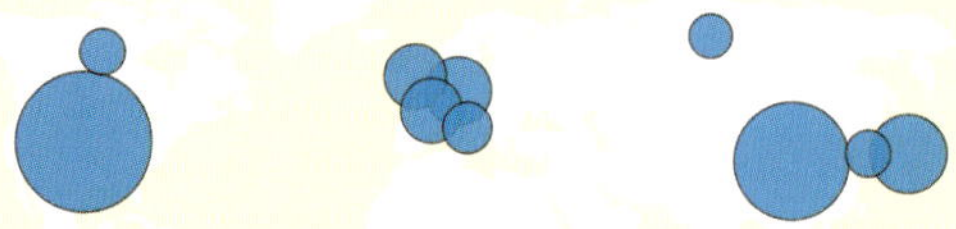

BUT THESE 10 CONTRIBUTE ONLY 7.3% OF THE PERSONNEL

WHO FUNDS MANPOWER?
33% OF PEACEKEEPERS COME FROM THE ASIAN SUBCONTINENT

	No. of peacekeepers
Nepal	6,124
Bangladesh	5,675
India	5,365
Pakistan	2,687
Sri Lanka	322
Bhutan	219

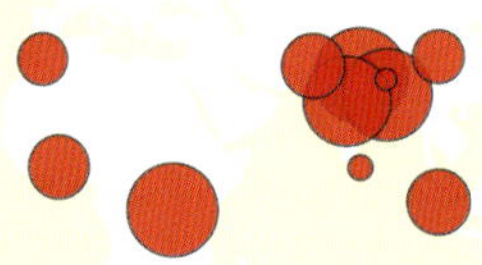

OTHER TOP CONTRIBUTORS	
Rwanda	5,891
Indonesia	2,747
Ghana	2,629
China	1,778
Morocco	1,710

Data source:
UN Peacekeeping,
as of 31 March 2025

60 | More Indians Die for World Peace than Any Other Country

UN peacekeeping began in 1948 to monitor the Arab–Israeli ceasefire. That mission remains unfinished—but since then, peacekeepers have been sent to over 70 conflict zones. Rich countries fund these missions, but the boots on the ground mostly come from the Global South.

India, historically the largest contributor, now ranks fourth—but still plays a frontline role. South Asia alone contributes 33% of all personnel. It has also made the highest sacrifice. Of 4,439 peacekeeper fatalities since 1948, India tops the list with 182 deaths, followed by Pakistan and Bangladesh.

Yes, these postings come with dollar paychecks—but how many people volunteer to die in obscurity for money? India's role in UN peacekeeping is both underappreciated and unmatched.

61 The Indian with the Most Nobel Nominations Isn't Gandhi

The Nobel Prize nominations are wrapped in secrecy—names are revealed only after 50 years. In 2025, that takes us up to the 1974 nominations. You cannot nominate yourself. Only select academics, parliamentarians, Nobel laureates, and award committee members can. Yet, for all the rigour, secrecy, and prestige, the awardee selection is opaque, bordering on biased. For example, up to the 1960s, the peace prizes went almost exclusively to Europeans and Americans. That's one reason why Mahatma Gandhi—nominated 12 times—never won. His first three nominations came from a Norwegian MP. Govind Ballabh Pant was also among his nominators.

Apart from pro-West bias, a former Nobel editor Øyvind Tønnesson mentioned two more possible reasons for denying Gandhi a Nobel: the committee couldn't grasp anti-colonial movements outside Europe, and they feared angering Britain. But Gandhi wasn't the most nominated Indian. That honour goes to Dr Sarvepalli Radhakrishnan, who was nominated 18 times for peace and literature, followed by Jawaharlal Nehru. Despite the few awards, India is one of only eight countries to have Nobel wins in all categories—a rare distinction.

166 NOMINATIONS BETWEEN 1929 AND 1974

Name	Nominations
Sarvepalli Radhakrishnan	18
Jawaharlal Nehru	13
C.V. Raman	12
Mahatma Gandhi	12
Satyendra Nath Bose	12
Vinoba Bhave	11
Sanjib Chaudhuri	10
Meghnad Saha	7
Mehr Chand Davar	7
Hari Mohan Banerjee	6
Upendranath Brahmachari	6
Homi Bhabha	5
Maharishi Mahesh Yogi	5
Others	42

9 WINNERS

ECONOMICS: **Amartya Sen** (1998), **Abhijit Banerjee** (2019)

PEACE: **Mother Teresa** (1979), **Kailash Satyarthi** (2014)

LITERATURE: **Rabindranath Tagore** (1913)

PHYSICS: **C.V. Raman** (1930), **Subrahmanyan Chandrasekhar*** (1983)

CHEMISTRY: **Venkatraman Ramakrishnan*** (2009)

PHYSIOLOGY/MEDICINE: **Har Gobind Khorana*** (1968)

*Indian-born US citizens
Data source: Nobelprize.org

62 The Changing Face of Our Currency

THE SHRINKING ROLE OF CASH?

- Between 2022–23 and 2024–25, currency in circulation grew at its slowest rate in four decades—maybe the first signs of digital payments eating into cash.
- If this trend holds, it could cut down India's currency printing cost—₹6,373 crore in 2024–25.

SMALL COINS, BIG EXIT

- Coins of 25 paise and below were withdrawn in 2011. In just one year, ₹720 crore worth of small change vanished from legal use.
- Older still were the 1-, 2-, and 3-paise coins and 'anna' system—one anna was 6.25 paise, 16 annas to a rupee. 'Char anna' and 'chavanni' still linger in Indian lingo.

Data source: RBI Handbook of Statistics

THE RISE, FALL, AND RISE OF BIG NOTES

₹1,000

notes were demonetised twice—in 1978 and 2016.

₹500

notes are now the backbone of currency circulation, with **85%** value share (up from 42% pre-demonetisation).

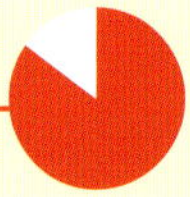

₹2,000

notes, introduced in 2016, were quickly withdrawn after briefly dominating the system.

₹100

notes once made up 19% of currency value; they're now just 6%.

63 Who Really Owns India Inc.?

The total value of all companies listed on the National Stock Exchange was just ₹6 lakh crore in 2000. By June 2025, it had surged to ₹457 lakh crore (higher than India's GDP)—a 76-fold rise in 25 years, which is roughly the same as doubling every four years. Beyond the massive wealth creation this represents (see Page 86), the shareholding patterns of nearly 3,000 listed firms also offer a rare window into who really owns India Inc. Ownership is broadly divided among three types of promoters and six categories of non-promoters. Over the past quarter-century, the share held by private promoters has stayed largely stable. The government's stake, however, has steadily declined, while mutual funds and foreign portfolio investors have nearly doubled their holdings. Here's what the ownership landscape looked like at the end of March 2025.

Promoters
50.1%

Non-promoters
49.9%

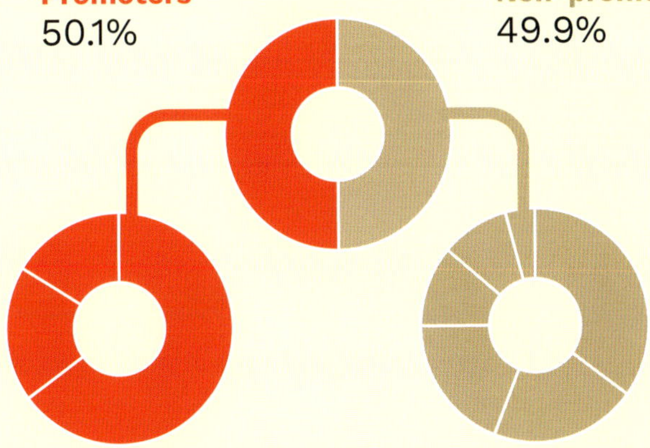

Promoters	
Private Indian promoters	32.5%
Government promoters	9.5%
Foreign promoters	8.1%

Non-promoters	
Foreign portfolio investors	17.5%
Domestic MFs	10.4%
Individual investors	9.5%
Banks, FIs, and insurance	5.6%
Other non-institutions	4.8%
Other institutions	2.1%

Data for financial year 2024-25, NSE listed companies

How many Indian districts saw population shrink in 2022?

- 5
- 10
- 14

Answer on Page 144

Future

UP + BIHAR + MP + RAJASTHAN (OR MAHARASHTRA) = 50%

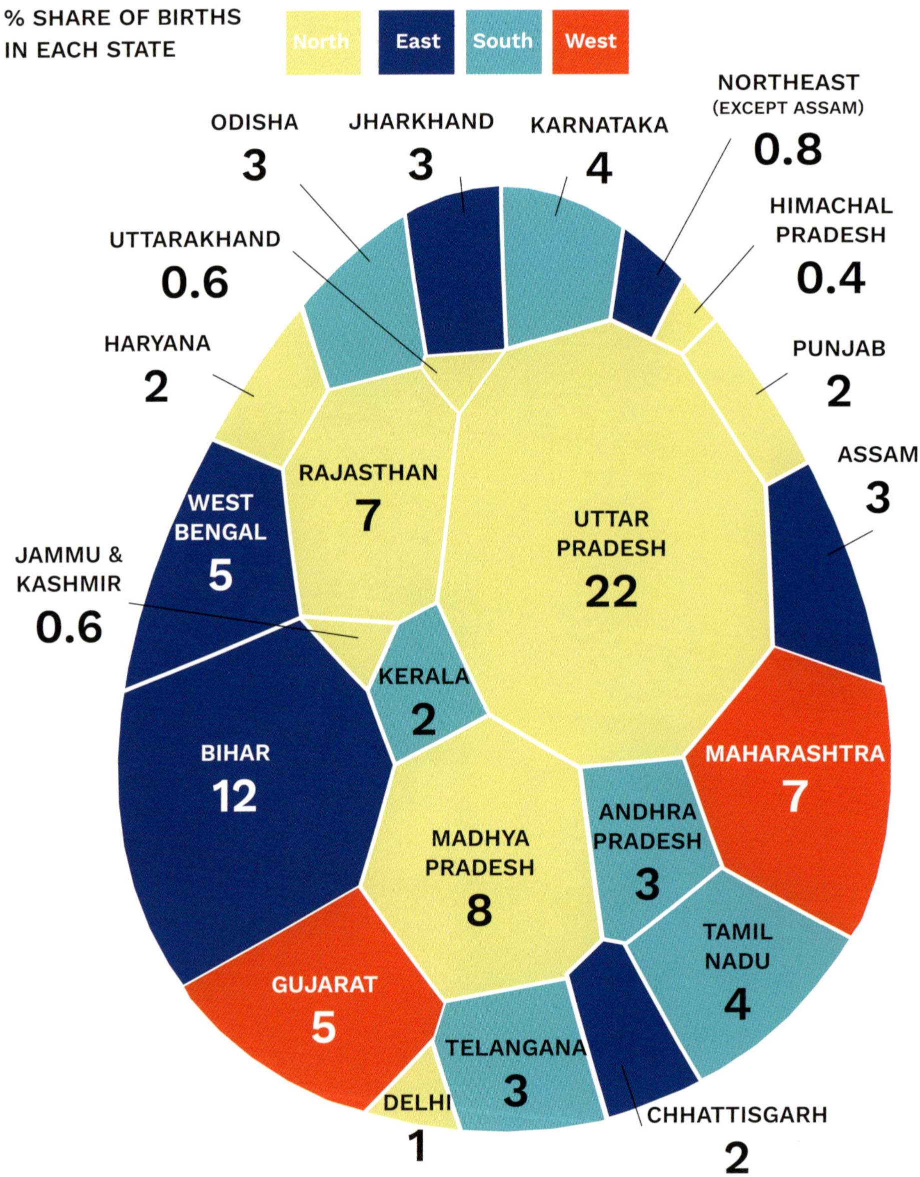

Calculations based on birth rate data from Sample Registration System (SRS) 2020.
Population from UIDAI. Figures are rounded to nearest whole number
Data source: Statsofindia.in, Sample Registration System (SRS) bulletin 2022

64

Where Will the Next 100 Babies in India Be Born?

Almost half of India's next generation is being born in just four states—call them the baby capitals of India. The other 26 states (counting Delhi and Puducherry) share the other half of the new arrivals. The skew in the population of newborns tells us what India will look like in the not-too-distant future.

The four baby boom states are home to 37% Indians today—13 percentage points less than their contribution to future population.

Of course, where you are born is not necessarily the place where you work or live. Not in a country where people are moving places faster than ever—e.g. labour mobility is on the rise. The states with the most people and highest birth rates are also India's biggest labour exporters. Uttar Pradesh and Bihar are the two biggest suppliers of labour and Gujarat and Maharashtra are the two biggest importers.

In the imaginable future, the Jhas, Mishras, Singhs, Yadavs—a sample of surnames from Uttar Pradesh and Bihar—from the north will not only speak fluent Tamil, Malayalam or Telugu, but could also be elected MLAs in these states. That would be the 'Kamala Harris effect' happening right here in India!

KNOW MORE

How fast does income double in India ● Page 75

65

What 25 Pyramids Say about India's Future

Look closely at a population pyramid and you'll see more than just age bands. You'll see where India's past was born, where the present works, and where the future is heading.

SHAPE OF INDIA...

PAST, PRESENT, AND FUTURE

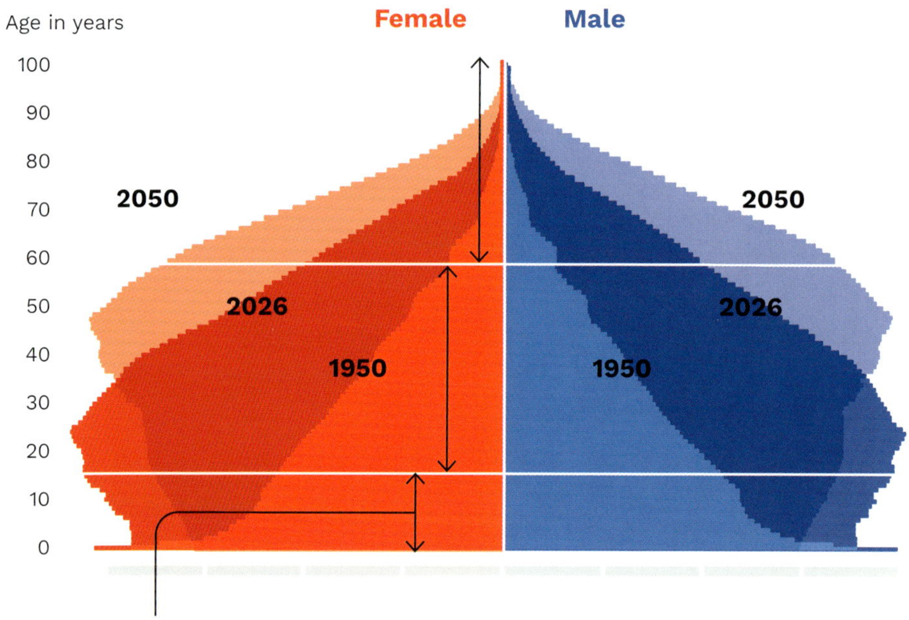

0–14 years: Wide base signals high fertility and a rapidly growing population

15–60 years: Working age; usually support both dependent groups

60+ years: Older adults; large numbers mean rising life expectancy, and need for care infrastructure

...AND 4 SHAPES OF INDIAN STATES

Some states still look like classical pyramids—wide base of children, narrowing towards the top. Bihar, UP, Jharkhand, Madhya Pradesh, Chhattisgarh, and Assam fall in this group. These states are younger, poorer, more fertile—and the largest exporters of people.

1. YOUNG, FERTILE, AND LABOUR-EXPORTING

Their widest pyramid bases make these states distinct. Bihar and Jharkhand are the youngest in this lot which explains their classical pyramid shapes.

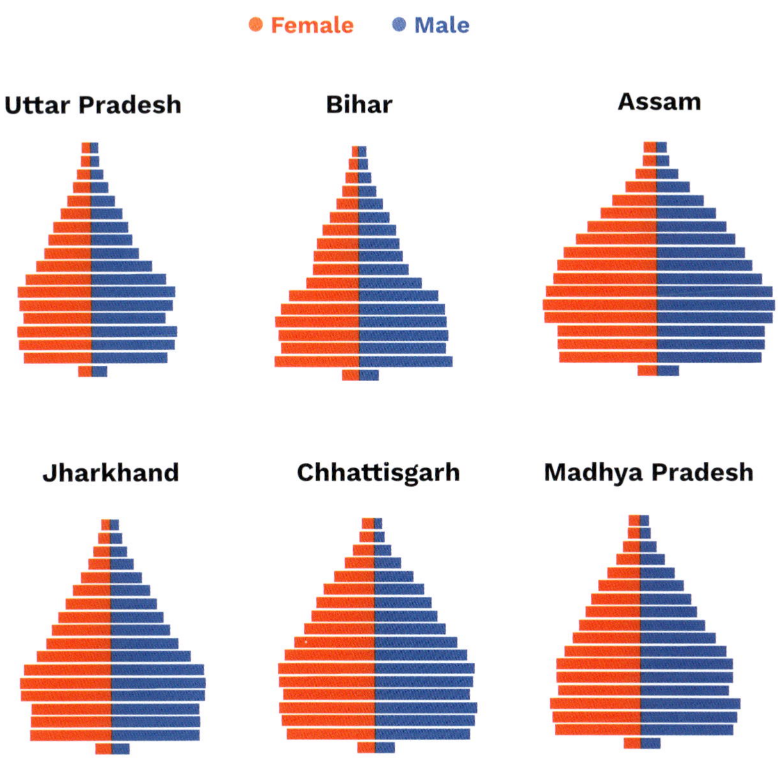

India pyramid shows data for all years (0–100); state pyramids are 4-year age groups.
All state pyramids are for 2026.

2. MIDDLE-HEAVY STATES

Punjab and Haryana show an unusual blue (male) bulge in their mid-sections—echoing their skewed sex ratios.

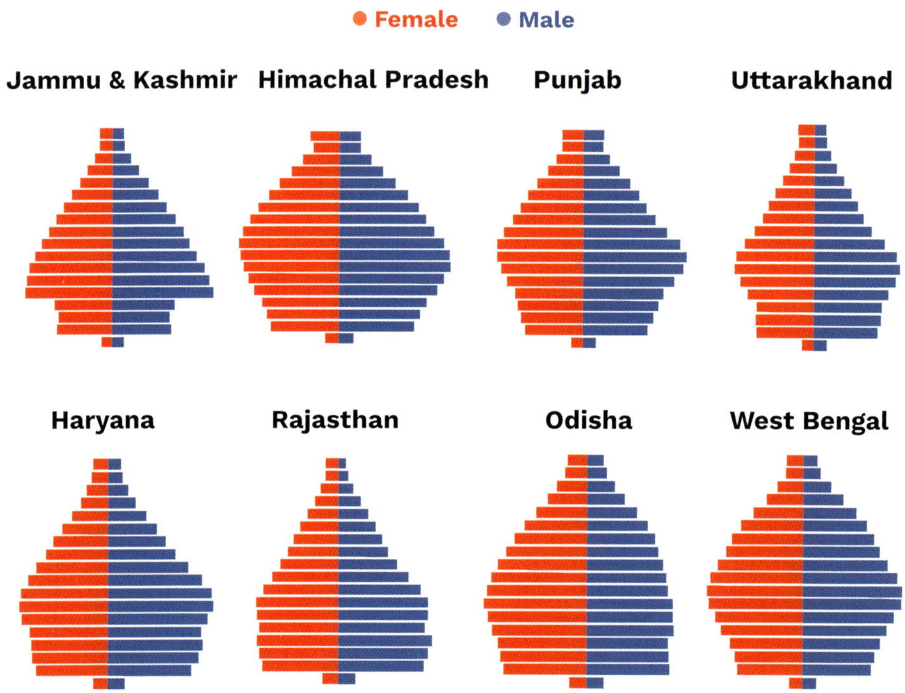

Then come the industrialised magnets—Delhi, Tamil Nadu, Maharashtra, Gujarat, and Karnataka. Their pyramids bulge in the middle: a concentration of working-age population. Migration and slower fertility have reshaped these regions. Somewhere in between are states like Punjab, Himachal Pradesh, West Bengal, and Uttarakhand. They are not industrialised at the same scale but have lower fertility. Their pyramids also bulge in the middle, for different reasons—outmigration of the young and aging populations staying behind.

Data source: UN World Population Prospects and Ministry of Health and Family Welfare.
Estimates not available for northeast states, Sikkim, and union territories.

KNOW MORE

How Delhi became Bihar's second-largest city ● Page 131

3. MIGRANT MAGNETS, INDUSTRIAL GIANTS

In this most homogeneous looking group,
Tamil Nadu's most pronounced mid-to-upper
bulge shows a higher share of people aged 50+

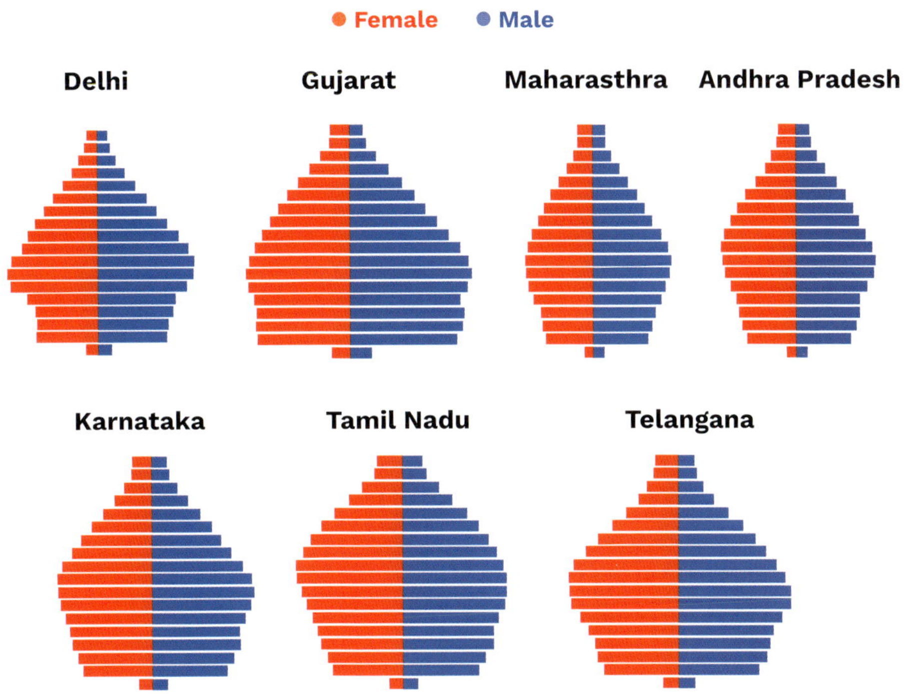

4. AGING STATES, GLIMPSE OF 2050

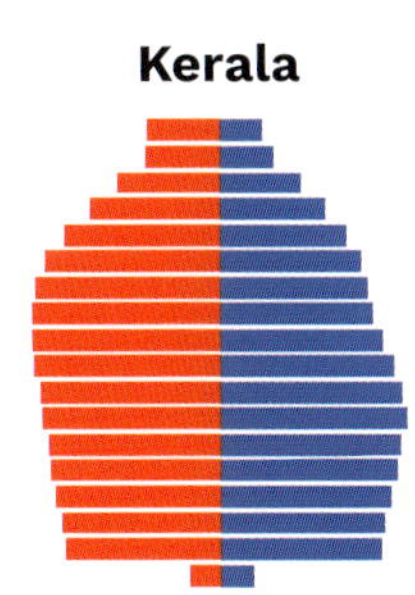

And then there is Kerala—a glimpse of India's 2050 and beyond. Its pyramid looks more like a square: nearly equal numbers across age bands. It mirrors what the pyramids of Germany and Japan look like today—aging but stable. A demographic dividend that has now entered maturity.

Each of these 25 pyramids offers a different forecast. Together, they form a mosaic of India's evolving soul.

ARE THE RED ZONES ON THIS MAP INDIA'S FUTURE?

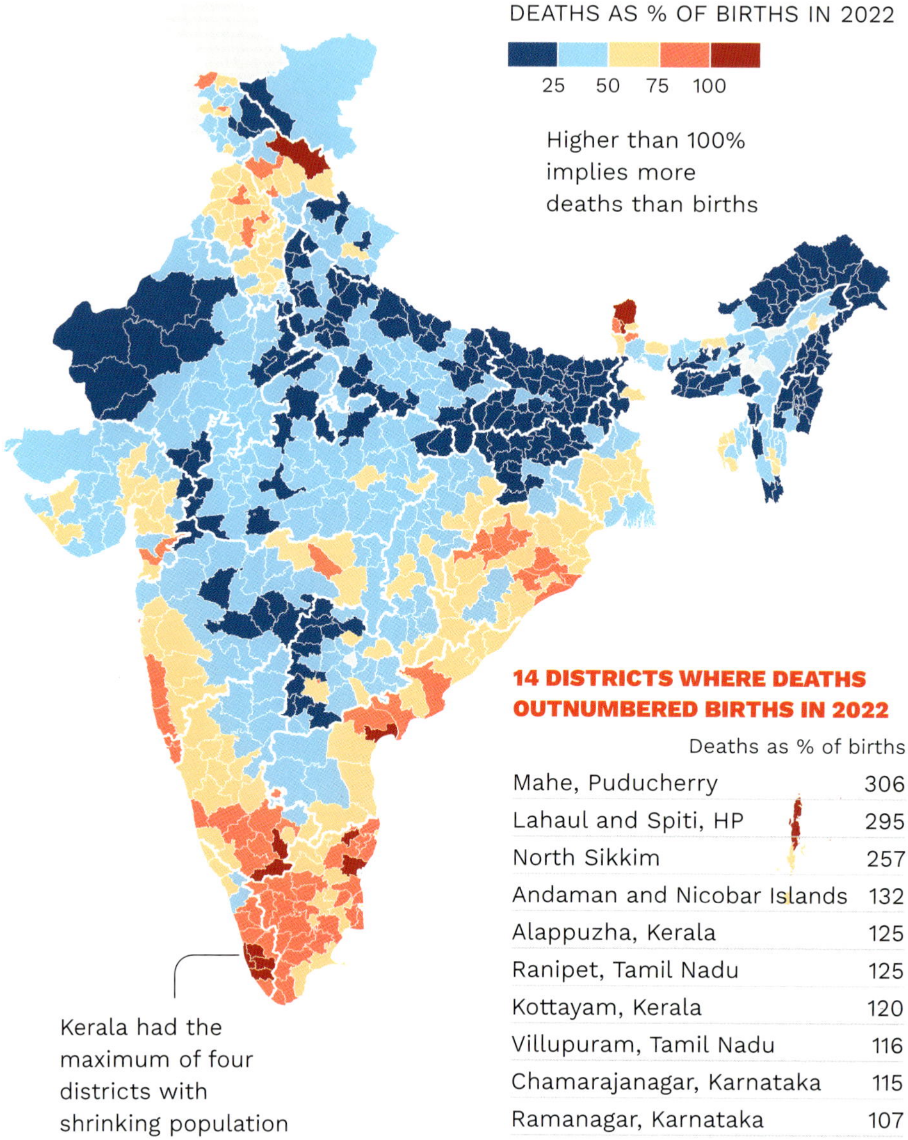

14 DISTRICTS WHERE DEATHS OUTNUMBERED BIRTHS IN 2022

	Deaths as % of births
Mahe, Puducherry	306
Lahaul and Spiti, HP	295
North Sikkim	257
Andaman and Nicobar Islands	132
Alappuzha, Kerala	125
Ranipet, Tamil Nadu	125
Kottayam, Kerala	120
Villupuram, Tamil Nadu	116
Chamarajanagar, Karnataka	115
Ramanagar, Karnataka	107
Bapatla, Andhra Pradesh	105
Pathanamthitta, Kerala	105
Kollam, Kerala	102
South Sikkim	101

Data source: Civil Registration System reports published annually by Census Commissioner

67

How Much Does it Cost to Raise a Child?

Inflation at the national level is not the same as inflation for a family—and even that changes with your age and stage of life. One of the ways to personalise this idea is to track the cost of raising a child from birth to adulthood. It also helps show how inflation affects affordability across 20+ years—building on the gap between real and nominal wages (See Page 92). Think of it this way: you can either buy a high-end car, or raise a child. Of course, a child brings far greater joy and change. But emotionally fulfilling as it is, it's also a huge financial commitment.

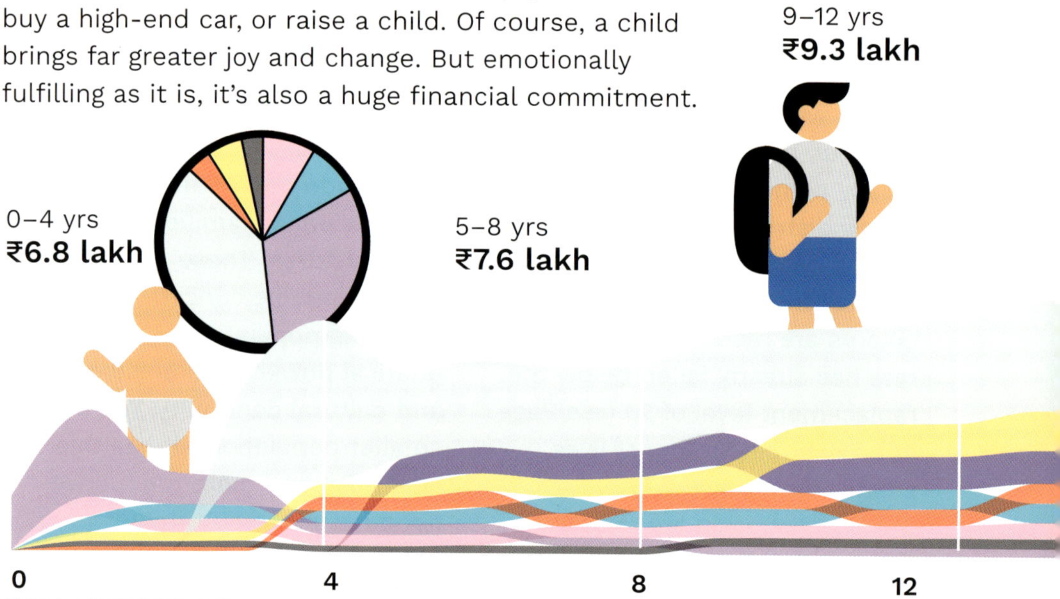

ASSUMPTIONS

The estimated cost of ₹74.3 lakh (max ₹1.8 crore, min ₹1.2 crore) is indicative and will vary by city and lifestyle. But it provides a useful ballpark for planning. Here's what it includes:

HOUSING: Renting or buying a larger house after the child is 4 will add to EMI or rent

FOOD: Higher early-life costs due to infant nutrition; modest share of overall total

CLOTHING: Includes all clothes, school uniforms, shoes—frequently replaced as kids outgrow them

HEALTHCARE: Prenatal to adolescence; assumes insurance and no major illness

₹74.3 lakh
From conception to college (21 years), at current estimates

₹1.16 crore
with 3% annual inflation

₹1.83 crore
with 6% annual inflation

CUMULATIVE BREAK-UP

59% of the total cost goes into education. This could be more in metros; varies hugely from public to private or boarding school

10% is spent on housing; a couple without children can live in a smaller home

9% on entertainment, which spikes during the teen years: birthdays, gadgets, hobbies, holidays with friends.

6% on clothing, followed by food, transportation, and healthcare—each contributing about **5%**.

EDUCATION: Private schools; includes fees, coaching, books, school trips (uniforms and shoes included)

TRANSPORT: To school/college, plus family holidays; may include a second vehicle

ENTERTAINMENT: Toys, books, internet, gadgets, holidays with friends

MISCELLANEOUS: Extra consumption (utilities, toiletries, and household help) from having one more person.

These estimates reflect urban upper-middle class spending patterns. For details on all assumptions, and yearly break-up of costs, scan the QR code on Page 182

1 million=10 lakh; 10 million=1 crore; details on Page xv

HOW CHINA WILL BE THE BIGGEST GAINER—AND LOSER—OF PEOPLE

TOP GAINERS (1950–2000)
Increase in population (million)

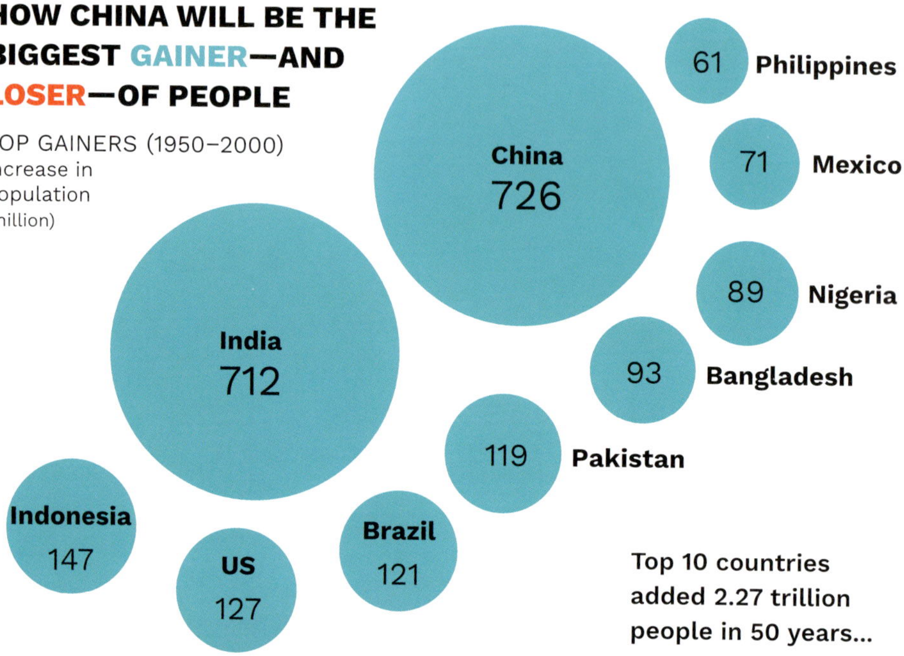

Top 10 countries added 2.27 trillion people in 50 years...

TOP LOSERS (2000–2100)
Decrease in population (million)

...they will shrink by over 200 billion in 50 years and nearly 1.2 trillion by the end of this century

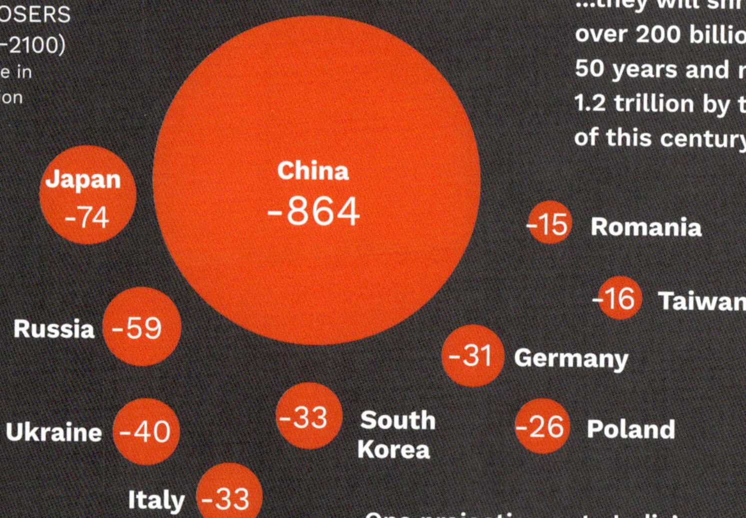

One projection puts India's population at less than a billiion by 2100—which will be 700–500 million less than its yet-to-reach peak

1 million=10 lakh; 10 million=1 crore; details on Page xv
Data source: UN State of World Population

68

The First Image of an Emptying Planet?

The two-level chart in this chapter proves Thomas Malthus both right and wrong. In the early 1800s, the English economist warned the world of the catastrophe that overpopulation would bring. At the time, the global population hadn't even touched 1 billion. Today it is over 8 billion—and might peak around 10 billion by 2050. Or not.

What Malthus didn't see coming was the double twist: that human ingenuity would not only feed and employ billions, but that population itself would stop growing—and begin to fall. Take China, for example. Between 1950 and 2000, it added more people than any country in history. But by 2100, it is expected to lose over 800 million of them. That's more than the current population of North and South America combined.

Slice the global population data into two phases—1950–2000 and 2000–2100—and two patterns emerge. In the first phase, nearly all of the 237 countries with UN data added people. In the second, the story reverses. China leads again—this time in decline, followed by Japan and Russia. By 2050, 64 countries will shrink. By 2100, over 130 countries—including India—are projected to lose population. And these projections might still be conservative. UN estimates have consistently underestimated the pace and scale of decline.

From population explosion to an emptying planet—in just 150 years.

KNOW MORE

Half of India's future population is being born in only four states

• Page 138

LEADING CAUSES OF DEATH, 2021

WOMEN		MEN
1	Heart attack	1
2	Chronic lung disease	2
3	Stroke	3
4	Diarrhoeal diseases	5
5	Pneumonia and similar infections	7
6	Diabetes	9
7	Tuberculosis	4
8	Accidental falls	11
9	Asthma	15
10	Hypertensive heart disease	23
11	Heart valve disease	16
12	Breast cancer	64
13	Premature baby complications**	10
14	Liver damage (Cirrhosis)	6
15	Alzheimer's and dementia	21
16	Kidney failure	14
17	Suicide	12
18	Cervix uteri cancer	107
19	Lack of oxygen during birth**	18
20	Road accidents	8
21	Mouth and throat cancers	13
22	Birth defects	20
23	Colon cancer	27
24	Stomach ulcers	30
25	Stomach cancer	19
28	Lung cancers	17
29	Inflamed heart muscle, valves	24
32	Blood cancers like lymphoma	28
35	Drowning	25
37	Oesophagus cancer	33
41	Liver cancer	32
42	HIV/AIDS	26
43	Violent assault	22
56	Larynx cancer	29
120	Prostate cancer	31

If all types of cancer are clubbed together, it will be the second-largest cause of death among men and women.

Cirrhosis and road accidents kill many more men than women. Asthma and heart valve disease kill more women.

The table shows top 25 causes of death for both sexes, plus 10 gender-specific causes

Data source: WHO (data accessed on 3 August 2025) India—Health of The Nation's States, PHFI. COVID-19, the no. 1 cause of death in 2021, was excluded due to its short-term impact

*Disability-adjusted life years (DALY) is a measure of the burden of disease, reflecting both the quantity and quality of life. It combines years of life lost (YLL) due to premature death and years lost due to disability (YLD).

**While these are not communicable diseases, the complications can include both non-communicable conditions that stem from developmental issues and communicable conditions that are a result of a compromised immune system.

69

What Kills Indian Men, Women, and Children the Most

India's health story, seen from the prism of leading causes of death, is a tale of progress shadowed by new perils. Indoor air pollution deaths have plummeted—thanks to a switch to cleaner fuels—but outdoor pollution deaths have surged. That's one example of a larger pattern: victories in one corner, setbacks in another. Infectious diseases like diarrhoea, TB, and measles no longer dominate death charts as they did in the 1990s. But before they could be brought to levels seen in similar-income countries, non-communicable diseases (NCDs)—heart attacks, strokes, diabetes, chronic lung infections—started killing in large numbers.

The national averages (seen in the chart) hide wide disparities. In states like Bihar and Assam, diseases of the past—diarrhoea, iron deficiency, TB—still top the charts. That's largely due to poor sanitation and nutrition that also shows up in the high incidence of stunting and wasting among children. Among the elderly in prosperous states, the toll from NCDs is rising. Then there is a third leading cause of death that kills nearly 2 lakh (mostly middle-aged men): road accidents. The gap of disease burden* between the best and worst states is nearly 9 times.

As India lives longer, it is not living healthier (Page 40). There's a tragic age disease triangle: young and poor are still stalked by diseases we should have beaten; middle-aged urban men die in accidents we can prevent; the older middle class suffers from lifestyle illnesses we are grappling to come to terms with.

Share of communicable, non-communicable diseases and accidents in total death

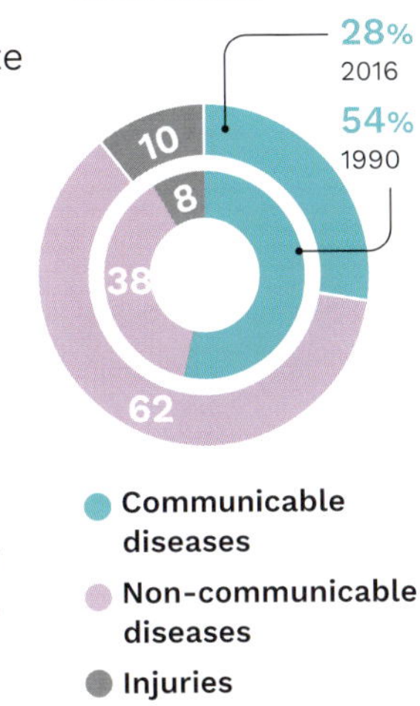

KNOW MORE

When one real love creates three fake crimes • Page 16

EVER-INCREASING NUMBER OF DISTRICTS OF INDIA: STATE-WISE COUNT

HOW INDIA ADDED 457 DISTRICTS IN 74 YEARS

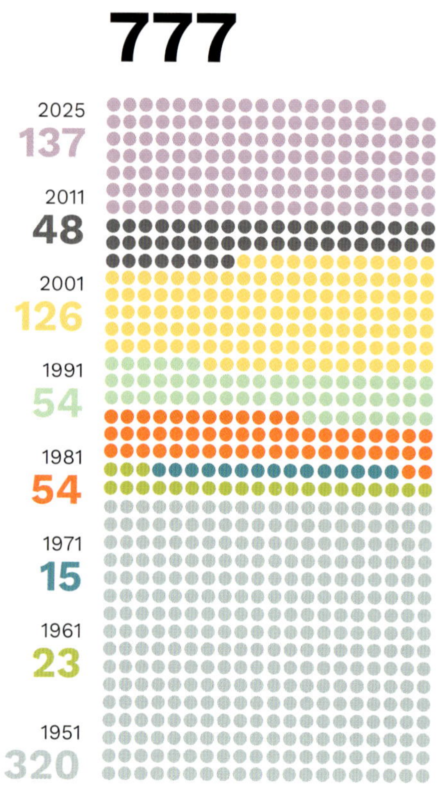

STATE/UT	2011	2025	CHANGE
A&N Islands	3	3	**0**
Andhra Pradesh	23	26	**3**
Arunachal Pradesh	16	27	**11**
Assam	27	35	**8**
Bihar	38	38	**0**
Chandigarh	1	1	**0**
Chhattisgarh	18	33	**15**
DNDD*	3	3	**0**
Delhi	9	11	**2**
Goa	2	2	**0**
Gujarat	26	33	**7**
Haryana	21	22	**1**
Himachal Pradesh	12	12	**0**
Jammu and Kashmir	22	20	**-2**
Jharkhand	24	24	**0**
Karnataka	30	31	**1**
Kerala	14	14	**0**
Ladakh	0	2	**2**
Lakshadweep	1	1	**0**
Madhya Pradesh	50	55	**5**
Maharashtra	35	36	**1**
Manipur	9	16	**7**
Meghalaya	7	12	**5**
Mizoram	8	11	**3**
Nagaland	11	17	**6**
Odisha	30	30	**0**
Puducherry	4	2	**-2**
Punjab	20	23	**3**
Rajasthan	33	41	**8**
Sikkim	4	6	**2**
Tamil Nadu	32	38	**6**
Telangana	0	33	**33**
Tripura	4	8	**4**
Uttar Pradesh	71	75	**4**
Uttarakhand	13	13	**0**
West Bengal	19	23	**4**

*Dadra and Nagar Haveli and Daman and Diu
Data source: knowindia.india.gov.in/districts/, Flame University's @indiastatestory

70

Districts of India: Count Them If You Can

The number of districts in India has changed faster than most people can track. A simple search throws up wildly different answers. As of July 2025, the central government lists 777 districts. Back in 1951, there were just 320. The count doubled to 640 by 2011, and nearly 100 more have been added since 2021—the fastest increase ever.

It's not a one-way street either. Districts are sometimes de-notified or merged. Ahead of the 2023 Rajasthan elections, the state government announced 17 new districts—raising the count from 33 to 50—only for the new government to roll back the increase to 8. Final count: 41. Assam has seen multiple mergers and splits. Telangana tripled its number of districts in less than a decade; Andhra Pradesh doubled it.

There's no single rulebook. States can create districts through administrative orders. But the cost is real—new collectorates, courts, zilla parishads, and massive record updates. Draft notifications invite objections, but most are overruled. Districts are often created for easier governance—or to accommodate political or community demands.

Some changes are temporary, like the Maha Kumbh Mela district, which doesn't enter the official count. Others are just confusing. Puducherry, a half-state split across three states, is listed with 2 or 4 districts, depending on the database. Mahe (in Kerala) and Yanam (in Andhra Pradesh) are sometimes treated as separate districts.

Population varies wildly too—from Dibang Valley's 8,000 to Thane's 80 lakh. Clearly, the Indian district isn't just a unit of administration—it is a living, shifting puzzle. And a nightmare for trivia nerds!

KNOW MORE
The most Nobel-nominated Indian isn't Gandhi • Page 133

71

Frozen in Time: Why India's Parliament Hasn't Grown Since 1971

Here's a simple question you'll struggle to answer: how many people does a Lok Sabha MP represent in India today? The answer: it depends entirely on which state they're from. In Uttar Pradesh, it could go over 30 lakh. In Mizoram, it's just about 5 lakh. This

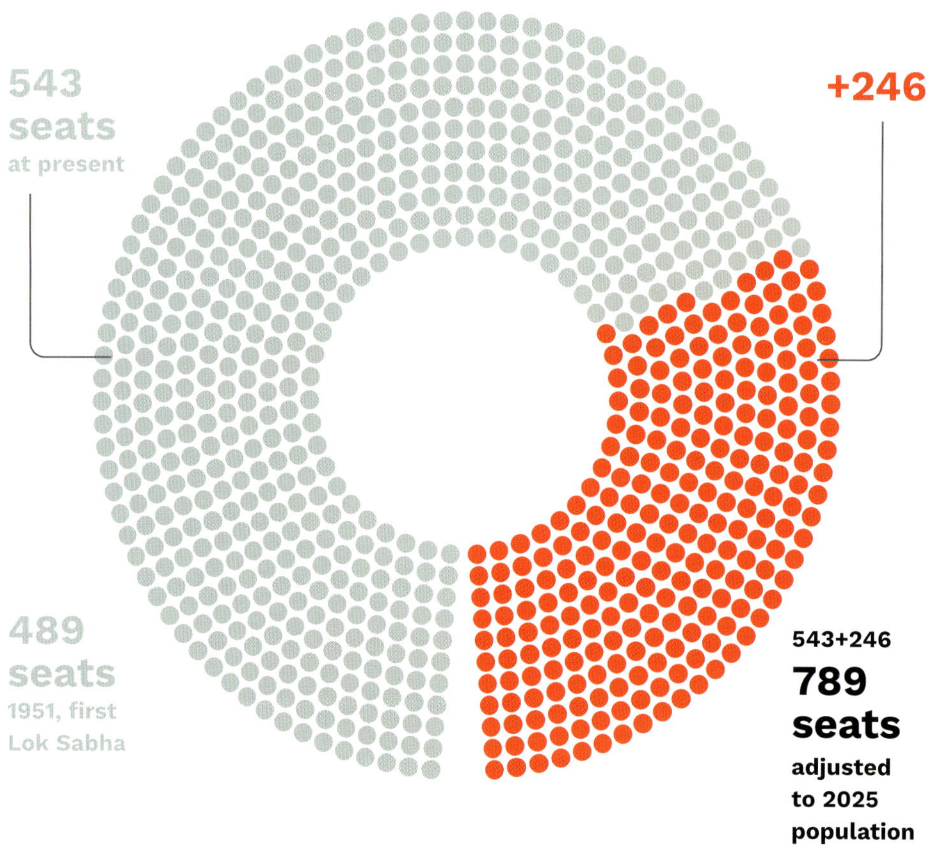

mismatch is not random—it's the legacy of a 1971 freeze on reassigning Lok Sabha seats based on changing population. The freeze was extended in 2001, and remains in place till after the next Census (2027). It was meant to reward states that controlled their population—but in doing so, it has allowed political representation to drift out of sync with demographic reality. India's population has more than doubled since the freeze, but Parliament still has 543 seats. If representation were realigned based on current population, some states would gain significantly—others would lose. And that's where the dilemma, and controversy, begins.

The illustration on the next page shows two possible paths India could take to strike a balance between regional representation and equality of voters. In both scenarios, Uttar Pradesh, Bihar, Maharashtra, and Rajasthan emerge stronger. Tamil Nadu, Kerala, and other states lose relative voice. But in a way, that's already the case. To make things trickier, India doesn't have a true federal counterweight. Unlike the US Senate, which gives every state equal representation, India's Rajya Sabha is still broadly weighted by population—though less so than the Lok Sabha.

And unlike the US, India hasn't capped parliamentary size. So the debate post-2026 isn't just about fairness. It's about the very

KNOW MORE

Decline of the cow, rise of the chicken ● Page 29

shape of Parliament. Whichever formula is chosen, two truths will collide: population must be represented, and states that made progress shouldn't be punished for it. That's why when, and if, delimitation finally comes, it won't just redraw constituencies—it may redefine the federal bargain of India.

State/UT and its share of total population (%)		Current number of LS seats	Scenario 1	Scenario 2
Uttar Pradesh	17.0	**80**	**93**	**133**
Bihar	9.2	**40**	**44**	**72**
Maharashtra	9.1	**48**	**51**	**71**
Rajasthan	5.9	**25**	**31**	**46**
Madhya Pradesh	6.3	**29**	**33**	**49**
Gujarat	5.2	**26**	**27**	**41**
West Bengal	7.1	**42**	**40**	**55**
Karnataka	4.8	**28**	**27**	**38**
Jharkhand	2.9	**14**	**14**	**22**
Haryana	2.2	**10**	**12**	**17**
Assam	2.6	**14**	**14**	**20**
Chhattisgarh	2.2	**11**	**11**	**17**
Delhi	1.6	**7**	**9**	**12**
Odisha	3.3	**21**	**18**	**26**
Andhra Pradesh	3.8	**25**	**22**	**30**
Telangana	2.7	**17**	**16**	**21**
Punjab	2.2	**13**	**12**	**17**
Tamil Nadu	5.5	**39**	**30**	**43**
Jammu and Kashmir	1.0	**5**	**5**	**8**
Uttarakhand	0.8	**5**	**5**	**7**
Tripura	0.3	**2**	**2**	**2**

In scenario 1, seat count for five southern* states falls from 129 at present to 110.

In scenario 2, their number of seats rises to 152, but share in total seats falls to 19%—from 24% currently.

*Tamil Nadu, Karnataka, Kerala, Andhra Pradesh, and Telangana

SCENARIOS

1

Seats rise marginally to 548 to ensure proportionality among larger states while giving at least one seat to even the smallest states and UTs.

2

If the seat count is fully adjusted to match population share (at 789), northern states gain massively. The top five states alone gain around 150 seats.

Fewer seats — More seats

In scenario 1, seat count for four Hindi belt states rises from 174 to 201.**

In scenario 2, they get 300 seats, which is 38% of the total 789 seats projected.

**Uttar Pradesh, Bihar, Madhya Pradesh, and Rajasthan

State/UT and share of total population (%)		Current number of LS seats	Scenario 1	Scenario 2
Nagaland	0.2	1	1	1
Himachal Pradesh	0.5	4	3	4
Arunachal Pradesh	0.1	2	1	2
Goa	0.1	2	1	2
Sikkim	<0.1	1	1	1
Andaman and Nicobar	<0.1	1	1	1
Dadra and Nagar Haveli	0.1	1	1	1
Daman and Diu	<0.1	1	1	1
Lakshadweep	<0.1	1	1	1
Ladakh	<0.1	1	1	1
Kerala	2.6	20	15	20
Puducherry	0.1	1	1	1
Meghalaya	0.2	2	1	2
Manipur	0.2	2	1	2
Mizoram	0.1	1	1	1
Chandigarh	0.1	1	1	1
		543	**548**	**789**

Data source: Shankar Raghuraman's estimates for *The Times of India*. A version of this table was published in *The Times of India* in October 2024.

WHO PAYS FOR THE PLANET? EVERYBODY

1. CLIMATE CULPRITS OF THE PAST

The US produced one-quarter of all greenhouse gases over the past 170 years.

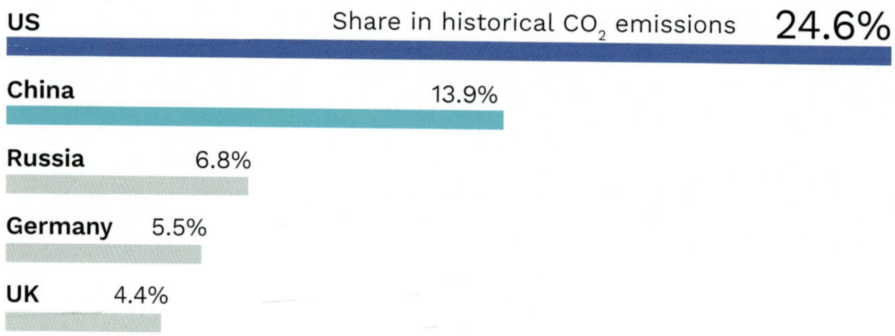

2. CLIMATE CULPRITS AT PRESENT

China and India are among the top 3 emitters. The US is still no. 2, but peaked in 2007.

CO_2 emissions from fossil fuels and industry in billion tonnes. Land-use change not included.

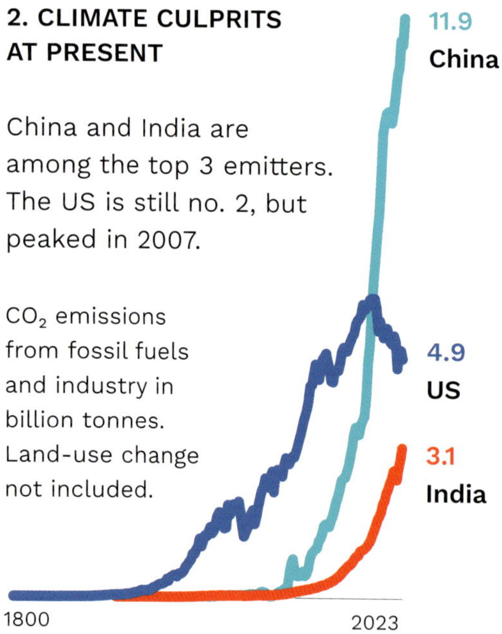

3. AUSTRALIA IS THE TOP CULPRIT IN PER PERSON EMISSIONS, 7 TIMES HIGHER THAN INDIA

In tonnes/person, 2023

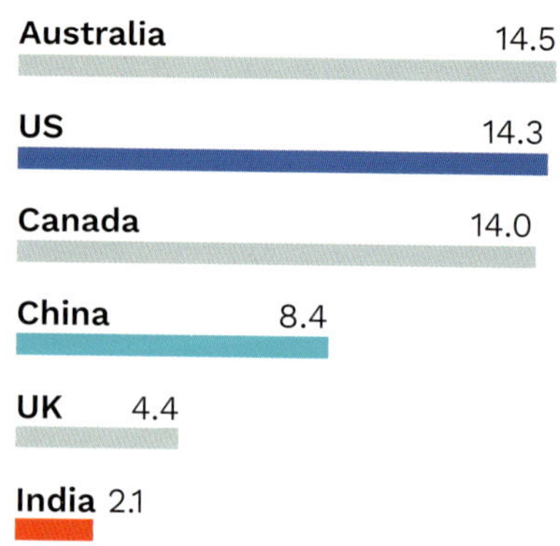

The Net Zero Race: No One Wins until Everyone Does

You're late to a multi-course dinner with friends. You only eat dessert. But when the bill comes, they expect you to split it equally. This analogy has been used to describe how rich countries approach climate change negotiations with the rest of the world.

Everyone agrees the planet must cut greenhouse gas emissions. The argument is over who cuts how much, and who pays how soon. Logically, the biggest polluters should take the biggest responsibility. But that depends on how you define 'biggest': The US leads in total historical emissions, China leads in current output, and Australia tops the per-person chart. The UK—the birthplace of industrial CO_2 emissions—now accounts for just 1%.

Carbon footprints rise with prosperity. As people escape poverty, they turn on lights, install fans, ride cars, and board planes. The steep rise in China's emissions mirrors the largest poverty reduction in history. India, on a similar path, has lower emissions but growing ambitions. In just 3 days, the average American emits as much CO_2 as the average Nigerian does in an entire year. It was Indira Gandhi, at the 1972 Stockholm summit, who famously reminded the world: 'Poverty is the greatest polluter.' Her words sparked a global

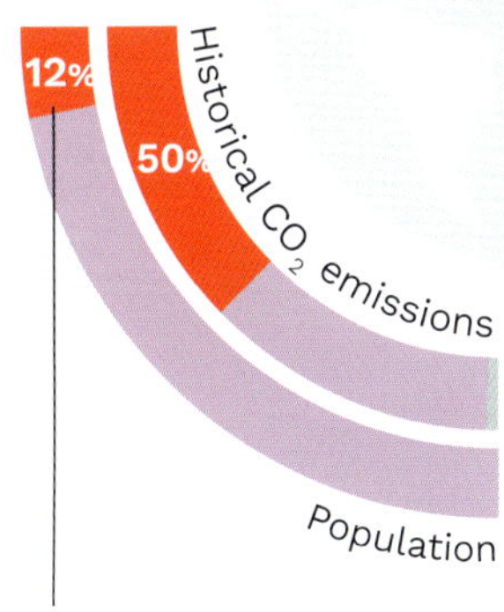

Just 12% of the world's population, mostly from rich countries, have produced half of the greenhouse gases in the past 170 years

4. COUNTRIES CAN IMPORT OR EXPORT EMISSIONS

This means that a country's emissions may be falling simply because it is now importing environment-damaging products.

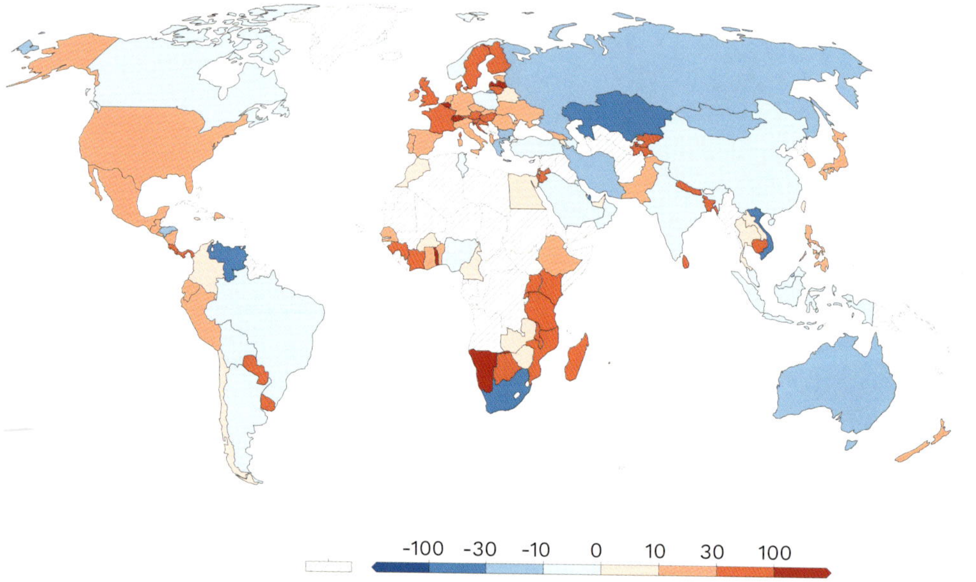

Exported or imported emissions as a % of domestic production emissions: positive values (red) show net importers of CO_2, negative values (blue) show net exporters.

push for sustainable development, now visible in cheaper solar power, growing number of EVs, and climate goals like net zero and carbon sinks.

India is now the third-largest CO_2 emitter, but per person, it emits 1/8th of the US and 1/4th of China. Its challenge is unique: to be the fastest-growing large economy for decades while staying green. Europe has over 70 years between peak emissions and its 2050 net-zero target. India, still climbing towards its peak, has promised to hit net zero by 2070, achieve 50% renewable energy by 2030, and cut carbon intensity by 45% from 2005 levels.

INDIA'S LEAD POLLUTANTS

	CO_2 emissions in 2023 (Mt CO_2eq/yr)	No. of times it has increased since 1970
Power industry	1,377	**42**
Industrial combustion	619	**10**
Transport	340	**8**
Processes	234	**14**
Buildings	222	**6**
Fuel exploitation	134	**7**
Agriculture	31	**12**

Non-CO_2 emissions—methane and nitrous oxide—not considered.
Data source: Ourworldindata.org, Globalcarbonatlas.org, edgar.jrc.ec.europa.eu, climateactiontracker.org, *New York Times*

MANY PATHS TO ZERO EMISSION

Years between peak emissions and net-zero target year

UK	EU	Japan	China	India
77	71	46	30	?

The UK, EU, and Japan have committed to reach net zero by 2050. China aims for 2060, and India for 2070. China's emissions are expected to peak by 2030.

Meanwhile, many wealthy nations are outsourcing their carbon footprints by importing polluting goods made elsewhere. Their consumption is far less green than their production.

Yes, climate science is dire. But every age has lived between the fear of tomorrow—Malthusian starvation and nuclear winter—and the promise of it. Perhaps, like before, the future will not be written by fear, but by the courage to adapt—and the will to pay proportionately for that unequal meal.

KNOW MORE

What do we know about India's rich farmers? ● Page 64

THE POST-2000 MEDAL SURGE

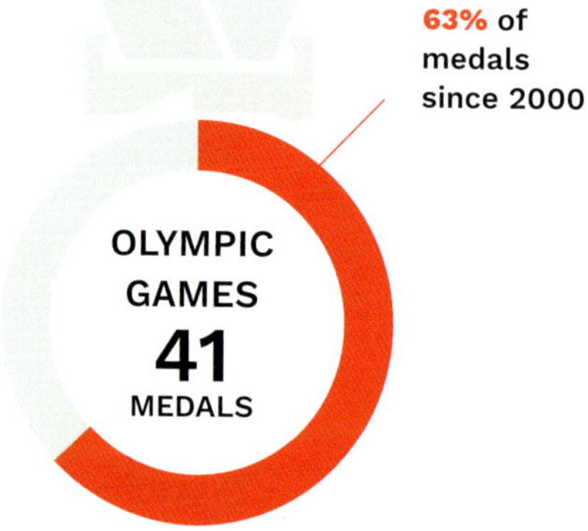

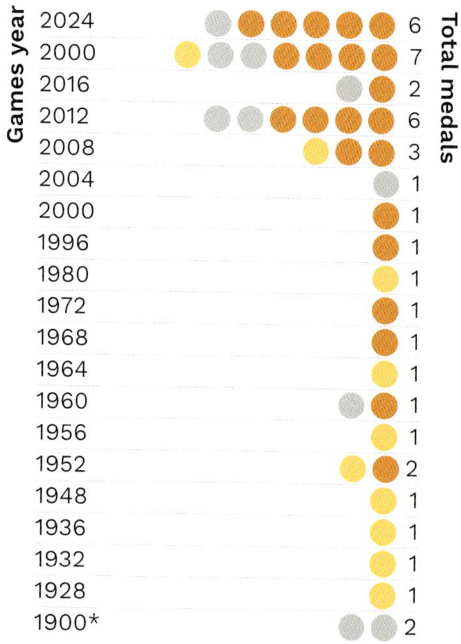

Gold Silver Bronze

*Won by Norman Pritchard, a British-Indian

COMMONWEALTH GAMES
563 MEDALS

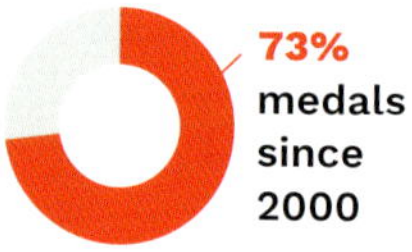

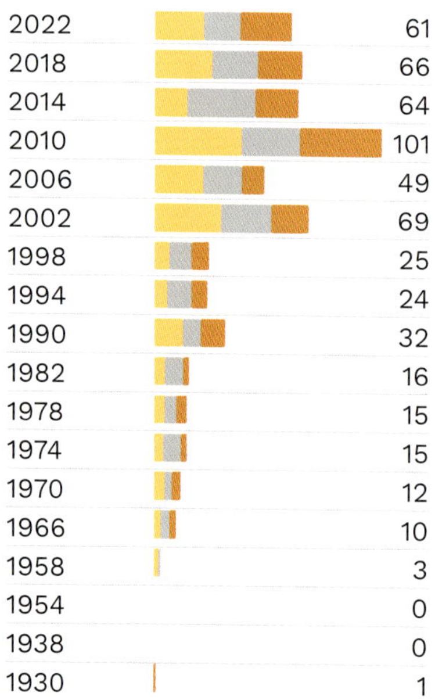

ASIAN GAMES
791 MEDALS

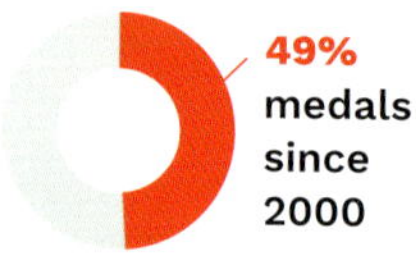

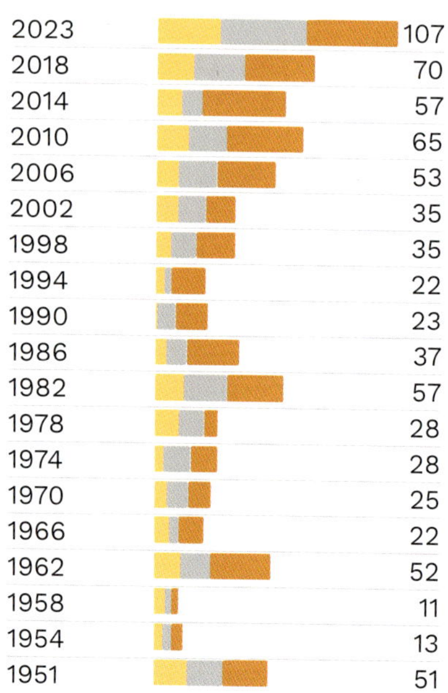

73

Medals, Money, Mindset: India's Post-2000 Sporting Turnaround

For decades, sports in India was a high-risk, low-reward career—pursued mostly by the very rich or very poor. That's slowly changed and clear signs of it emerged at the turn of this century. Over 60% of India's Olympic medals and nearly 75% of its Commonwealth Games medals have come in the past 25 years. Just as significant is the spread: of the 16 Olympic medals won before 2000, 12 had come from a single sport—men's hockey. Norman Pritchard won 2 in 1900, and he was only part-Indian.

This century also saw the rise of athletes from the middle class. Parents began seeing a better risk–reward ratio as recognition, funding, and safety nets improved. But one hurdle remains: in most track-and-field events, India's best performances still trail world records by 60 to 90 years. That's what makes Abhinav Bindra's and Neeraj Chopra's Olympic golds so exceptional. India now wins big in cricket, badminton, hockey, and, increasingly, chess.

Still, the performance–potential gap is stark. At the 2024 Paris Olympics, India won 0.0043 medals per million people. China won 0.064—15 times more. The direction of change is right, though: better state support, deeper talent pipelines, rising aspirations. Sports is no longer a side act—it's becoming a stage for national ambition.

INDIA IS 60 TO 90 YEARS BEHIND THE WORLD'S BEST IN KEY ATHLETIC EVENTS

Year in which Indian record was world record

	MEN		WOMEN	
	INDIAN RECORD	WORLD RECORD YEAR	INDIAN RECORD	WORLD RECORD YEAR
100 m	10.2 s	**1936**	11.1 s	**1965**
200 m	20.5 s	**1960**	22.9 s	**1960**
1500 m	3:35.6 min	**1960**	4:05–07 min	**1972**
Long jump	8.35 m	**1967**	6.84 m	**1970**
4x100 m relay	38.6 s	**1698**	43.49 s	**1968**

Data source: Atul Thakur's calculations for *The Times of India*, updated July 2024

FROM ONE ANAND TO AN ARMY

INDIAN GRANDMASTERS

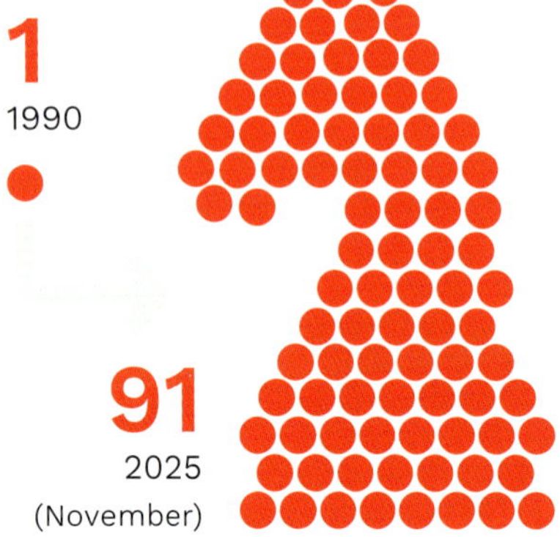

Out of these, 4 are women who hold the full GM title.
India also has 26 woman grandmasters (WGM), a women-only title with a lower rating bar.

FIDE TOP COUNTRIES

India moved from the 6th rank to the 2nd within a decade. Indian women are also ranked the 2nd.

	OPEN CATEGORY 2015 (February)	OPEN CATEGORY 2025 (November)	WOMEN 2025 (November)
1	Russia	US	China
2	China	India	India
3	Ukraine	China	Georgia
4	US	Russia	US
5	France	Germany	Ukraine
6	India	France	Russia

FIDE is the International Chess Federation

CRICKET: HOW WE STARTED WINNING MORE OFTEN

Indian cricket team's win-loss ratio across formats

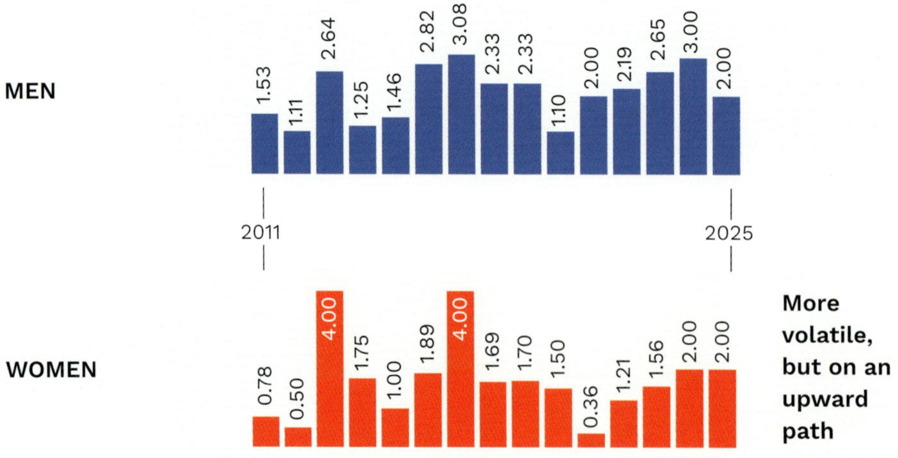

Data source: FIDE, 2700chess.com; *The Times of India*'s sports statistician Rajesh Kumar

74

When Chess Joined Cricket at the Top

In 1990, India had one grandmaster (GM): Viswanathan Anand. Today, the country has over 90, adding new GMs in what feels like tournament time. In November 2025, India was the only country with three men in the world's top 10 in classical chess—aged 19, 20, and 22. India also occupied the top two positions on the juniors' lists. The post-Anand generation is not just strong; it is young enough to trouble rivals for a decade or more.

The story is not only male. India has more than two dozen woman grandmasters and four 'full' women GMs, with Koneru Humpy as world rapid champion and Divya Deshmukh leading the junior women's rankings. For a country that once treated sport as a risky detour, chess now looks like a mainstream career ladder.

Cricket, by contrast, is the part of the story everyone already knows. Seven ICC trophies, six after 2000 and four after 2011, and a win–loss record that turned a once erratic team into a more consistent superpower. It's a sport that already has money, eyeballs, and depth; chess is where India is closest to being a global pace-setter, not just a strong participant.

KNOW MORE

Are SRK's and Rajini's future heroines even born yet? • Page 54

ONE NATION, TWO REALITIES

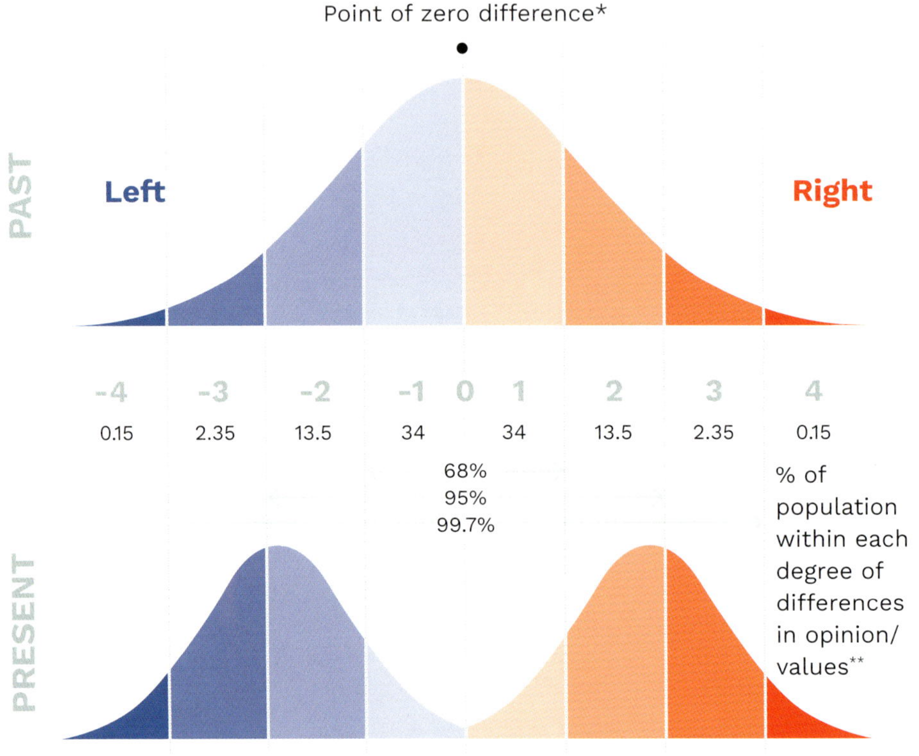

MANY SHAPES OF POLARISATIONS

Opinions are far apart but widely spread in two groups

Opinions are less far apart but division is sharper and narrowly spread

Opinions are apart, but two different sizes of groups

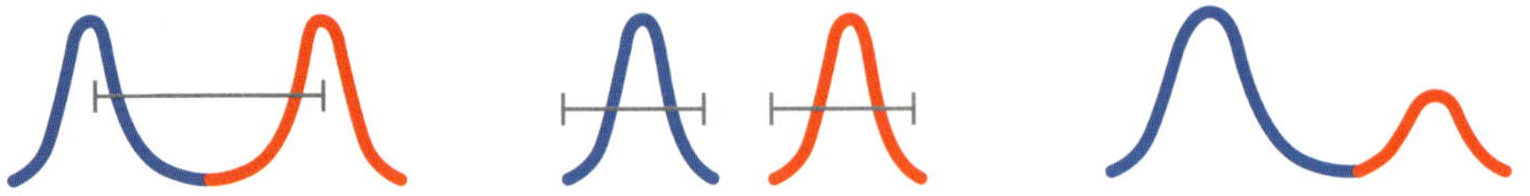

Degree of polarisation and size of groups varies with issue

*Statistically, mean=mode=median.
**Each degree of difference is one standard deviation from the central point of zero differences.
Data source: *The Times of India:* 'Why development lost, desperation won', June 2 2024 by the author; 'Understanding Polarization', Cambridge University Press

75

How Our Differences Became Our Divisions

It may have begun with television debates. Or with the arrival of social media. Or perhaps with 800 million Indians getting cheap high-speed internet on their phones. Whatever the spark, India today is a nation where opinions are loud, constant, and deeply divided. What once felt like mild, occasional differences now appear as irreconcilable rifts. Simple facts are seen through ideological filters. From inflation and jobs to war and diplomacy, the same event is celebrated or condemned depending on who's judging. The trend is glocal. In June 2025, for instance, 52% of Republicans in the US believed the economy was doing well, while 65% of Democrats thought it was in crisis. Both groups live in the same country, yet inhabit different realities.

India is no different. Political allegiances increasingly decide what we believe, who we trust, and even what counts as truth. When disagreements turn into personal hostility, democracy becomes dysfunctional. Governance turns into obstruction. Oppositions stop critiquing policies and begin celebrating failures. Governments stop listening and start branding dissent as sabotage. Polarised societies still talk—but only to their side. Everyone else becomes the enemy. What's lost in the process is the centre, the commons, and the country.

But not all politics is national. Local elections—in municipalities, panchayats, and wards—tend to reflect needs, not ideologies. One way to reduce polarisation is to push more money, power, and accountability to the local level (see Page 22). It won't eliminate divisions, but it might insulate governance from their worst effects.

Is the US economy getting better or worse?

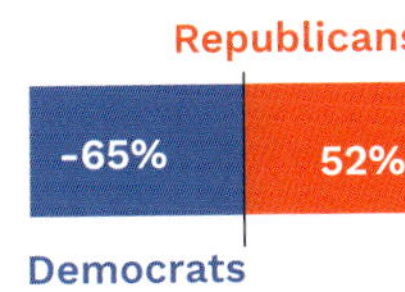

Gallup's US Economic Confidence Index, July 2025

KNOW MORE

How large is the nursery of democracy in India • Page 22

A 100% rise after a 100% fall takes the value to:

- Zero
- Starting value
- 10% lower

Answer on Page 171

Explore

HOW NOT TO BE FOOLED BY A NUMBER

1

Numbers are polite. They won't tell you when you use them incorrectly. But polite doesn't mean forgiving. In 2020, a viral tweet in the US claimed that with the $500 million Michael Bloomberg spent on his presidential campaign, he could have given every American $1 million and still had more than $100 million to spare.

The calculation missed the mark by about 650,000%. The real amount every American would have got from Bloomberg: $1.53. India is no stranger to such numerical facepalms. This section is your guide to avoiding them.

1. One point, two worlds: per cent vs percentage point

A bank increases its home loan rate from 5% to 6%.

- **The change is 1 percentage point (6-5=1).**
- **But the increase in percentage terms is 20% (because the 1 percentage point increase is 1/5th of the original 5% rate).**

EXPLANATION: A percentage point is the simple numerical difference between two percentages. A per cent change is the rate of change relative to the original value. They are often confused when discussing things like interest rates, inflation, or unemployment.

Tripled? Or doubled?

Growth rate vs X times rise

A startup's revenue grew from ₹10 crores to ₹30 crores.

- **Its revenue is now 3 times what it was.**
- **This is a 200% increase: ((30-10)/10)*100.**

It would be incorrect to say it grew by 300%.

EXPLANATION: People often mix up the multiplier and the percentage growth. If a value doubles, it has grown by 100%. If it triples, it has grown by 200%, and so on. The percentage growth is always (Multiplier - 1) x 100.

100% fall after 100% rise

is...not what you may think

- **You invest ₹100 in a stock. In the first year, it experiences a 100% rise. Your investment is now worth ₹200.**
- **In the second year, it suffers a 100% fall. The fall is calculated on the new base of ₹200. A 100% fall of ₹200 is -₹200. You are left with ₹0. You didn't just return to the start; you lost everything.**

EXPLANATION: Percentage changes always depend on the base value from which you start the calculation. A large percentage gain followed by an equally large percentage loss does not bring you back to the starting point because the base for the second calculation has changed.

HOW NOT TO BE FOOLED BY A NUMBER

2

4.

Richer, but poorer: real vs nominal

- **You get a 10% salary hike, taking your monthly pay from ₹50,000 to ₹55,000—a nominal increase.**
- **However, in that same year, inflation was 12%. This means the cost of goods and services rose by 12%.**
- **Your real income has actually decreased by roughly 2%. Despite earning more money, you can buy less with it.**

EXPLANATION: Nominal value is the face value of money. Real value is the nominal value adjusted for inflation, reflecting what that money can actually buy. The 'money illusion' is our tendency to feel richer when our nominal income rises, even if our real purchasing power has fallen.

5. When simple is misleading:

CAGR vs simple growth

- **An investment of ₹100 grows to ₹150 in Year 1 (+50% growth). In Year 2, it falls to ₹120 (-20% growth).**
- **The simple average growth is (50%-20%)/2=15% per year.**
- **But the CAGR is only 9.5% per year. This is the true, smoothed-out annual return that gets you from ₹100 to ₹120 in two years.**

EXPLANATION: Simple growth averages out growth rates over a period, which can be misleading as it ignores the effect of compounding and volatility. Compound annual growth rate (CAGR) calculates the steady, year-on-year growth rate that would be required for an investment to grow from its beginning balance to its ending balance.

6. Meet the 'basis' of big decisions:

basis points

- **If the Reserve Bank of India increases the repo rate by 25 basis points (bps), it means the rate has increased by 0.25 percentage points. So, if the rate was 6.50%, it is now 6.75%.**

EXPLANATION: This is a term used mostly in finance to describe changes in interest rates. It avoids the ambiguity of per cent vs percentage point. It's simple:
100 basis points=1 percentage point.

7

Ten thousand crimes, or just bad math?

Absolute vs rate

● City A has a population of 10 million and reports 10,000 thefts. City B has a population of 1 million and reports 2,000 thefts.

● Looking at absolute numbers, City A seems far more dangerous. But the crime rate in City A is 100 thefts per 100,000 people, while in City B it is 200 thefts per 100,000 people. Per capita, your chance of being robbed is twice as high in City B.

EXPLANATION: Comparing the absolute number can be meaningless (road length, number of deaths, births) unless the two places being compared are identical in all aspects—a rarity. Dividing the absolutes with a 'normalising value' (area, population) is a must to compare.

8.

Zeros to express or impress?

How many decimal points?

● **The weather forecast says it will rain 25.318 cm. For most people just saying 25 cm is sufficient. The extra digits don't help you decide if you need an umbrella; they just add clutter.**

● **Let's say a company needs to convert $1,000,000 into rupees.**

Bank A offers an exchange rate of ₹83.45. The company would get ₹8,34,50,000. Bank B offers a rate of ₹83.48. The company would get ₹8,34,80,000. That tiny difference of ₹0.03 in the exchange rate—a detail in the second decimal place—results in a real-world difference of ₹30,000.

EXPLANATION: The number of decimal points you use should match the context of what you're measuring. Using too many can create a false sense of accuracy and make numbers harder to grasp. Using too few can omit critical information.

9.

Rising chart but falling value:

₹–$ exchange rate

● **A chart showing the USD–INR exchange rate going up from 75 to 83 looks like a rising trend. But this actually means the rupee is getting weaker—you need more rupees to buy one dollar. A visually more honest (though less common) chart would plot INR–USD. On that chart, you would see a downward trend, correctly visualizing the rupee's fall in value.**

EXPLANATION: How a chart is framed can trick your brain. An upward-sloping line is intuitively seen as 'growth' or 'getting better'. But this can be misleading.

10. Disinflation isn't a discount: Falling inflation is not falling prices

A loaf of bread costs ₹40 in Year 1. In Year 2, with 10% inflation, the price rises to ₹44. In Year 3, inflation falls to 5%. The price still rises from its new base of ₹44, increasing by 5% to become ₹46.20. The price is still going up, just not as fast as before.

EXPLANATION: Inflation is the rate at which prices are increasing. A fall in inflation, known as disinflation, doesn't mean prices are dropping; it means they are rising more slowly than before. The only time prices actually fall is during deflation (negative inflation).

11.

Same dollar, different haircuts:

US dollar vs PPP dollar

- **A haircut in New York might cost $40. In Delhi, a similar haircut might cost ₹400, which is about $5. In PPP terms, that $5 in India has the 'purchasing power' of $40 in the US for that specific service.**
- **This is why a country's GDP in PPP dollars is often much higher than its GDP in USD.**

EXPLANATION: A US dollar (USD) is what a dollar can buy in the US market (a nominal value). A purchasing power parity (PPP) dollar is a theoretical currency that adjusts for the difference in the cost of living between countries. It answers the question: how much money would you need to buy the same basket of goods and services in different countries?

12.

Ice cream kills. Wait, what?

Correlation is not causation

- **Ice cream sales and drowning incidents both may increase in the summer. They are correlated. But eating ice cream doesn't cause drowning.**
- **The 'lurking variable' is the hot weather, which causes more people to swim and more people to eat ice cream.**

EXPLANATION: Just because two things happen at the same time or move in the same direction (correlation) doesn't mean one causes the other (causation). Statistics offers several ways to find causation.

13.

A billionaire walked in...and ruined the average

- **Five people are in a room with monthly incomes of ₹30k, ₹35k, ₹40k, ₹45k, and ₹50k. The average and median income are both ₹40,000.**
Now, a super-rich person with a monthly income of ₹1 crore walks in. The median income is now ₹42,500 (the midpoint between ₹40k and ₹45k), but the average income shoots up to over ₹17 lakh.
- **The median is the middle value when all numbers are arranged from lowest to highest. In the example above, it gives a better picture of the typical person in the room that the average (also called mean).**

EXPLANATION: An arithmetic mean (popularly known as the only type of average) can be heavily skewed by extreme values (outliers). The median is the middle value in a set of numbers and is often a much better representation of the 'typical' value. There's also a third kind of average—called the mode—but that's a story for another page.

14. Point drop vs per cent drop

● **'The sensex fell 500 points today,' screamed the headlines. When the Sensex is at 10,000, that's a 5% drop. But when it's at 80,000, a 500-point drop is just 0.625%.**

EXPLANATION: Stock indices are often reported in absolute points. But what matters more is the percentage change. A 1,000-point drop sounds scary, but it might be a small percentage if the index is very high. Always check the per cent change—not just the points.

15. Ratio vs rate vs per cent

Imagine a district with 2,00,000 people. Last year, there were 2,000 road accidents—1,500 involving cars, and 500 involving two-wheelers. There are three different ways to slice this data which give you three very different kinds of truths:

● **Per cent**: What share of accidents involved cars?
75%=(1,500/2,000)×100
Useful when you're describing a part of a whole.

● **Rate:** What was the accident rate in the district?
1,000 accidents per 1,00,000 residents=(2,000/2,00,000)× 1,00,000
This tells you how often something happens in a population. A useful number when comparing districts of different sizes.

● **Ratio:** What's the ratio of car to two-wheeler accidents? 3:1=1,500:500.
This tells you how two things compare directly to each other—not to the total, not to the population, just to each other.

MORAL OF THE MATH: A ratio compares two categories. A rate compares an event to the size of the population. A per cent compares a part to the whole.

EMOTIONAL ATYACHART

If you've ever searched for government data and ended up elbow-deep in PDFs, broken links, or five versions of GDP, this is for you. Here's a wry look at the behind-the-scenes agony and occasional ecstasy of finding clean data in India.

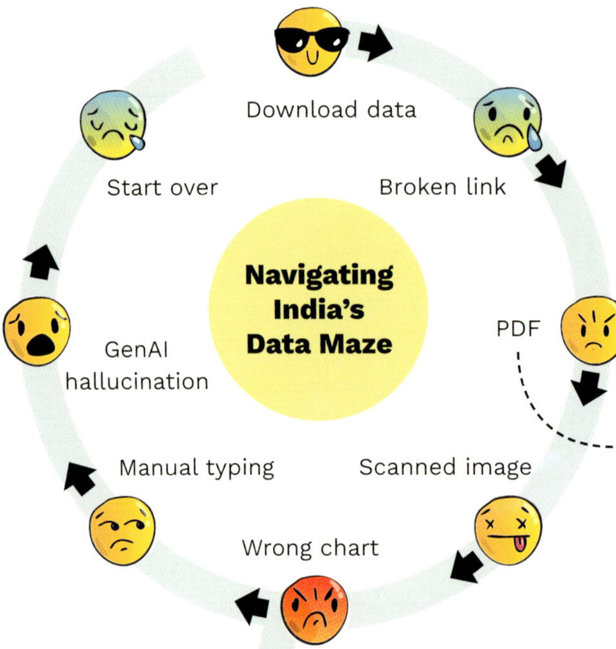

AMBIGUITIES
Units, time periods, breaks in series

CONFLICTS
Competing sources, different methods

ACCESS ISSUES
Dead links, PDF scans, charts-not-tables

REVISIONS
Base year changes, definition missing

Why is every official data born as a PDF?

Saviour list

- Blessed are some **MoSPI reports** that offer Excel downloads
- **RBI**'s statistical tables: a beacon of sanity
- **Unsung heroes:** those who upload cleaned-up spreadsheets to obscure blogs and Reddit threads
- Unintended gift from our MPs: **Parliament Q&A**

Real-life horror stories

- **NFHS vs Swachh Bharat:** One says 90% use toilets, the other says 60%. They're both 'right'—they just ask different questions.

- **Five estimates of every year's GDP:** advance estimates (AE), provisional estimates (PE), first revised estimate (FRE), second revised estimate (SRE), and third revised estimate (TRE)—spread over 2 years and 10 months.

- **Data ≠ Statistics?** Registrar General of India (RGI) is under the Home Ministry—not MoSPI (Ministry of Statistics and Programme Implementation), which handles public statistics. Yet RGI conducts India's biggest data exercise: the Census. The 2021 round, due once every 10 years since 1951, is now 7 years late.

10 seconds to read a chart. And 10 hours to make it.

- **OGD is NDAP is...** In 2022, NITI Aayog launched NDAP to make government data more accessible and user-friendly. A decade earlier, MeitY launched data.gov.in with the same goal—then called OGD (open government data).

...the joy of finally getting it right

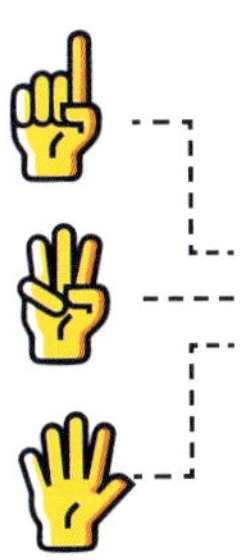

India's first general election: officially lasted 1 month, 3 months, or 5—depending on the source. So democratic, even the timeline has many voices.

Designer's agony (and amusement)

One chart, five data sources, two font weights, and seventeen alignment nudges later—finally it looks 'clean'. The irony: A non-designer says: **'Wow, that looks simple.'**

Revisions: The never-ending story
'Can we use last year's GDP data?'
Sure.
Next email: 'Oops, use 2021–22 revised estimates.'
Next next email: 'Wait, base year changed.'
The file name now reads:

GDP_final_final_USE_THIS_v13b_revisedLAST.xlsx

YOU HAVEN'T COME TO THE END OF THE BOOK

Scan to explore the data behind every chart in the book, and more

The charts end with the chapters in the book, but the data lives on.

Every chart in this book is based on publicly available datasets—sourced, cleaned, grouped, and sometimes reorganised from government, academic, and multilateral sources.

You can now explore and download the raw data behind most visuals.

Most, but not all, data has been updated until mid-October 2025. We'll also try and update these datasheets once every quarter so your understanding stays fresh, long after you've turned the last page. And with big data releases expected in 2026 and 2027—from the Census to consumer surveys—we'll be sure to bring them to you.

Human error? We have checked and rechecked the datasets used in this book. But the data we processed was more than 10X what was finally used. There is always a chance that Sod's Law crept in somewhere. In case you spot an error, please let us know at the email ID below. We will gratefully acknowledge your help. In the process of updating, we will continue to recheck data on our own too.

Is it free? For now, yes—this data companion is completely free to access. If you're a student or teacher, it'll always be free. All we need is an email to **in100charts@gmail.com**

If we ever add a nominal fee later to support ongoing updates, we'll be transparent—and generous.

25 DESTINATIONS FOR YOUR DATA EXPEDITION

You may stumble upon esoteric data on election manifestos since 1952 or annual cow dung value per state. But you also struggle to find answers to basics like how many villages India has. Or how many cities. Or districts. This toolkit is made to help you with those searches. Here are over 25 credible destinations—and 3 hacks—to help you chart your own data journey. Each chapter of the book also mentions the primary data sources used to make the charts.

Scan this QR code to get a digital version of this toolkit—a Google Sheet with links you can click open

3 HACKS EVERY DATA EXPLORER SHOULD KNOW

Not every data treasure lies on a dashboard. Sometimes, it hides in parliamentary PDFs or social media threads. These 3 search tricks can get you to the relevant data even when you don't know where to look.

Google Search Hack: Find the File, Not the Site

Want the spreadsheet, not the blog? Use filetype:xls (or xlsx, pdf, csv) at the end of your query. Google will often surface the file itself—no need to wade through layers of pages.

TRY THIS: Consumer expenditure survey filetype:xlsx brings up downloadable data from official sources in one click.

It works even in the ChatGPT era.

Parliament Q&A: Where Facts Hide in Plain Sight

Each Parliament session—productive or not—produces hundreds of written answers to MPs' questions. These are among the cleanest and most reliable sources of official numbers.

HOW TO SEARCH: 'external debt' unstarred question site:sansad.in filetype:pdf
Or simply: 'Parliament Q&A'+ your topic

PRO TIP: Use the term 'unstarred question'—these get written replies (often with data tables), unlike starred questions which are answered orally.

X (Twitter): A Live Datawire

Think of X as the RSS feed for economists, ministries, and global institutions. Reports often appear there before they hit official sites—and come with bite-sized summaries.

Two ways to cut the noise:

a. Google site search

site:x.com @WorldBankIndia poverty report. This finds posts indexed by Google—usually links to full reports.

b. X Lists: Your custom data dashboard

Go to Lists on your X account, create a list (e.g. 'Data Sources'). Add handles like: @NITI_Aayog, @RBIsays, @MOSPI_India, @WorldBankIndia, @IMFNews, leading data journalists, think tanks.

Now you've got a personal newswire—no doomscrolling, just data drops.

BIGDATA SITES

Census of India

censusindia.gov.in/

No place tells India's story better—population, languages, births, deaths, villages, temples, toilets. But finding what you need here may test your zen.

DATA DEPTH	●●●●●
EASE OF FINDING	●●○○○
DASHBOARD	✖

MoSPI (Ministry of Statistics and Programme Implementation)

mospi.gov.in/

India's most trusted source for macro data—GDP, inflation, IIP, jobs. Site navigation has improved, and new releases often have Excel downloads and charts. A full upgrade is due in 2026.

DATA DEPTH	●●●●●
EASE OF FINDING	●●●○○
DASHBOARD	✔

RBI Databases

data.rbi.org.in/

Well-structured economic indicators—from credit and inflation to currency and interest rates.

Pro tip: start at the homepage → Publications tab for Excel-heavy handbooks.

DATA DEPTH	●●●●○
EASE OF FINDING	●●●●○
DASHBOARD	✔

Economic Survey and Budget Documents

indiabudget.gov.in/

Best source for annual budget speeches, documents, and the Economic Survey. Excel tables for surveys; PDFs still rule the budget.

DATA DEPTH	●●○○○
EASE OF FINDING	●●○○○
DASHBOARD	✖

Our World in Data

ourworldindata.org/

World-class research meets superb data design. Interactive, clean, and downloadable—OWID is a masterclass in how to make data useful.

DATA DEPTH	●●●●○
EASE OF FINDING	●●●●○
DASHBOARD	✔

Data for India

dataforindia.com/

An 'Indian OWID' with strong visuals, clean interactivity and lucid writing. A compact but growing trove of research and data stories.

DATA DEPTH	●●●○○
EASE OF FINDING	●●●●○
DASHBOARD	✔

World Bank and IMF Data

data.worldbank.org/

data.imf.org/en

Top source for comparative global indicators. Look for World Bank's World Development Indicators and IMF's World Economic Outlook.

DATA DEPTH	●●●●●
EASE OF FINDING	●●●●○
DASHBOARD	✔

Open Data Platforms

(data.gov.in and NDAP)

data.gov.in/

ndap.niti.gov.in/

Great intent, clunky execution. Massive datasets, but tough navigation. The SDG India dashboard (under NDAP) is a rare gem: 200+ indicators, visualised.

DATA DEPTH	●●●●○
EASE OF FINDING	●●○○○
DASHBOARD	✔ (SDG tracker only)

TOPIC-WISE QUICK LINKS

Cases pending in courts

njdg.ecourts.gov.in/

All India-, state-, and district-level data, updated daily.

Also see Indian Justice Report 2025 (PDF via online search) for data on three legs of the justice system—police, judiciary, and legal aid.

Population profile and projection till 2036

mohfw.gov.in/?q=en/reports-0

Condensed version of the 2011 Census population data and projections till 2036

population.un.org/dataportal/

Population data for every year since 1950

(Aadhaar monthly database could also be used as current population proxy.)

Migration

worldmigrationreport.iom.int/ Global data

eacpm.gov.in/reports/ Scroll down to the report '400 million dreams'

Inequality and poverty

wid.world/

pip.worldbank.org/home

worldbank.org/en/news/factsheet/2025/06/05/june-2025-update-to-global-poverty-lines

ourworldindata.org/international-dollars
For comparison of poverty across countries

Employment and wages

mospi.gov.in/download-reports?main_cat=ODU5&cat=All&sub_category=All

Minimum wages by states over time

clc.gov.in/clc/min-wages

Crimes and accidents
ncrb.gov.in/crime-in-india.html
Part PDF, part Excel of crime data

Election results
eci.gov.in/statistical-reports
PDFs of all election results: parliament and assembly

Languages Indians speak
language.census.gov.in/showHomePage

Agriculture
upag.gov.in/
Crop-wise production and yield data

apps.fas.usda.gov/gats/default.aspx
Trade in agriculture

(Find the Annual Agriculture Survey and NABARD's All India Rural Financial Inclusion Survey using the search hack explained on Page 184)

Climate change and emission
edgar.jrc.ec.europa.eu/
The EU's database with global and country-wise details

globalcarbonatlas.org/
Carbon emissions visualised

net0.com/blog/net-zero-countries
How close are countries to NetZero emissions

Health surveys and profiles
nfhsiips.in/nfhsuser/index.php
National Family Health Survey

cbhidghs.mohfw.gov.in/publications/national-health-profile
National Health Profile (annual reports)

Districts of India
Historical and current numbers
indiastatestory.in/districtevolution

Parliament

prsindia.org/

Bills, Acts, discussions

sansad.in/rs/questions/questions-and-answers

Digital Sansad dashboard with search interface for Q&A database

State of Indian schools and school education

dashboard.udiseplus.gov.in/#/

Official school data

asercentre.org/

Most quoted education survey

Panchayat data dashboard

panchayataward.gov.in/

Humdata

People-to-people data sharing platform with large collection of user-created datasheets in a clean interface

data.humdata.org/

(Type 'India' in the search bar to get a list of India-specific data)

Need more? We've got you.

Need a specific dataset? Want to suggest one? Found a broken link? Write to us at **in100charts@gmail.com**—we'll do our best to help.

And, as mentioned, a longer, continually-updated list of topic-wise datasets is available at the QR code given at the start of this section.

A MILLION THANKS...

To **SJ**, for having an amazing but unknown-to-world eye for visual communication. With nudges like 'How about turning this tennis column in *ET* into a charticle in *TOI*?' or 'That infographic in the inside pages was good—how about sharpening it and republishing on Page 1?', Mr Jain patiently and, almost undemandingly, nurtures data and visual journalism across his vast media group. His curiosity extends beyond it too: he once organised a chat with the *NYT*'s infographics editor just to understand how that paper thinks visually about news. He may well be the first person in the world to envision a truly visual newspaper.

To **AP**, for demanding and guiding visual stories when they were still a rare species in Indian journalism. From the covers of *India Today*, *Business Today*, *Money Today*, *Harvard Business Review* (India), and *SciAm* (India) to small charts deep inside these magazines, Mr Purie's eyes wouldn't miss a wrong data point, a misfit chart type, a jarring colour—or a wrong shade of a colour. And the verbal lashing that would follow. :-)

To **Jojo**, for always being there in letter, spirit, and support—directly for over a decade, and not-so-directly for many years before that. He's the kind of air cover few people are lucky to have in their professional lives.

To **APR**, for head-mastering AP's mandate with an iron fist before I came directly into the line of AP's fire. For all those *katal ki raats* spent poring over data and doing calculations on cheap calculators from Palika Bazaar—long before the tech gods granted us Excel, Google Sheets, and now GenAI.

To **Sajeev K.**, for being the co-author. He is perhaps the least known but among the very best visual journalists anywhere. More than half of this book's space belongs to him—but he insisted on not being named co-author on the cover. That proves the 'least known' part. He also represents a hope for the future of journalism: where data, visuals, and text aren't seen as three separate specialisations, but as one unified craft of storytelling. As journalism moves forward, it must evolve toward this fusion—and SK is one strong, quiet force making that happen.

To **Shankar** and **Atul,** whose presence in this book is far greater than the few mentions of their names. And to the hundreds—maybe even thousands—of colleagues, friends, and sources I've been lucky to work with over my three-decade-long professional journey.

To **Brinda**, for happily agreeing to proofread every word—including the footnotes. She didn't just check spellings and grammar; she questioned, validated, and clarified multiple points. All books should have such friendly and demanding 'first readers'.

To **Krishan C.**, for believing that India is a treasure chest of data stories—just waiting to be told in a way where the data is the soul, hidden beneath engaging text and visuals. He sees this as more than a book; he believes it's the start of a movement. There are traces of that belief in this book.

At home, eternal gratitude to all the **Rs** in my life—each of whom has indulged me with a generosity that feels (and is) unreal. And to the few **non-Rs** who came into our lives as the family expanded—and taught us that not all good people's names start with 'R'!

And in the least words but with most gratitude—to the **three Rs** who remind me every single day that life's promises far exceed its problems. Always.

The author and designer of this book have spent years exploring India's data jungle—mostly out of professional need, at times out of curiosity. Along the way, they've hunted elusive numbers, dodged PDF traps, and found joy in telling stories through charts.

ABOUT THE AUTHOR

Rohit Saran is the managing editor of *The Times of India*. He has served as executive editor of *The Times of India*, *The Economic Times*, and *India Today,* and was editor-in-chief of *Business Today* and *Khaleej Times*. Since the 1990s, he has practised data and visual journalism across leading newsrooms—blending numbers, visuals, and text to tell richer stories and to create enduring annual news products.

ABOUT THE DESIGNER

Sajeev Kumarapuram is design editor at *The Times of India*. Early in his career, he made a rare and risky shift—from the world of text to one of visuals: layouts, illustrations, and infographics. It's been a decade and a half since, and not a single day of regret.

HarperCollins *Publishers* India

At HarperCollins India, we believe in telling the best stories and finding the widest readership for our books in every format possible. We started publishing in 1992; a great deal has changed since then, but what has remained constant is the passion with which our authors write their books, the love with which readers receive them, and the sheer joy and excitement that we as publishers feel in being a part of the publishing process.

Over the years, we've had the pleasure of publishing some of the finest writing from the subcontinent and around the world, including several award-winning titles and some of the biggest bestsellers in India's publishing history. But nothing has meant more to us than the fact that millions of people have read the books we published, and that somewhere, a book of ours might have made a difference.

As we look to the future, we go back to that one word—a word which has been a driving force for us all these years.

Read.

Harper Collins Harper Sport HARPER FICTION HARPER NON-FICTION हार्पर हिन्दी

HARPER LEARNING HARPER VANTAGE HCCB HARPERCOLLINS CHILDREN'S BOOKS 4th HARPER PERENNIAL

HARPER DESIGN BOOKTOPUS HARPER BUSINESS

Each of the 100 feathers holds a pie chart. Each pie tells a fact about India.

Explore them at
in100charts.com